I0715362

BANKSY'S LOST WORKS

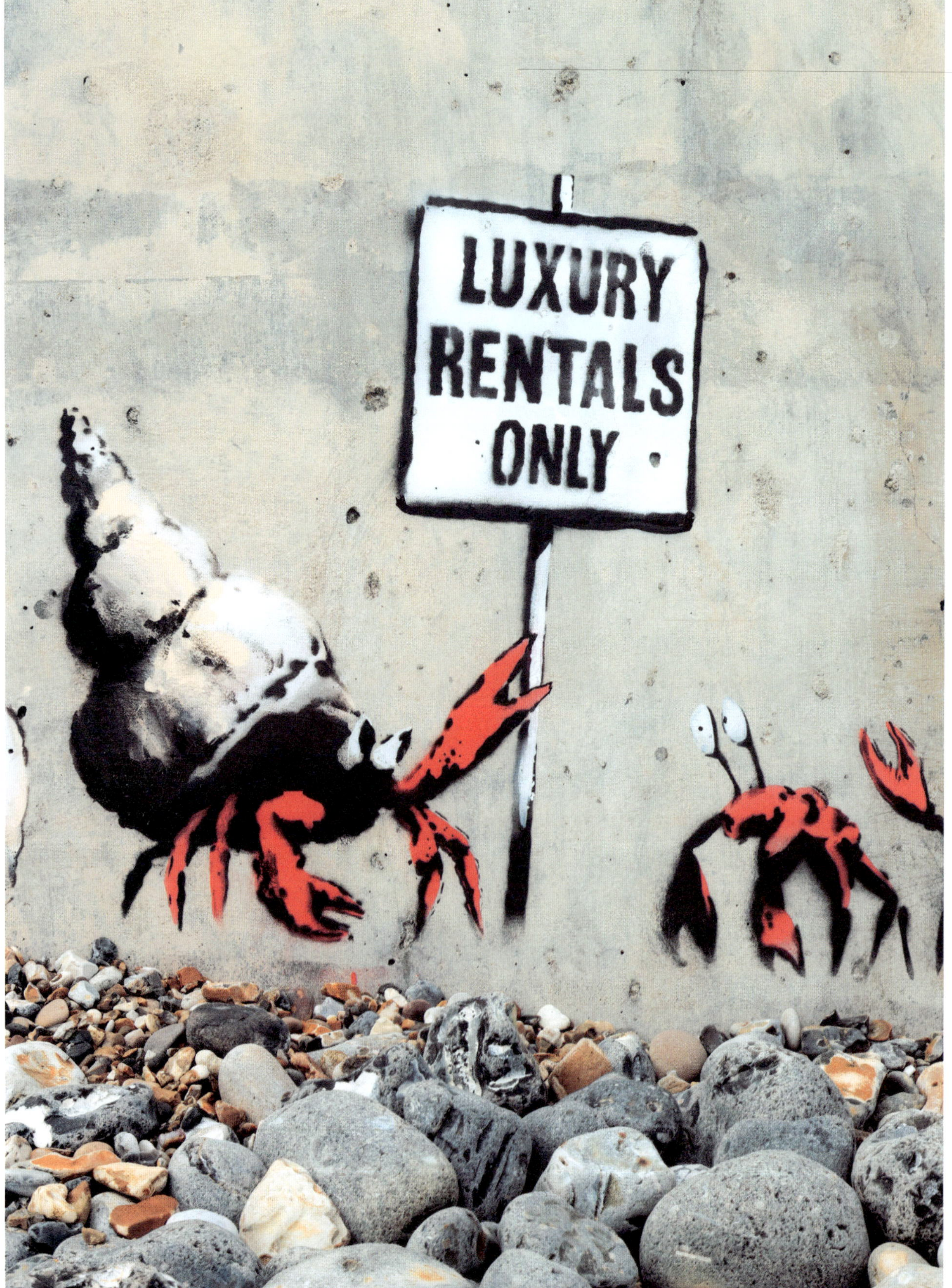

LUXURY
RENTALS
ONLY

WILL ELLSWORTH-JONES

BANKSY'S LOST WORKS

ON THE TRAIL OF HIS VANISHING STREET ART

CONTENTS

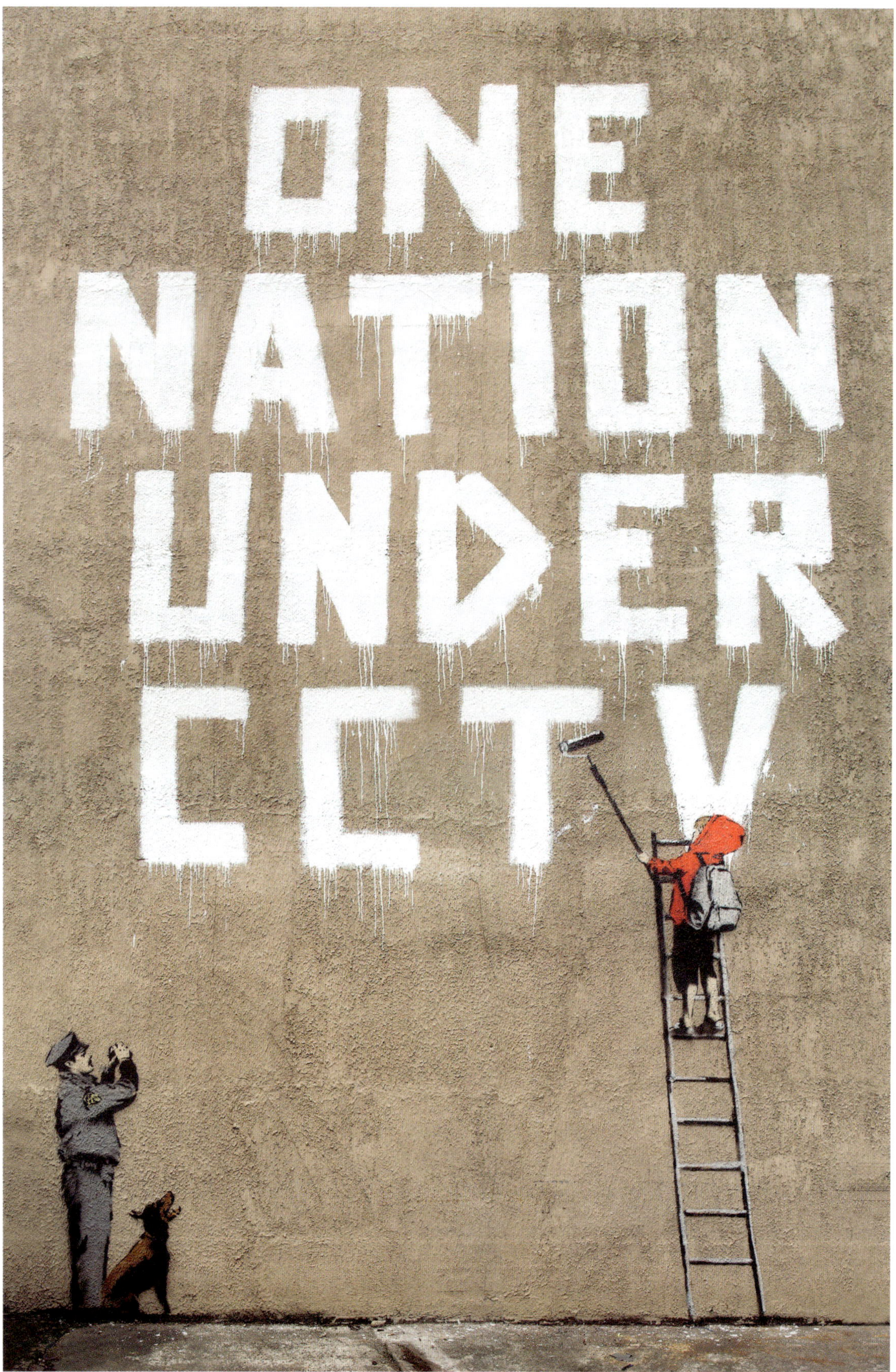

ONE
NATION
UNDER
CCTV

INTRODUCTION

During Banksy's 30 years as a street artist he has sprayed all kind of surfaces, primarily walls, obviously, but also doors – metal, roller and wood – pavements, traffic bollards, road signs, cars, vans, lorries, tube trains, balloons, bridges, Nelson's Column, Tate Britain, the National Theatre, skips, sheep, cows, pigs, one elephant, a farm gate, a boat, a beach wall, a breakwater, a model village, a cash machine, a water tank, a pub, a petrol station, a wheel clamp and a New York anti-graffiti sign, to list just some of his canvases. Yet today, sadly, very little of his work actually survives on the street in anything like its original form. He is a street artist whose pieces have gone absent without leave.

It has come to the point where even in his home town of Bristol, where he has painted 30 or perhaps 40 pieces over the years, Banksys are now few and far between. It is easy to reel off the favourites – *Well Hung Lover*, *Mild Mild West*, *Girl with a Pierced Eardrum*, and a couple more that are still there… just – but after that it is only in the safety of a school playground, a tattoo parlour and a museum that they have survived. And what is true of Bristol is equally true of other cities, like New Orleans, New York, Los Angeles, Toronto or Detroit, where his pieces have been and now are gone. London hardly fares any better.

So this is an unusual if not unique guidebook to the places where you can no longer see his masterpieces – and the sometimes incredible, sometimes laughable and sometimes sad stories of what happened to them. As Banksy says in

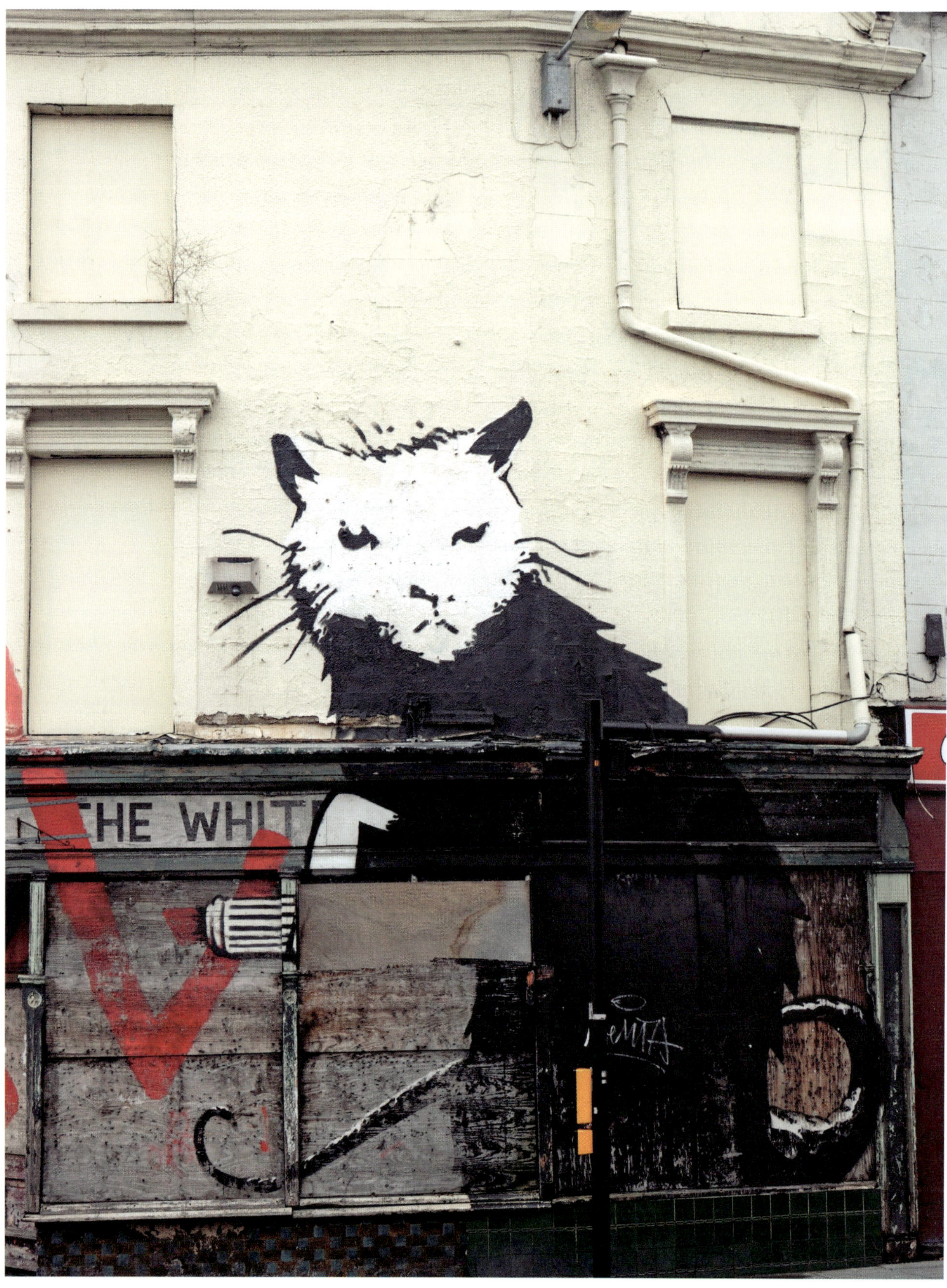
THE WHIT

Cut & Run, the book that accompanied his exhibition in Glasgow in 2023, 'It's got to the point where I'm not sure what part of this is the "art" any more. It doesn't seem to be about the painting so much as events that unfold around it.'

Graffiti has always been a transitory art but with Banksy it has become something of a split-second art. Blink and it is gone. Of course, in his early days he faced council clean-up teams eager to exterminate graffiti despite whoever painted it. But today local councils tend to fall at his feet, taking pride in the fact that they have their own Banksy bestowed upon them. Now he has new enemies, different but equally effective. One set, the dealers, who take his work off the wall both to preserve it and sell it. The second set are other graffiti artists – not all of them, but some – who would never use a stencil and regard him an outcast, a 'toy' painting for the masses instead of his self-absorbed peers. They want to destroy his work, not sell it.

His problems with dealers began almost 20 years ago when he painted a piece of graffiti called *WHAT?* on the back of a stall on London's Tottenham Court Road. The stallholder happily accepted £1,000 cash for the back of his stall. It soon sold again for £250,000. Banksy had been monetized and there was no turning back.

How sad. For he brings art, comment, laughter, a hint of something different to out-of-the-way places (easier to paint there) which need a bit of all that. I remember the joy of being among the crowds looking at and discussing his *Slave Labour* on the wall of a Poundland store in a slightly obscure part of North London – the excitement, the vitality of a mini gallery amid a everyday shopping street. And then it was gone, sold to America.

But it is also understandable. How can a painting by Banksy, protected by nothing but Perspex, sit on a wall in full view of every passer-by when other paintings by him are selling in auction rooms for millions? It is just not human nature to resist such temptation. Building owners and their agents will literally take off the whole side of a property if necessary to get to a Banksy. In Margate, for instance, where he painted a battered housewife on the end wall of a Victorian terraced house, they first had to take out the hallway floor and the stairs down to the cellar and up to the first floor. Only then, by dismantling the inner layer of the cavity wall, could they get to the back of the wall the piece was painted on. Then, the old grouting on the

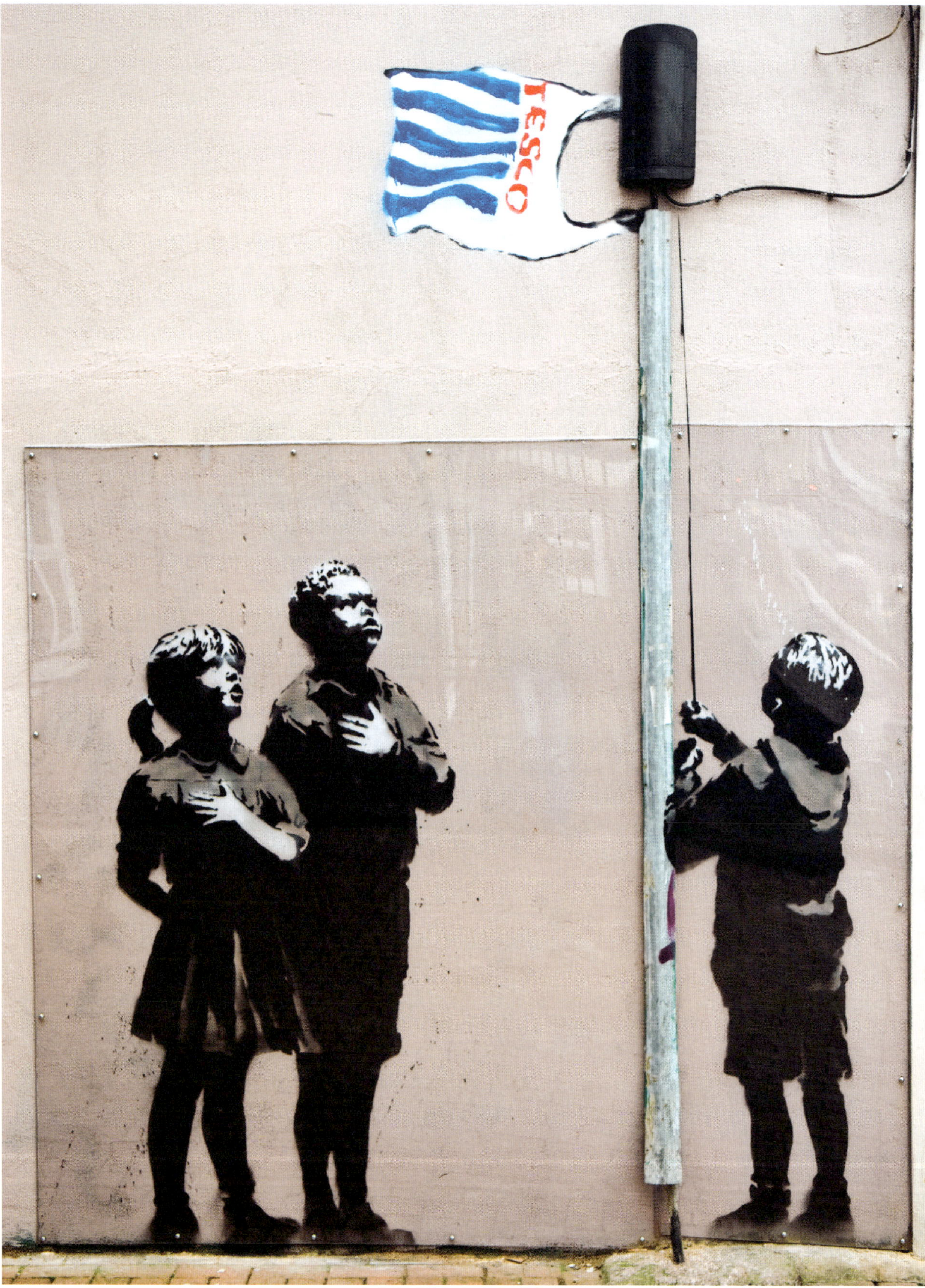

TESCO

outer wall was replaced by cement foam to stabilize the bricks and this in turn was covered by a tongue-and-groove backing board. Next came the steel and on it went until the wall was in a fit state to be cut out. Of course, once the housewife had gone everything had to be replaced or rebuilt. The bill for all this, including security, transport and restoration, was £205,000 and counting.

Banksy has always tried to keep his pieces where he painted them by refusing to authenticate any of his work taken off the street. He set up the appropriately named Pest Control to separate fakes from the real thing, and Pest Control will not give any pieces that are taken from the street their stamp of approval. Without that stamp the big auction houses will not touch them. So even though he has announced the arrival of a new work on Instagram and often pictured it later in his books, they still will not get the precious certificate of authenticity. The slight risk that the buyer may not be getting the real thing lowers the price accordingly and on occasions makes a piece impossible to sell.

Originally, my own slightly muddled view was that Banksy was wrong and the owners of the wall and the dealers were right: if Banksy's work is as good as I think it is, then it is worth saving for generations to come.

What changed me was a work on an isolated chunk of wall in an abandoned car factory in Detroit 'rescued' by a small, non-profit, art gallery. The wall it was painted on was soon to be demolished along with the rest of the factory, and the gallery saw itself as acting like a museum, preserving the Banksy for posterity. Yet five years later the gallery sent the wall to California for auction. Yes, the money was for a good cause, but Banksy's wall was lost to anyone but the buyer and his friends. His street art is better left to live and die in the context in which it was painted rather than being treasured by a private buyer or preserved – however painstakingly – by a museum.

Stephan Keszler, who for a time was the go-to dealer for anyone having a wall to sell in the USA and made big money out of it, disagrees quite heatedly. 'Eighty per cent of his works on the street have been destroyed by other street artists. I ask you: What is better, that the work is destroyed or that it is in someone's house or a museum or a gallery? I have some pieces which are still in my possession. If I did not have them they would have been destroyed... What we did to preserve

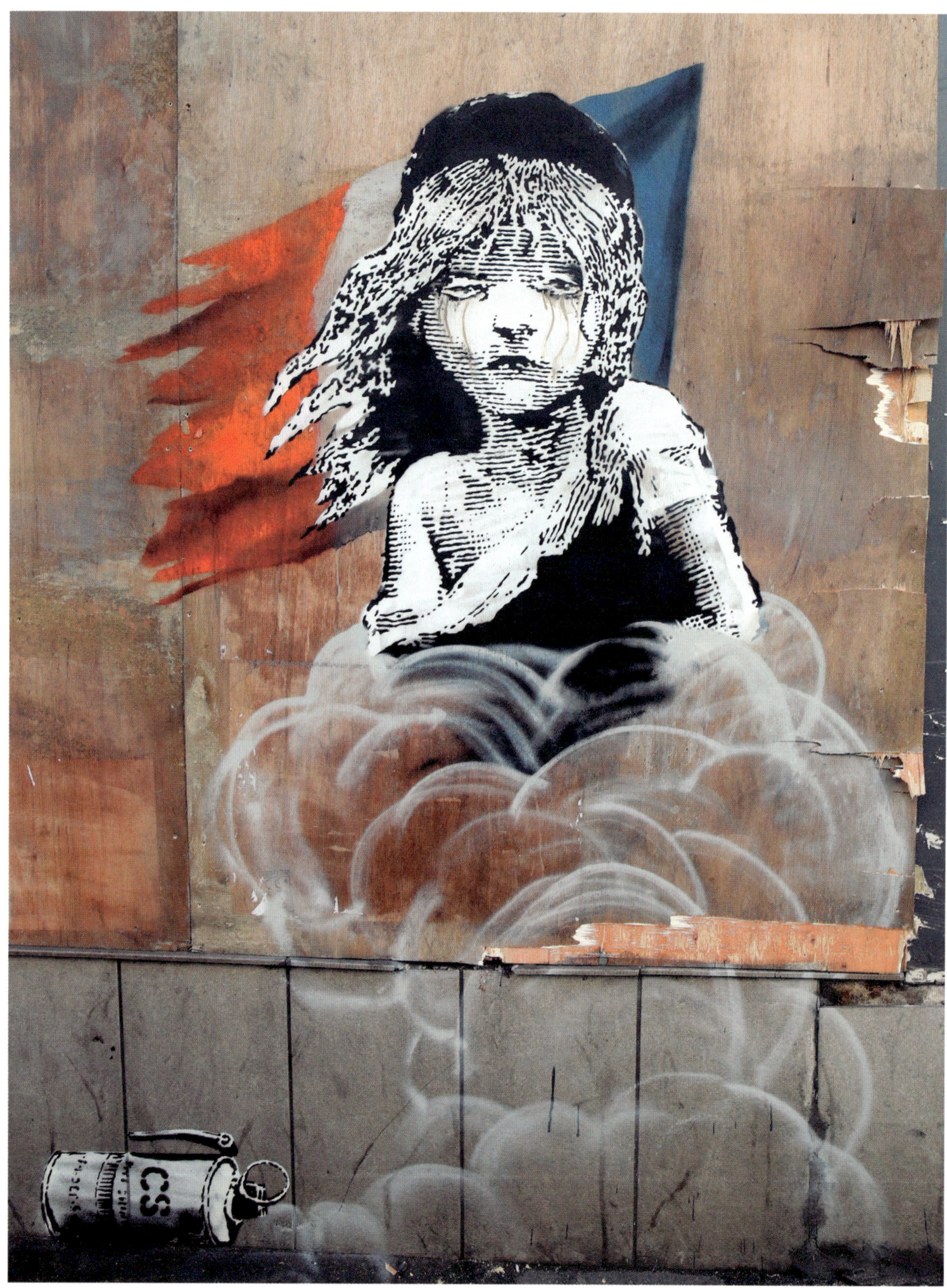

this work, you cannot even value it, it is unbelievable what good things we did. Thank God we were there and thank God we did it.'

Mr Keszler suggests 80 per cent of Banksy's works have been destroyed by other artists, but actually as no one has kept a tally, no one knows for sure although it is certainly a very large number.

Some graffiti artists enjoy putting their own tag across other people's work, a bit like a dog leaving its mark, and this is often the result of rivalries between graffiti crews, or else just jealousy. Others go over pieces because they want to paint the wall themselves – create their own 'burner' – and once they have painted it they know someone will come after them and repeat the process. It is simply part of life on the streets. But with Banksy it is different, and the difference is the venom with which they do it. They are not after a good wall to paint, they are after Banksy. Part of this, surely, has to be about pure envy at his success. But piled on top of this comes a long-running dispute with a prominent London graffiti artist, King Robbo, who died ten years ago. Banksy was accused of disrespecting him for painting over a piece of his which, remarkably for any piece of graffiti, had survived for 25 years. In return, followers of Robbo, or perhaps more accurately enemies of Banksy under the Robbo tag, are simply out to destroy him. In most cities around the world, if Banksy has been there, then sooner or later the Robbo tag will follow.

At the end of *Cut & Run*, Banksy says: 'The canvases, the prints, all the "proper" art I've made doesn't matter. Only the streetwork will last.' Taken literally this would mean that soon there will be nothing left of Banksy. But I think what he actually means is that the street is where the heart of his painting is, it is the vital context, it is where it matters. Take his work away from there and it is a far lesser creature.

Going to the opening of an exhibition, put on by his former agent in Mayfair, I was painfully aware of the difference between street and gallery. On display were some of his works sprayed on canvas, where the images were often the same as those on the streets, only smaller. The first-night sun-dried tomatoes and ricotta, the bubbly and the raw tuna probably did not help, but these works just did not have the same impact or importance as Banksy in his natural environment – even though it is these canvases that make Banksy his money.

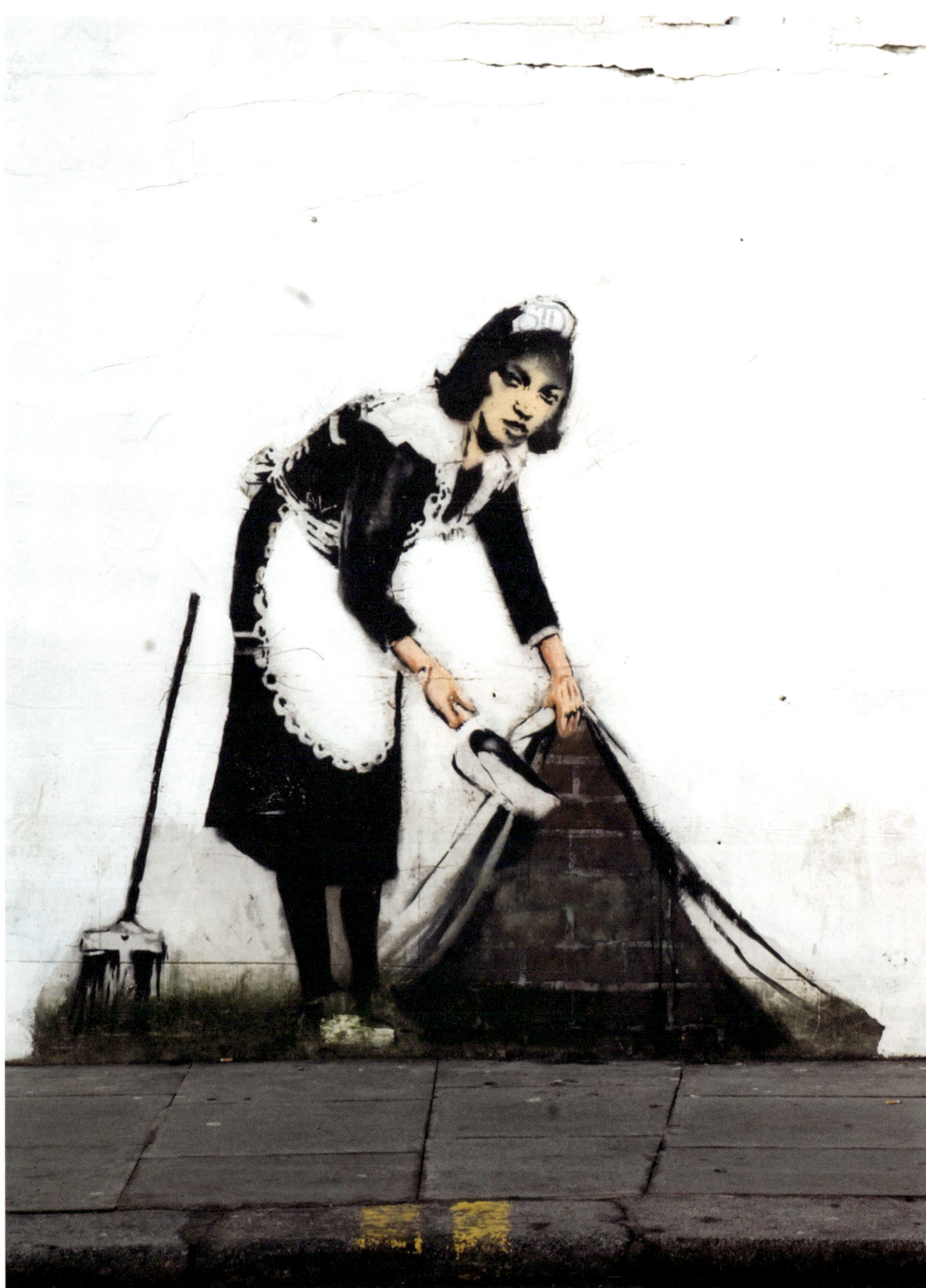

But at least the work on display was actually by Banksy, unlike the exhibition which opened at the 'Banksy Museum' in New York in May 2024, where there were 160 or so Banksys on the walls, but none of them by the artist himself. To explain: ten anonymous street artists had been hired to reproduce his work on the walls, and the museum came complete with noises from the street, hazard markings and police sirens in an attempt to give it the right edgy feeling. 'It has been our goal to present the art in the way that is as close to what the artist originally intended,' said the museum's executive director. 'We believe in the power of this art and that it has a spiritual quality unlike any other.' Quite apart from the spiritual quality of this work, it is hard to imagine that Banksy could ever have dreamt that his work would be copied into a 'museum' all in the name of preserving street art.

Even trying to retain and safeguard his work on the street is problematic. In Venice, for example, there has been a fight over *Migrant Child*, a piece on the waterline of the busy Rio Novo canal, between those who believe it should be preserved and those who feel it should be allowed to fade away naturally, helped by the waves of passing boats.

Banksy now appears fairly phlegmatic about all such arguments, although it is noticeable that many of his key later works have not been graffiti but huge and very successful installations, like *Dismaland* in Weston-super-Mare, *The Walled Off Hotel* in Bethlehem, or *Cut & Run* in Glasgow, where he retains total control of his work.

It would be impossible to cover every lost Banksy in one book but what I hope this guided tour will achieve is to document some of the key pieces that have vanished and the reasons – worthless or righteous – for their disappearance. As Banksy himself says, art comes alive in the arguments you have about it. Although he might hope that the arguments are about art, in many cases they are much more about money; but art, money or both, they are always compelling. Will his street art be remembered in a hundred years' time? Yes, I think so, but it shouldn't need a large chunk of wall carved from the street and expensively preserved in a museum for that to happen.

01
DROPPED WHILE
SHE SHOPPED

BRUTON LANE, LONDON W1J 6QH

When Banksy painted *Shop 'til you Drop* impossibly high up an office building in London's Mayfair, little could he or anyone else have imagined that it would be taken off the wall in one piece 12 years later to be put on the market with an asking price of $5 million.

The graffiti itself is a tribute to his chutzpah, his ingenuity and his skill with stencils. He painted it in broad daylight over a weekend. One Saturday morning in November 2011, professional scaffolders turned up outside the disused office building, erected the scaffolding, then finished it off with tarpaulin to cover the areas where Banksy was working. There was even some sort of 'security guard' protecting it. By 5pm on Sunday the scaffolding was gone, along with the security guard and all that was left was the Banksy on the wall.

The height of the building helps emphasize the obsession of the shopper, clutching her supermarket trolley whatever the cost to herself, and the shading he carefully created behind both the woman and her trolley makes it feel as though she really *is* falling. It is, or rather was, an amazing piece.

This height not only made the image work but serendipitously it protected the piece. Rival graffiti artists might have wanted to wipe it out but they were not going to hire the scaffolding needed to do so. It remained untouched and there were no tags from other artists that needed to be cleaned off.

When the building came down in 2023 (it is expected that a hotel will replace the office) the company demolishing it knew exactly what they had got and what condition it was in. They fitted a cage around the whole piece so that a crane could lift it off and take it into storage.

Now all that is needed is a buyer. Someone who has several million dollars to spare and room for a piece of art weighing just over 10 tons and measuring four metres square – probably the largest of all the Banksys to be taken off the wall in one piece.

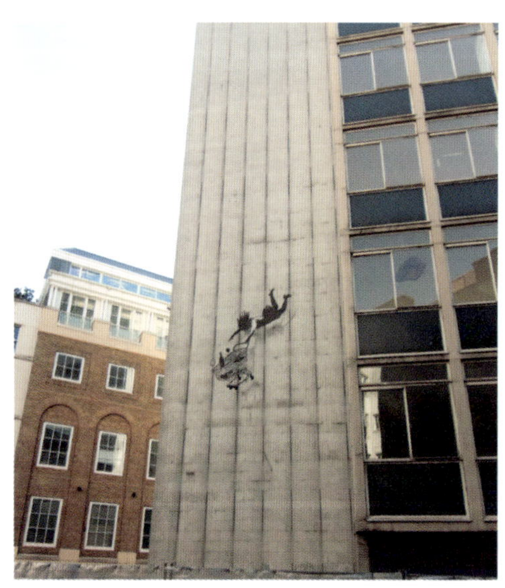

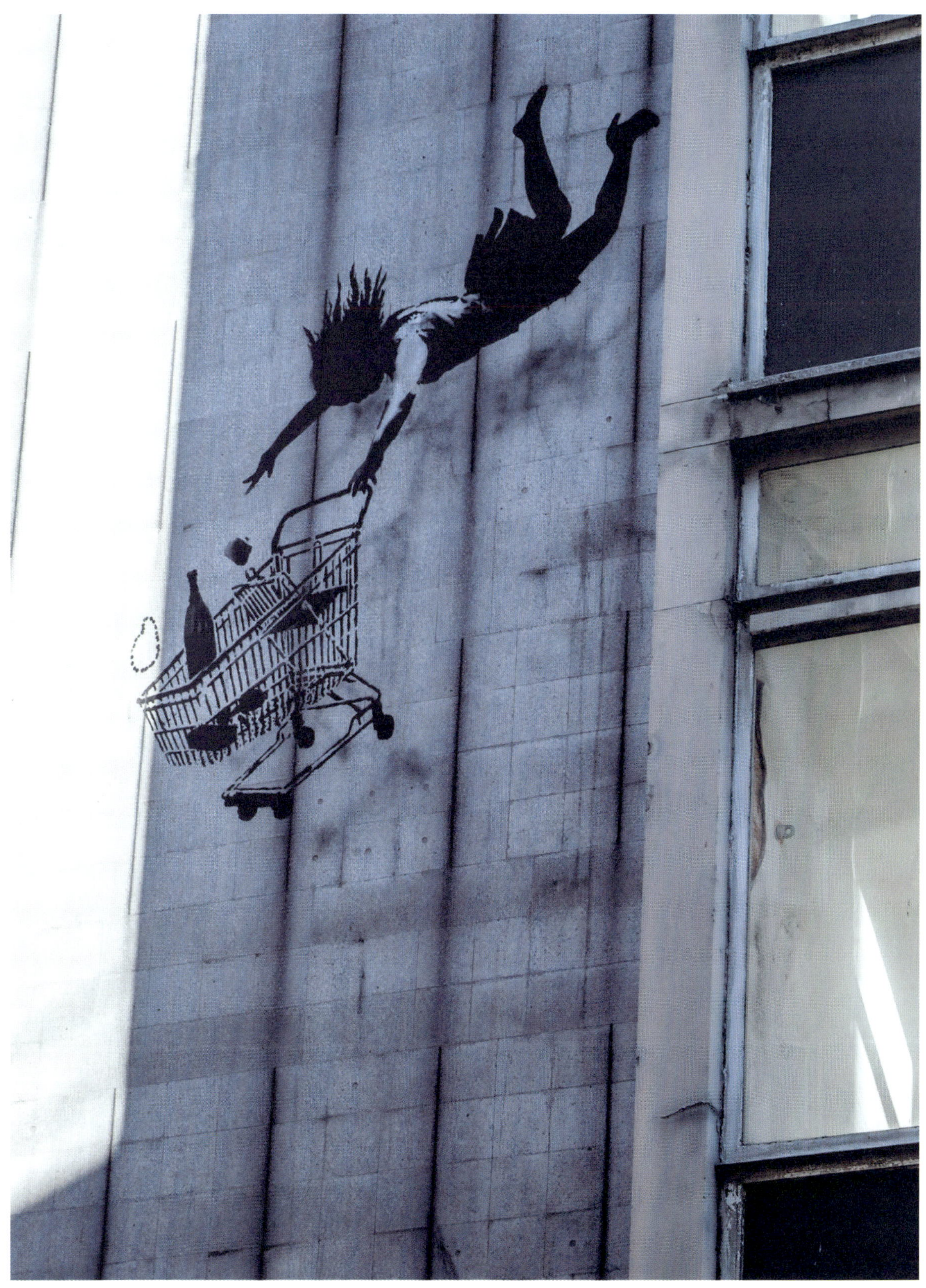

A COSTLY MISTAKE

TOTTENHAM COURT ROAD, LONDON W1T 1AP

It was 5am one morning in May 2006 and Banksy was at work at the back of a news-stand on Tottenham Court Road in central London. He had already got as far as stencilling a picture of a boy with a dripping paint brush in both hands, a paint pot beside him. This was an image he had used before, but each time he used it he changed the text that the boy was painting.

Before he left home he had copied down what he calls a 'rather clever quote' he had found, but when he reached in his pocket to get the quote, he remembered he had left it on the kitchen table.

As the city began to wake up, his lookout was getting increasingly antsy. 'What are you going to write?' the lookout asked him anxiously. 'What?'

'Good idea,' Banksy replied. 'I will paint that.'

So 'WHAT?' was exactly what the boy wrote in giant pink letters, and it seemed just right. A question for which neither the puzzled-looking boy nor anyone else had the answer.

The stall was owned by a street trader named Sam Khan, who knew all about tourist knick-knacks, football scarves and luggage but nothing about Banksy. So when he was offered £1,000 for the back of his stall, he took the money. By the time he realized his mistake, it was far too late. 'I've had people coming up to me saying, "How did you not know who Banksy is?" and "Why didn't you go on the internet?" I'm on the stall for twelve hours a day. I don't follow these things.'

From there *WHAT?* made its way to Robin Barton, who had just opened a small Notting Hill art gallery called Bankrobber and was beginning to realize how much money there was to be made out of Banksy's works taken off walls, stalls, wherever, even if Banksy refused to authenticate them. Just 18 months after *WHAT?* had been painted, Barton was standing in front of Matthew Freud, founder and head of Freud Communications, who asked him, 'Why should I buy this work?'

Barton wrote later, 'I had prepared to roll out my laboured and much rehearsed pitch, the art bullshit. But instead I falter, hesitate and turn theatrically to point at six partially obscured letters crudely stencilled to the front of the paint pot that read: "BANKSY". '

That was enough to do it. The work was sold to Freud for £250,000 and it is now part of an entertainingly diverse collection which greets visitors to Freud's office in London's Fitzrovia. Freud got a bargain, but what this sale did was open everyone's eyes to what a Banksy on a wall could be worth. From then on, wherever and whatever surface Banksy painted he had to recognize that the chances of his work staying there were small.

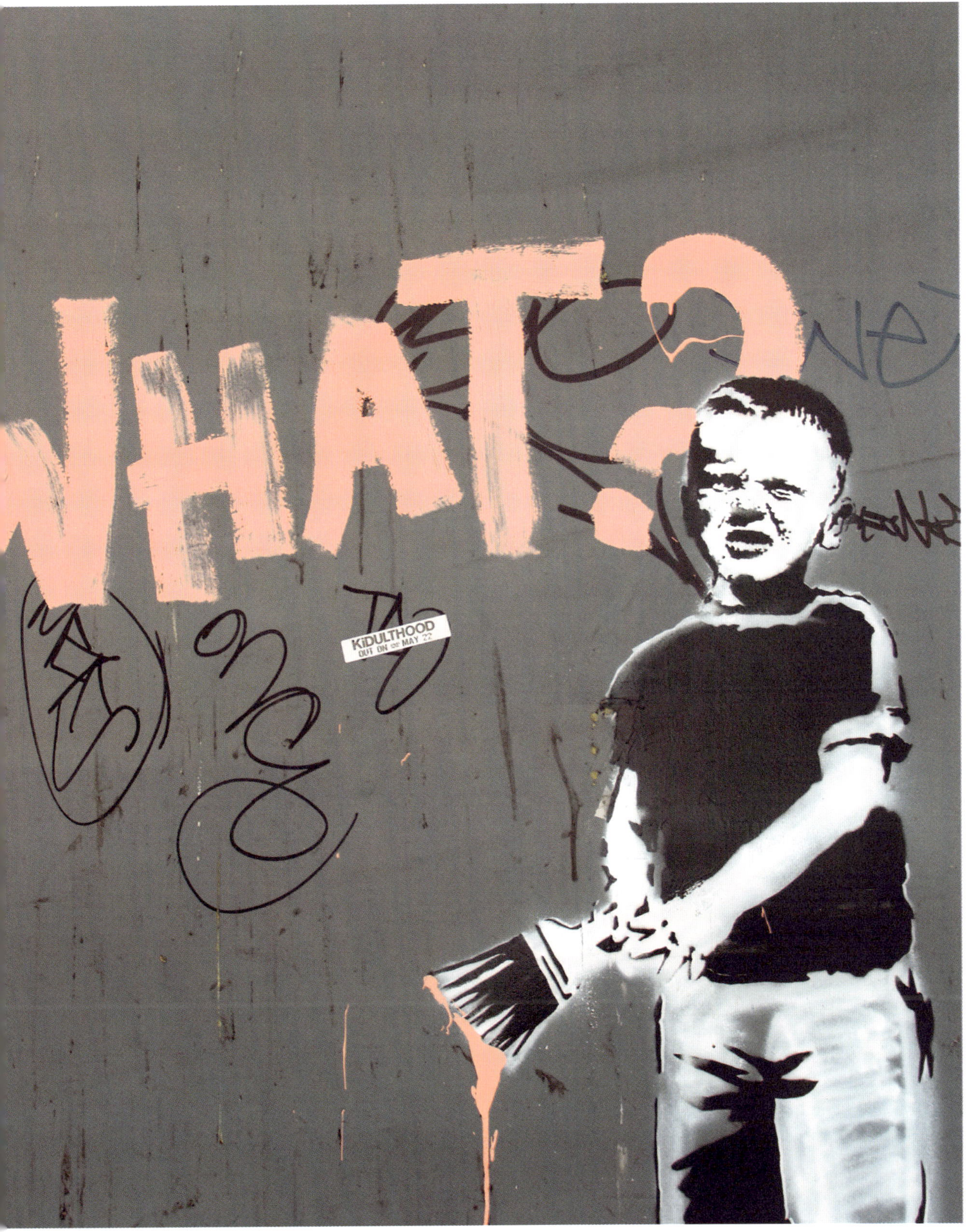

WHAT?
KiDULTHOOD
OUT ON DVD MAY 22

PARIS BANDITS

📍 PASSAGE ST-PIERRE-AMELOT, 75011 PARIS

In January 2019 three men drove their large white Citroen van down the narrow Passage St-Pierre-Amelot in Paris and stopped right outside an emergency door of the Bataclan nightclub.

This was the door that concert goers had used to escape from the terrorist attack on the Bataclan four years earlier which left 90 dead and more than 300 injured. It was the door on which Banksy painted *Sad Young Girl* in June 2018. It was lucky it had survived at all because the door was a regular spot for graffiti, which was always painted over by the club, but this time a manager at the Bataclan had said, 'Hang on, this looks pretty unusual.' Instead of being destroyed it quickly became a moving memorial to all those who had lost their lives.

Unfortunately, this was the door the three men wanted. Armed with a crowbar and angle grinder, it took them no more than three or four minutes to take the door off its hinges and escape with it in their van. It was four in the morning and no one was around, and although CCTV captured every move they made, including the sparks from the grinder, they were hooded and the van's number plate was blanked out.

From Paris the door went south to the Alps, then over the border to Italy. There it sat, first in the cellar of a hotel in the seaside town of Tortoreto in Abruzzo, before being hidden in the attic of a farm in Sant'Omero, 15 minutes away.

After 18 months the French and Italian police – tipped off by the ex-girlfriend of one of the thieves – caught up with the door, which they found in surprisingly good condition.

The problem for the thieves had always been not stealing the piece but selling it. The man who reluctantly helped hide it told the thieves, 'You've gone and stolen the only unsellable Banksy in the world.' The lawyer for one of the eight men eventually charged and convicted either of the theft or receiving stolen goods said, 'It would be like trying to re-sell the Mona Lisa.'

During the time the door was missing, it became something more to France than a piece of graffiti; it was as if the thieves had stolen a gravestone. So in a ceremony with honours that would be worthy of the Mona Lisa, it was handed back to France by the Italian police on Bastille Day 2020.

Did everything end happily ever after? No. Sadly, as can often happen where Banksy and money are involved, the owners of the building and the city of Paris engaged in a protracted legal wrangle over who owned the door. It was only settled in 2024 when an appeal court ruled in favour of the owners. After the verdict, one of the owners said that the door would never leave France and that if they sold it the city of Paris would have first refusal – a measure of just how important a symbol the Bataclan Banksy had become.

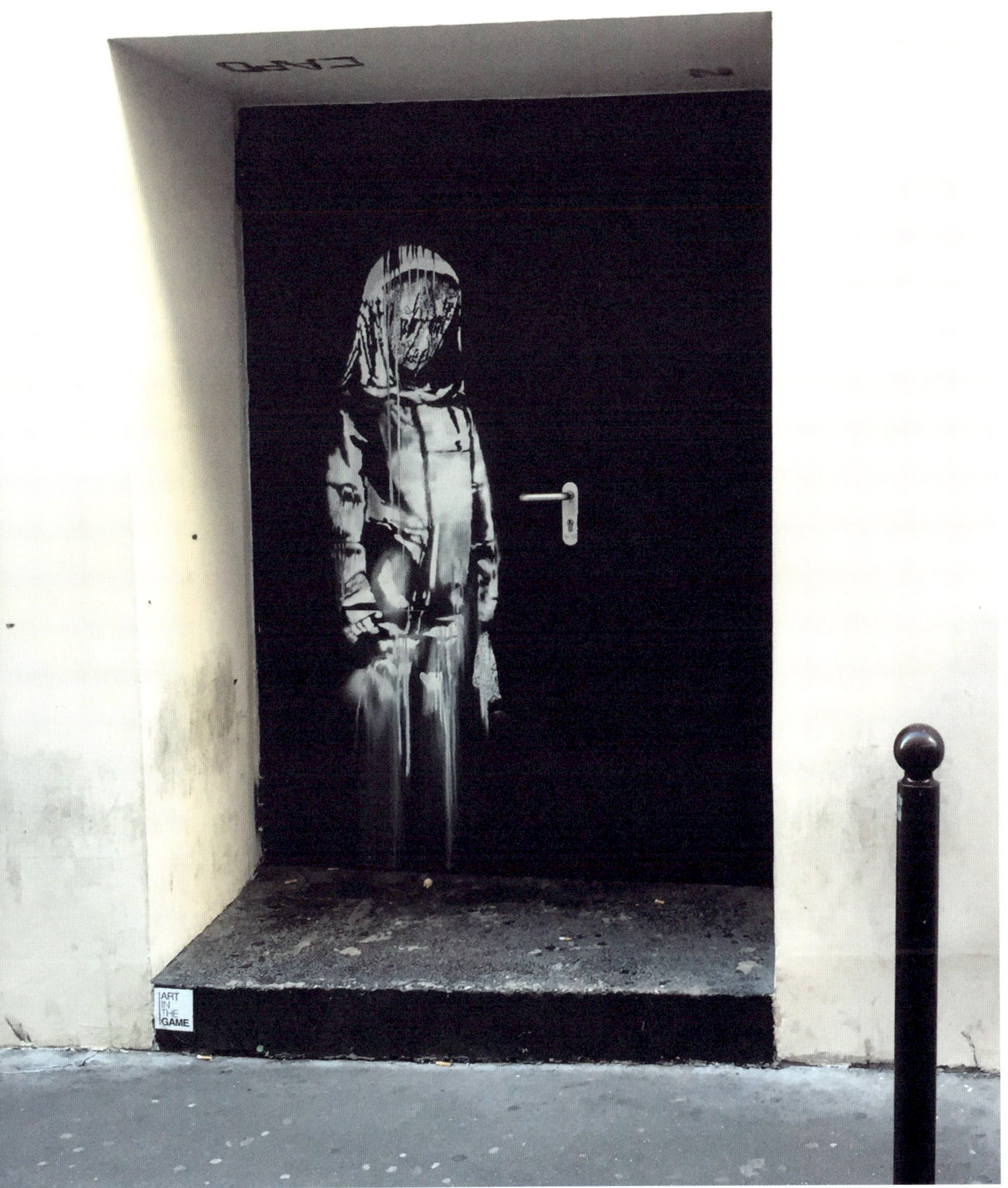

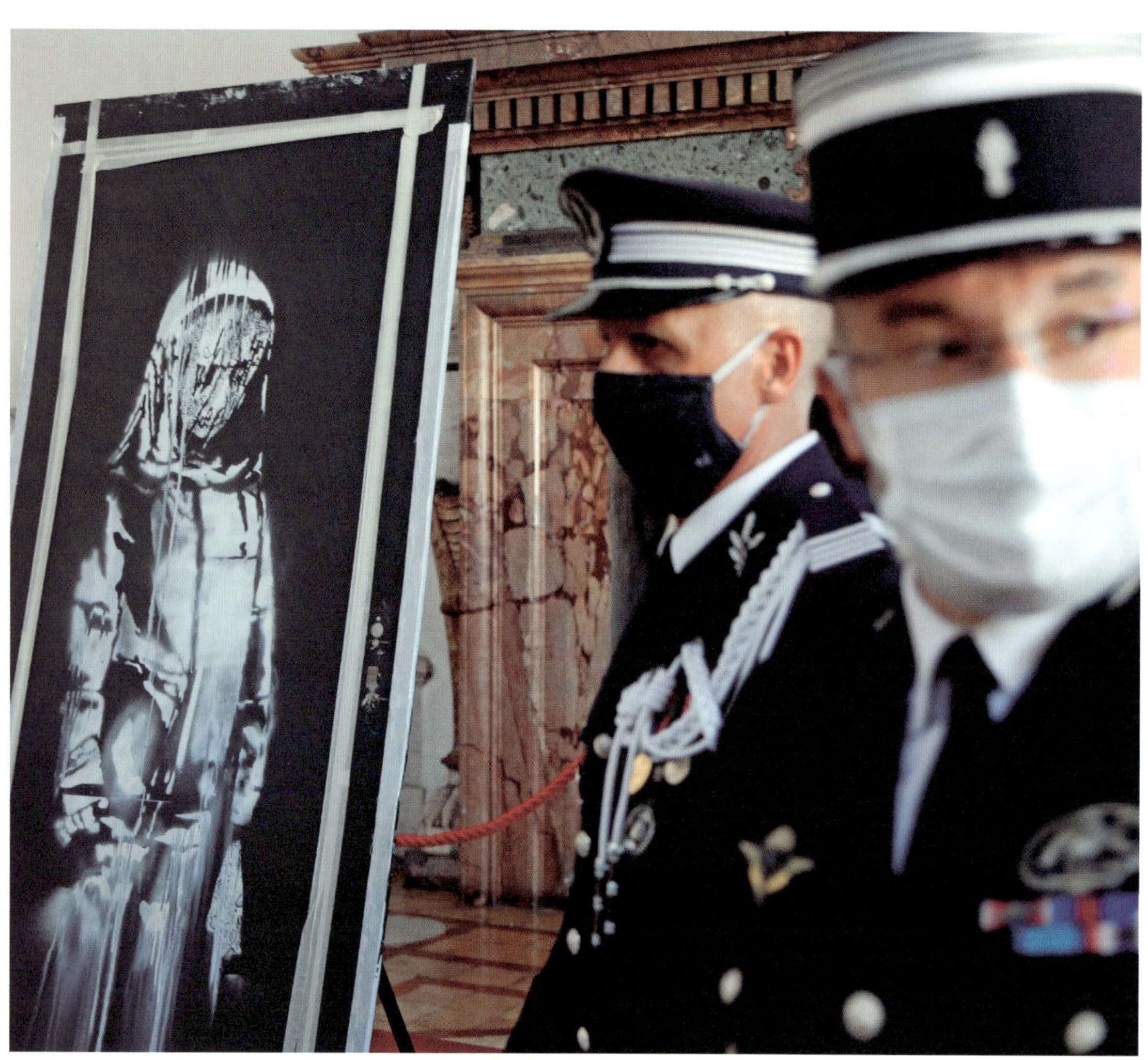

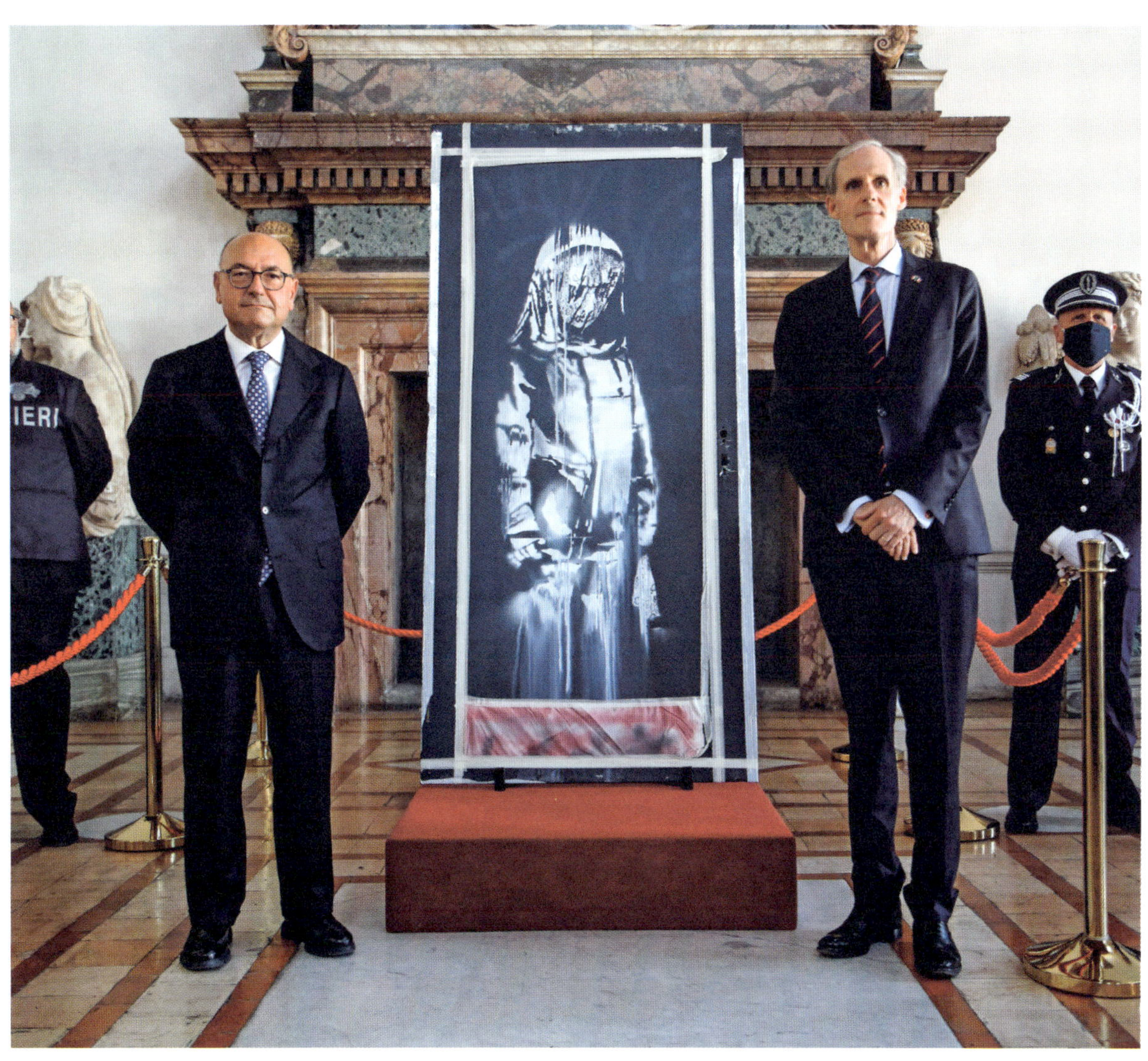

TRAPPING AN ELEPHANT

⚲ PACIFIC COAST HIGHWAY, BETWEEN CHAUTAUQUA BOULEVARD AND TEMESCAL CANYON ROAD, NEAR SANTA MONICA

This water tank turned elephant sitting in the foothills alongside the Pacific Coast Highway between Malibu and Santa Monica had a short life: from elephant to scrapyard within ten months.

In 2011, days before the Oscars, with Banksy's film *Exit Through the Gift Shop* up for an award, he arrived in Los Angeles to publicize the film in his own unique way. He saw in the water tank what no one else had ever seen: the tank, with its dangling spout/trunk, did look just a little bit like an elephant.

Rather than painting a couple of unimaginative elephant ears on it, he simply wrote across the tank, 'This Looks A Bit Like An Elephant', then put a picture on his website.

Two very keen Californian Banksy fans, Tavia and Christian, both in their twenties, went after it in a very determined, efficient American way.

Tavia told me, 'We wanted it so bad. We were both huge Banksy fans and we wanted to be a part of the whole Banksy movement.' They recruited two friends to join them. These friends ran a waste-disposal business and therefore had access to the heavy-lifting equipment they needed. They researched the ownership of the tank and bought it off the City of Los Angeles for several thousand dollars. (What their research did not

show them was that a homeless man had been living in it only months before it was cut down.)

In just over two weeks the elephant had been cut down, put on a truck and sent to a warehouse for storage. Their motives, it seems, were mixed. Tavia said they were on a rescue mission; they saw it as 'a very special piece, different from anything else he had ever done.' But having saved it, they wanted to sell it.

It was only when they put their elephant up for sale that they discovered that Banksy refused to authenticate any piece taken off the street, whether it be an elephant or a car door. 'There were buyers who were willing to throw money at us, but they needed that piece of paper,' said a very frustrated Tavia. Storage costs mounted so fast that by the end of the year they had to scrap the elephant.

Tavia and Christian were unsuccessful front-runners – too early for their own good. There was absolutely no doubt at all that it was a Banksy and a few years later, when extracting Banksys from the street and selling them without authentication had become quite common, they could have sold their elephant. Instead they were left with a large bill and, as Tania said, feeling 'super-sad.'

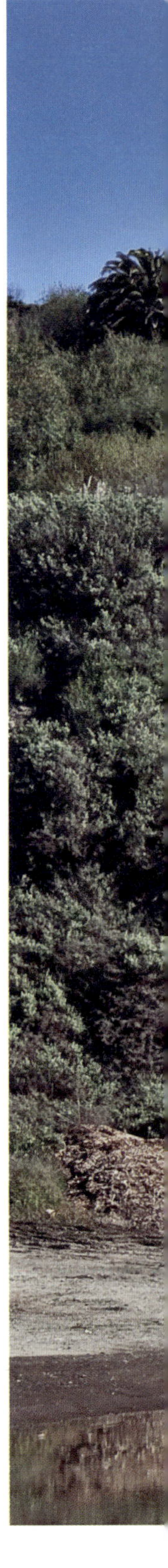

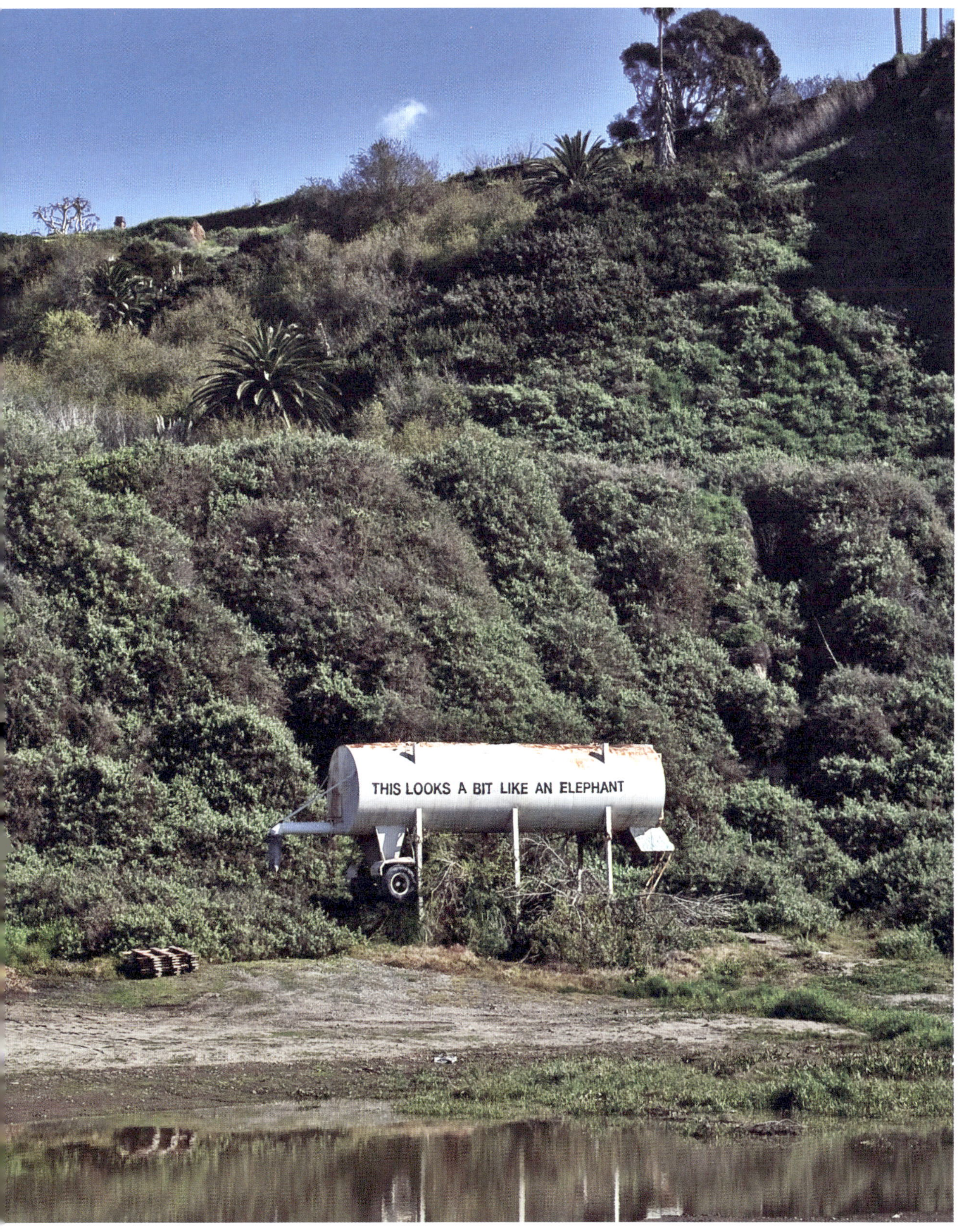

THIS LOOKS A BIT LIKE AN ELEPHANT

STREET FIGHTERS

⦿ REGENT'S CANAL TOWPATH, LONDON NW1 9LP

To an outsider the feud between the old-school graffiti artist King Robbo and the new kid on the block, Banksy, must be difficult to comprehend. But its effect has been long-lasting. Quite simply, if there had been no feud there would be many more Banksys surviving on the walls. Even now, ten years after Robbo's death, if his followers hear of a new Banksy, they make it their mission to find and destroy it.

In 1985 Robbo painted *Robbo INC*, a large, colourful piece, on a wall beside the canal very close to Camden Lock in London. It was difficult to get at and so there it stayed, scrawled on but never obliterated. To stay undefeated on a wall this long is, in graffiti terms, almost a miracle. And there it probably would have stayed but for some sort of late-night macho argument between Banksy and Robbo in a bar in Shoreditch – 'He was a cocksure young toy', Robbo told me. According to Robbo, Banksy claimed to have no idea who he was, so 'I went bang and give him a backhander' and told him, 'You might not have heard of me, but you'll never fucking forget me, will you?' Banksy denied all this, and when Robbo's version of the dispute got out some years later, he decided it was time to get his own back. He cleverly transformed the original piece, stencilling a workman to make it look as though Robbo had done nothing more than a quick wallpaper job.

In turn, Robbo crossed the canal early on Christmas morning, using a blow-up mattress and a wetsuit, and did his own transformation, leaving the stencilled workman but changing what he appeared to be pasting up to KING ROBBO. This was too tempting for Banksy, who simply added FUC to KING to make FUCKING ROBBO.

It might seem that the graffiti world is a lawless one, but there are rules, and one of them is that you respect your elders – the Kings – and particularly any long-surviving piece of theirs. As a stencil artist Banksy has always been anathema to the pure graffiti world, and being such a successful stencil artist makes it even worse. Robbo declared, 'He started it, I'm going to finish it', and he and his team went round London defacing any Banksy they could find – usually leaving a 'Team Robbo' tag just to emphasize what they had done and who they were doing it for. His death, after a fall on the steps to his home, has stopped nothing, for Team Robbo is more than just friends of Robbo – it is anyone in the enclosed, macho graffiti world who sees Banksy as a sell-out.

Ironically, the feud lifted Robbo out of the 'pure' graffiti world and into the world of Shoreditch galleries. But for Banksy the feud was just trouble: hard enough being a street artist anyway; even harder if your work is going to be prised off the wall or tagged, 'Team Robbo', or both.

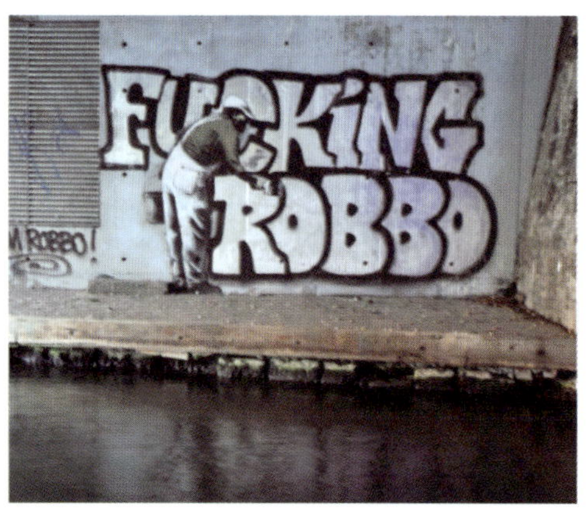

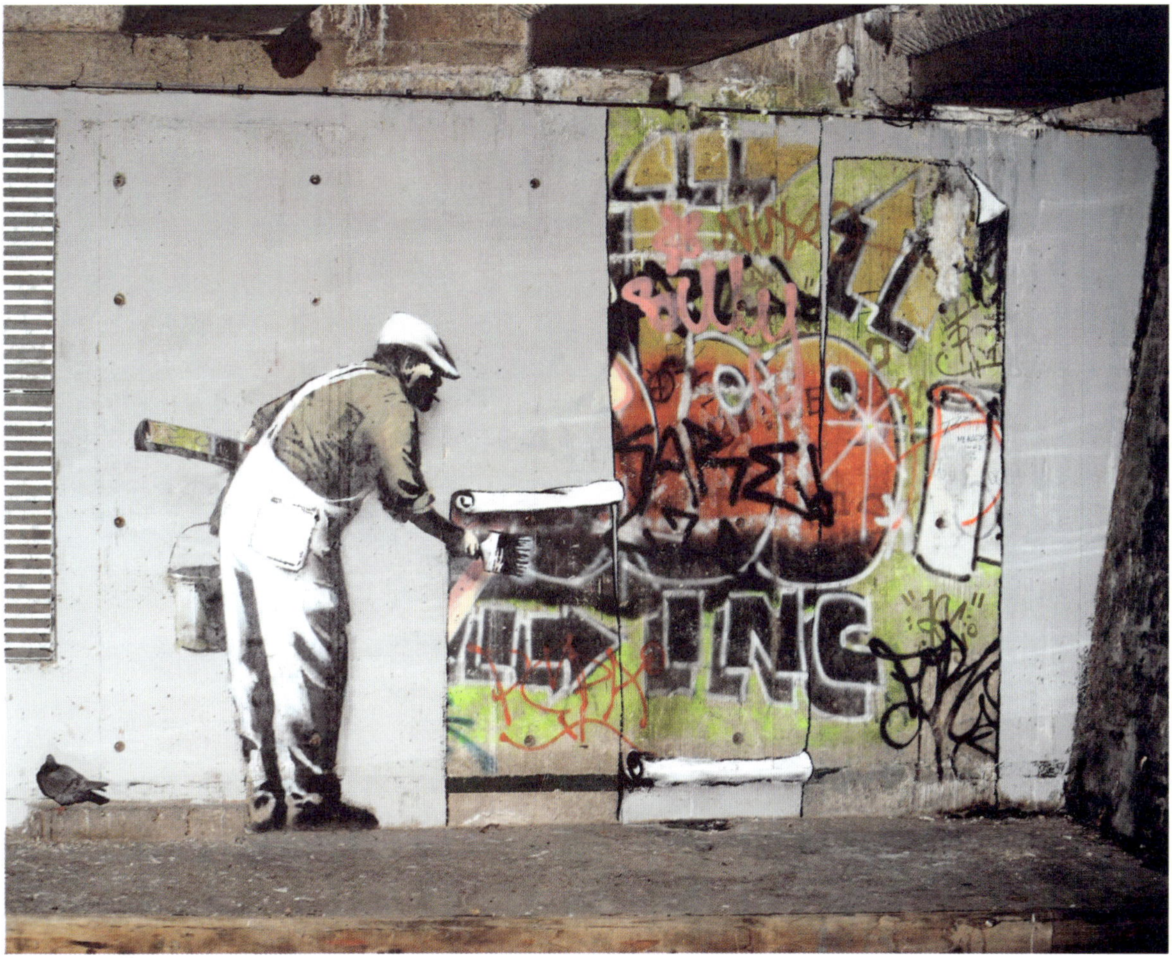

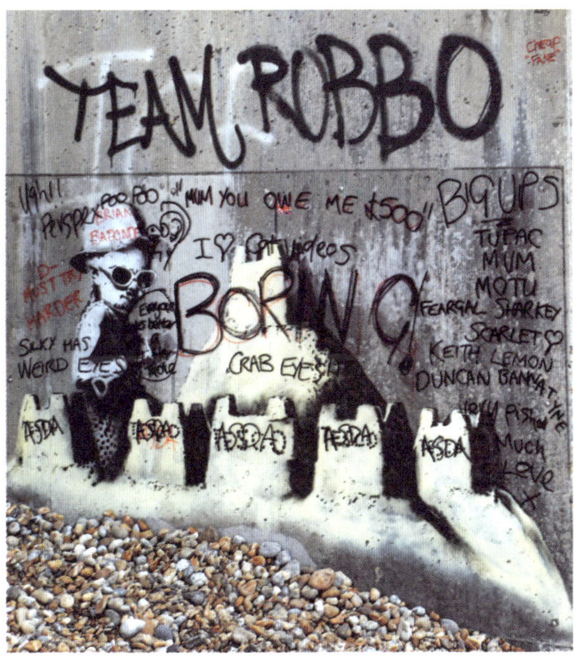
TEAM ROBBO
MUM YOU OWE ME £500
BIG UPS
TUPAC
MUM
MOTU
FEARGAL SHARKEY
SCARLET
KEITH LEMON
DUNCAN BANNATYNE
CRAB EYES
ASDA
ASDA
ASDA
ASDA
ASDA

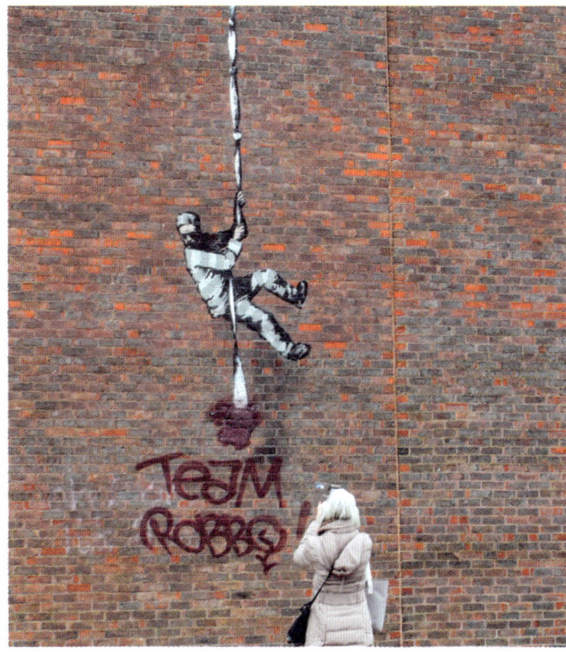
TEAM
ROBBO

THE DOCTOR WON'T SEE YOU NOW

CHINATOWN EASTERN BAKERY, 720 GRANT AVENUE, SAN FRANCISCO CA 94108

In the notes that went with his exhibition in Glasgow in 2023, Banksy is quite starry-eyed about this doctor. 'I first painted this character in downtown San Francisco, the birthplace of peace and love. He's been preserved there ever since complete with a sign asking people not to damage because it's very hard to get one [a doctor]'.

Perhaps Banksy's view of San Francisco dates back to the 1960s when it was all long-haired flower power rather than the reality of today's rougher city. The *Peaceful Hearts Doctor* used to sit on the wall of the Eastern Bakery in Chinatown, but far from being preserved over time, Banksy's doctor was defaced many years ago. Now it is Bruce Lee who has replaced him and, although he was much more than just a martial-arts film star, he was certainly no cardiologist.

Orlando Kuan, the owner of the Eastern Bakery, is not sure how long the doctor survived. Looking back 14 years after it was painted, he thought it might have been about four months, but actually it was considerably more than that, although nothing like the time that Banksy suggests. Soon after it was painted it was covered with a protective screen. It was not Mr Kuan who put the screen up, but he says the Chinese sign might be his because 'sometimes I like to do that'. It was painted in April 2010, and within 18 months the doctor was surrounded by two huge dragons snarling away. Although they rather overwhelmed the doctor, they did not quite trespass into his territory. But within two years the doctor had been obliterated by black paint poured between the wall and the protective screen.

'I don't think they were specifically attacking Banksy,' says Mr Kuan. 'They just like to erase everything.'

Bruce Lee has been up for about two years and so far he has managed to survive, although his time will come too. His survival is probably accounted for by the fact that he was born in San Francisco, his films were so popular and he has become something of an Asian-American icon. Whatever the reason, Mr Kuan says he seems rather more popular than Banksy's peaceful doctor.

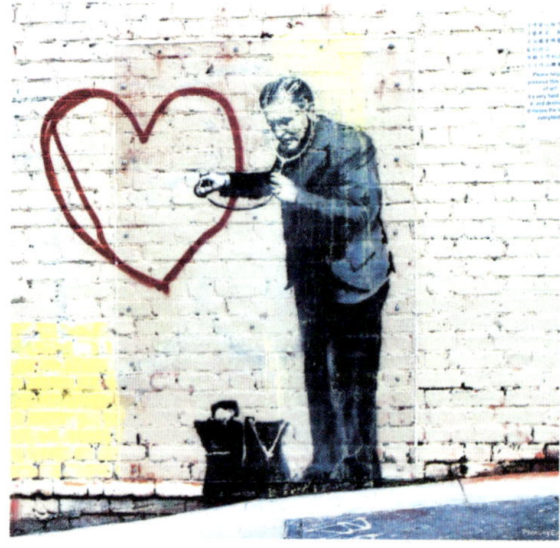

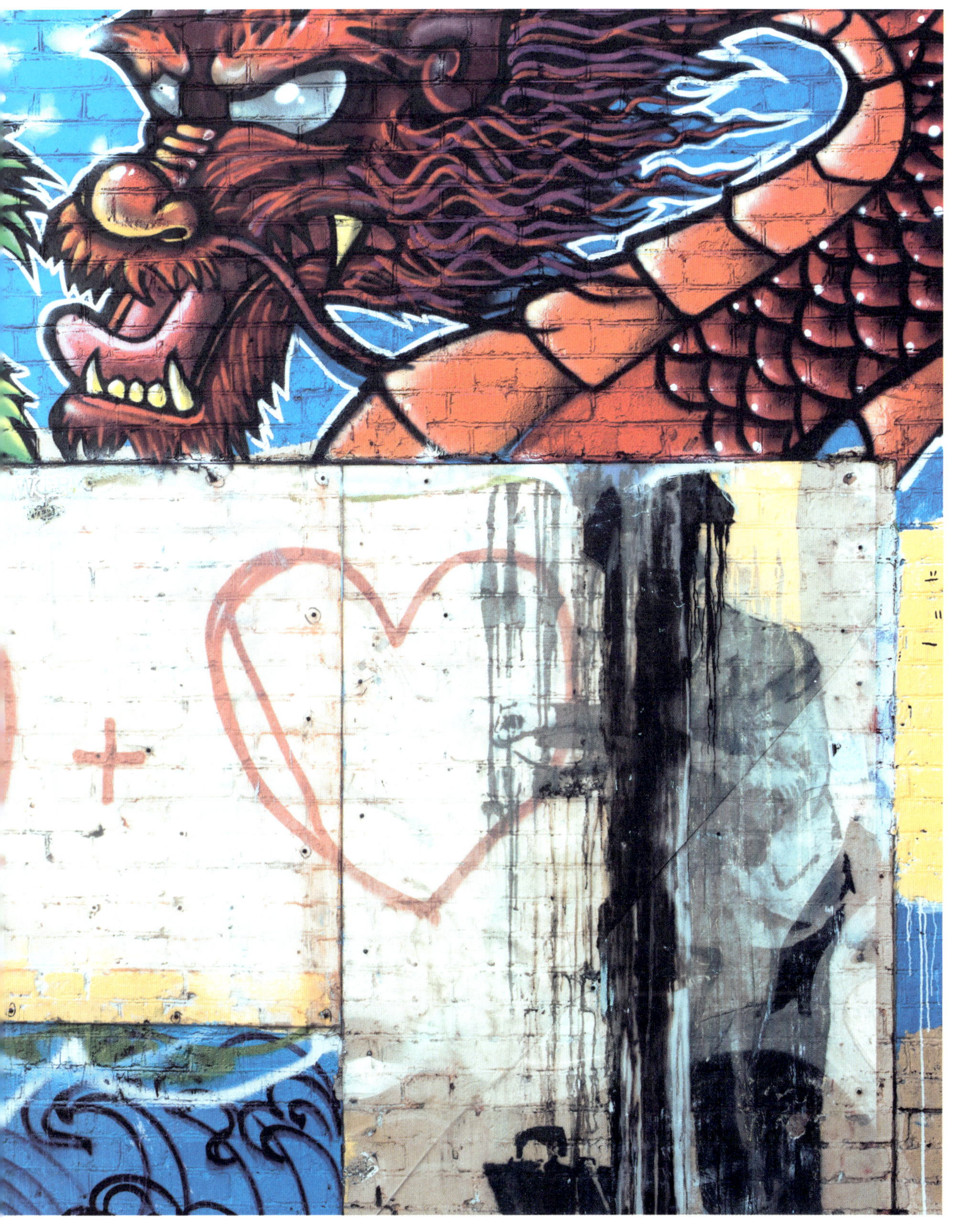

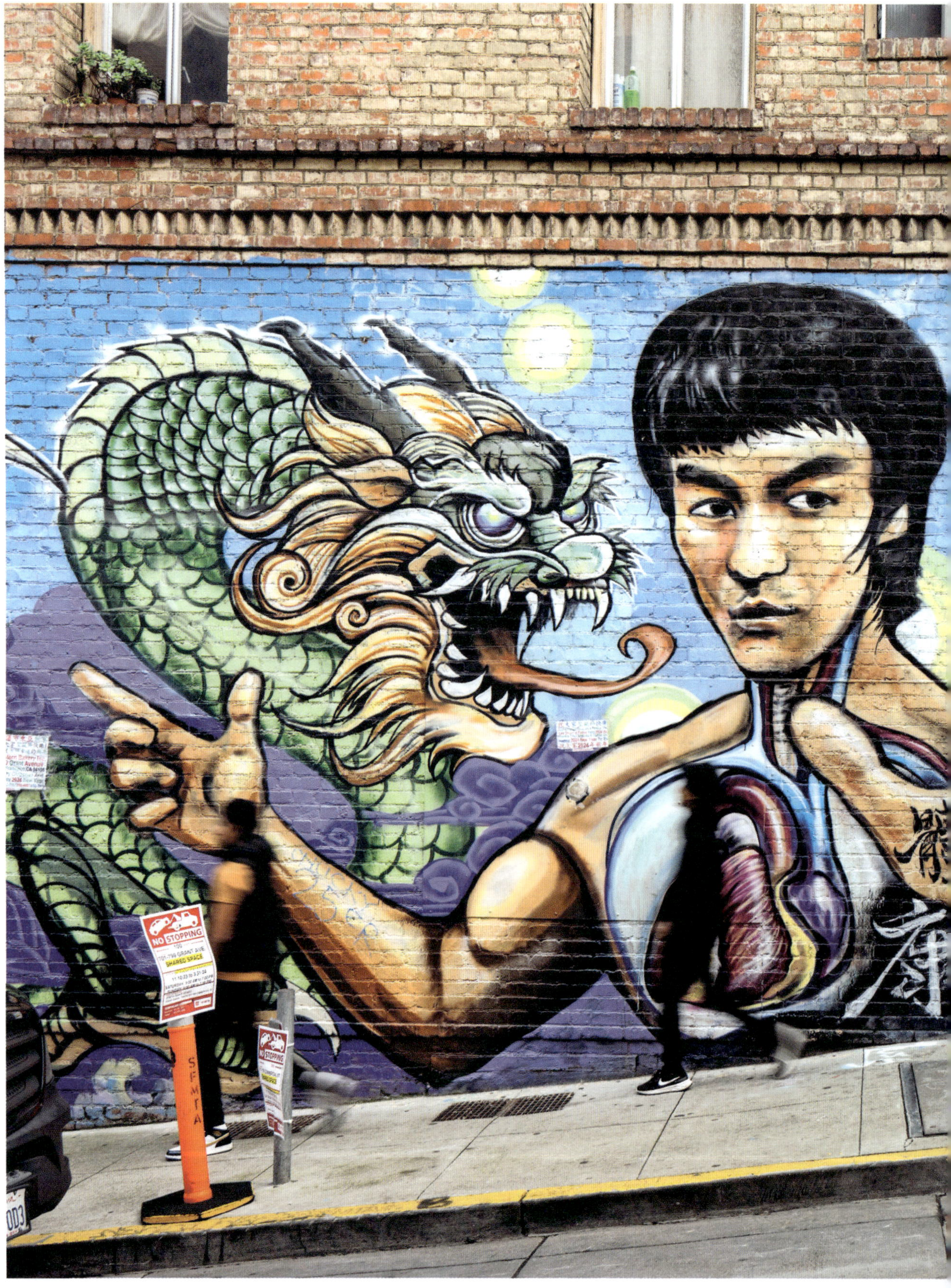

NO STOPPING
701-799 GRANT AVE
SHARED SPACE
SFMTA

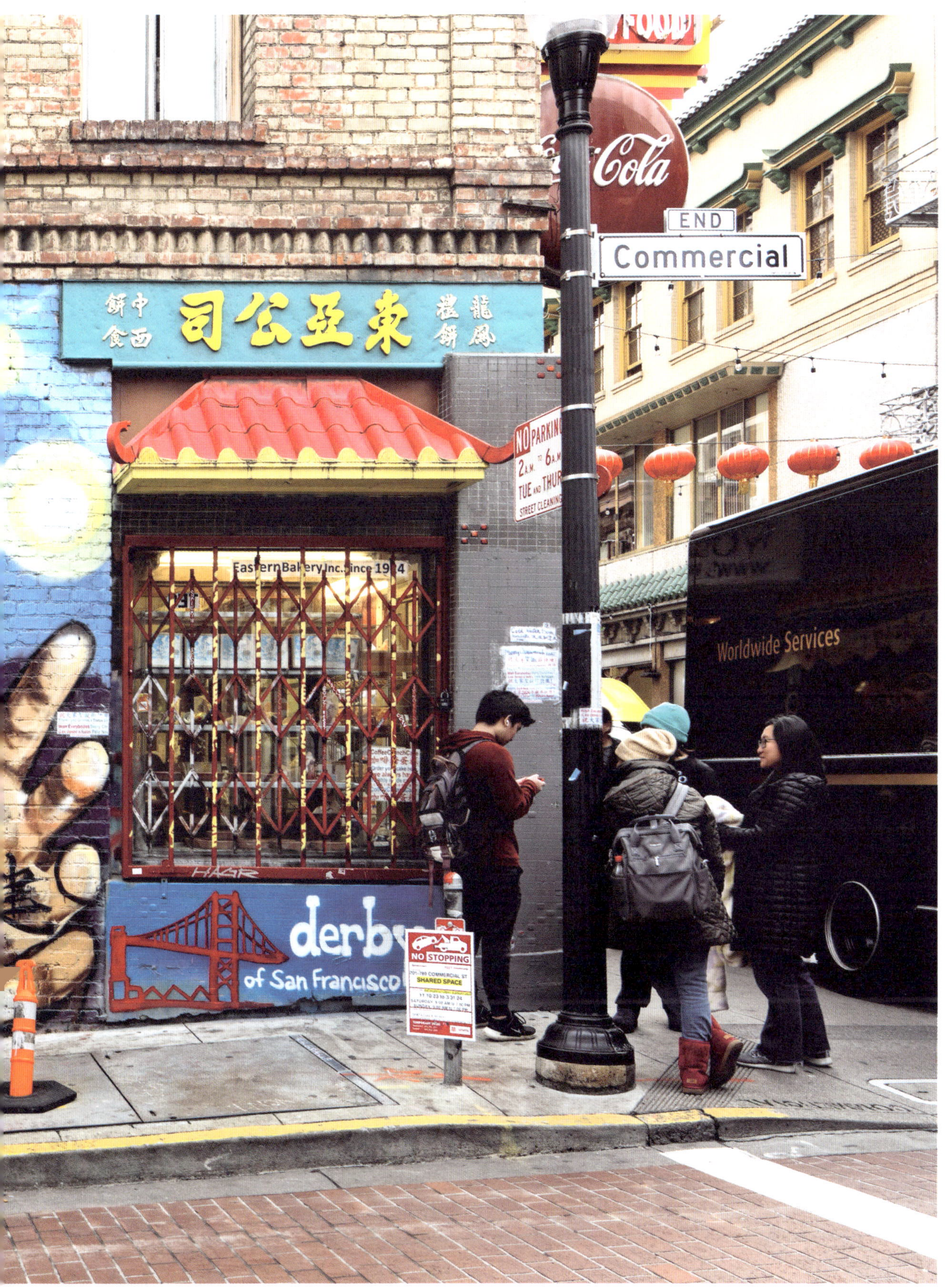
餅中
食西
龍鳳
司公亞東
禮餅
Coca-Cola
END
Commercial
Eastern Bakery Inc. since 1924
NO PARKING
2 A.M. TO 6 A.M.
TUE AND THUR
STREET CLEANING
HAGR
derby
of San Francisco
Worldwide Services
NO STOPPING
701-799 COMMERCIAL ST
SHARED SPACE
FOOD

THERE'S A LEOPARD UNDER THE BED

◯ PEMBROKE ROAD, BRISTOL BS8 3BE

Banksy's *Barcode Leopard* has been prowling around quite a few cities over the years. There have been at least two in Bristol, one in Brick Lane, London, and another in Manchester. But this Leopard, in the Bristol suburb of Clifton, is probably the original one and certainly the only one to survive, albeit under a bed rather than on a wall.

It was painted around 1998 on a wall which was all that was left of an end-of-terrace Georgian house that had been bombed during World War II. In 2010 the architect for the new town house to be built there got permission from his client, the owner of the site, to take the leopard off the wall before it was destroyed. He spent just three or four hours one Bank Holiday weekend getting it off. 'The render was about four inches thick so I took a disc cutter and some tools and cut a 100mm channel around it and then just slowly eased it off.' Amazingly it came off in one piece – he did not need the black gaffer tape he had stuck across the front in case it started to break up.

He wrapped it in a blanket, put it in his car and drove home. There he hid it under the bed and set off for a family camping holiday, all in the same day.

The architect prefers not to be named – but he says, 'We have no shame about owning a Banksy, we just don't want nutters at the door.' Why did he do it? 'To me it was more about the technical challenge of doing it than anything else.' He says, quite rightly, that it is not 'the greatest quality Banksy ever done', but he sees it as a sort of 'historical' piece. He has been offered substantial sums of money for it but 'that's not what it's all about.'

The first anyone knew he had it was in 2014 when his wife took it to the school where she worked as a teacher, in Nailsea near Bristol, to help promote the school open evening. He offered it to Bristol Museum on a sort of permanent loan but was told the museum already had a couple of Banksys and did not need any more. He then lent it to the Art of Banksy exhibition, first in Manchester and then in London. 'I know Banksy has this philosophy that street art is for everybody to see, so I thought it would be nice if people could go to see it.' Did he get paid for this? 'No, they do pay but I didn't think it would be right to take any money. I just asked them to insure it.'

So what next? 'I don't really know what to do with it, to be honest. I think I will let it become my children's problem.'

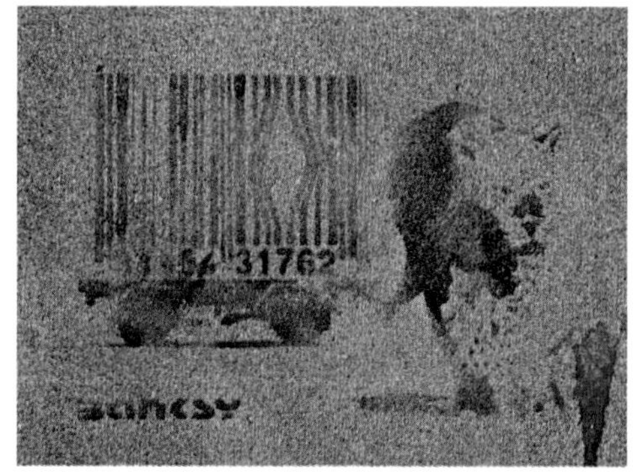

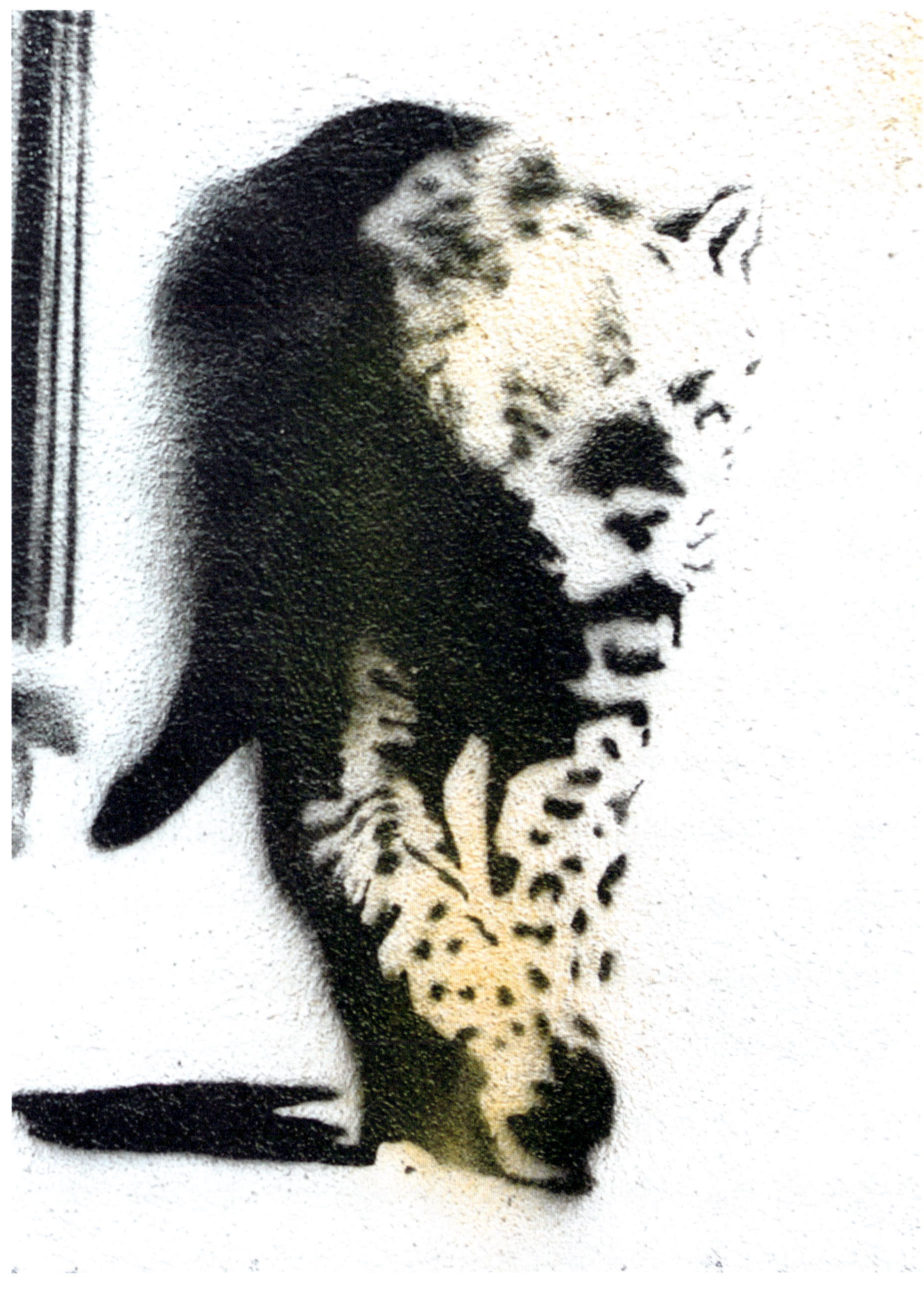

STARS OF BETHLEHEM

HEBRON STREET, BETHLEHEM (*STOP AND SEARCH*)

The listing on eBay in late 2008 was intriguing to put it mildly: 'We can deliver anywhere in the world two works by the most famous artist in the world just $2 million American dollars for two paintings... call George.'

The artist was, of course, Banksy, and for Robin Barton, the swashbuckling dealer who specializes in unauthenticated Banksys, this was too tempting an opportunity to miss.

George, it turned out, was a carpenter in Bethlehem, who knew much more about Banksy and what he was worth than his neighbours. In one of the two works, *Stop and Search*, Dorothy from *The Wizard of Oz* has an Israeli soldier literally up against a wall while she frisks him. Banksy had painted it on the wall of a butcher's shop in 2007, and George had swapped the Banksy wall for a new wall complete with a new doorway, much to the butcher's delight. The second piece, *Wet Dog*, possibly interpreted as a dog shaking off the oppression around him rather than the rain, was taken from a dilapidated bus shelter, also in Bethlehem.

They were both undoubtedly Banksys. The two million dollars was soon negotiated down to a more reasonable $40,000, half to be paid in cash on inspection and the other half to be paid once the two pieces had left Israel.

Once Barton's agent had handed over a brown envelope full of $100 notes, the two walls, weighing almost four tons in total, started on their way. The journey almost ended as soon as it had begun, when *Wet Dog* slipped its harness and fell to the ground as it was being transferred between two lorries. Somehow the wall remained in one piece and they both made it first to Newhaven and then to a picture restorer in Kent. When Barton saw them there, he writes in his book *Robin Banksy*, he sensed for the first time 'the artist's message of hope hijacked by my own selfish and avaricious intent.' But it was too late for any doubts.

The two pieces were next shipped to The Hamptons on Long Island where, in August 2011, Barton, together with fellow New York dealer Stephan Keszler, put them on show, offering *Stop and Search* for $450,000 and *Wet Dog* for $420,000. Banksy's Pest Control issued a warning against buying unauthenticated Banksys, and for good measure suggested that 'these works will come back to haunt' the pair of dealers. They were not haunted but instead swamped by the untimely arrival of Storm Irene, and neither piece sold.

So the next stop on their long travels was Miami, and eventually the two pieces did sell, *Stop and Search* for $420,000 and *Wet Dog* for $350,000. They were bought by the owner of an American football team who, like Banksy, prefers to remain anonymous; *Wet Dog* later ended up in the hands of Sylvester Stallone. It is all far, far away from the butcher in Bethlehem.

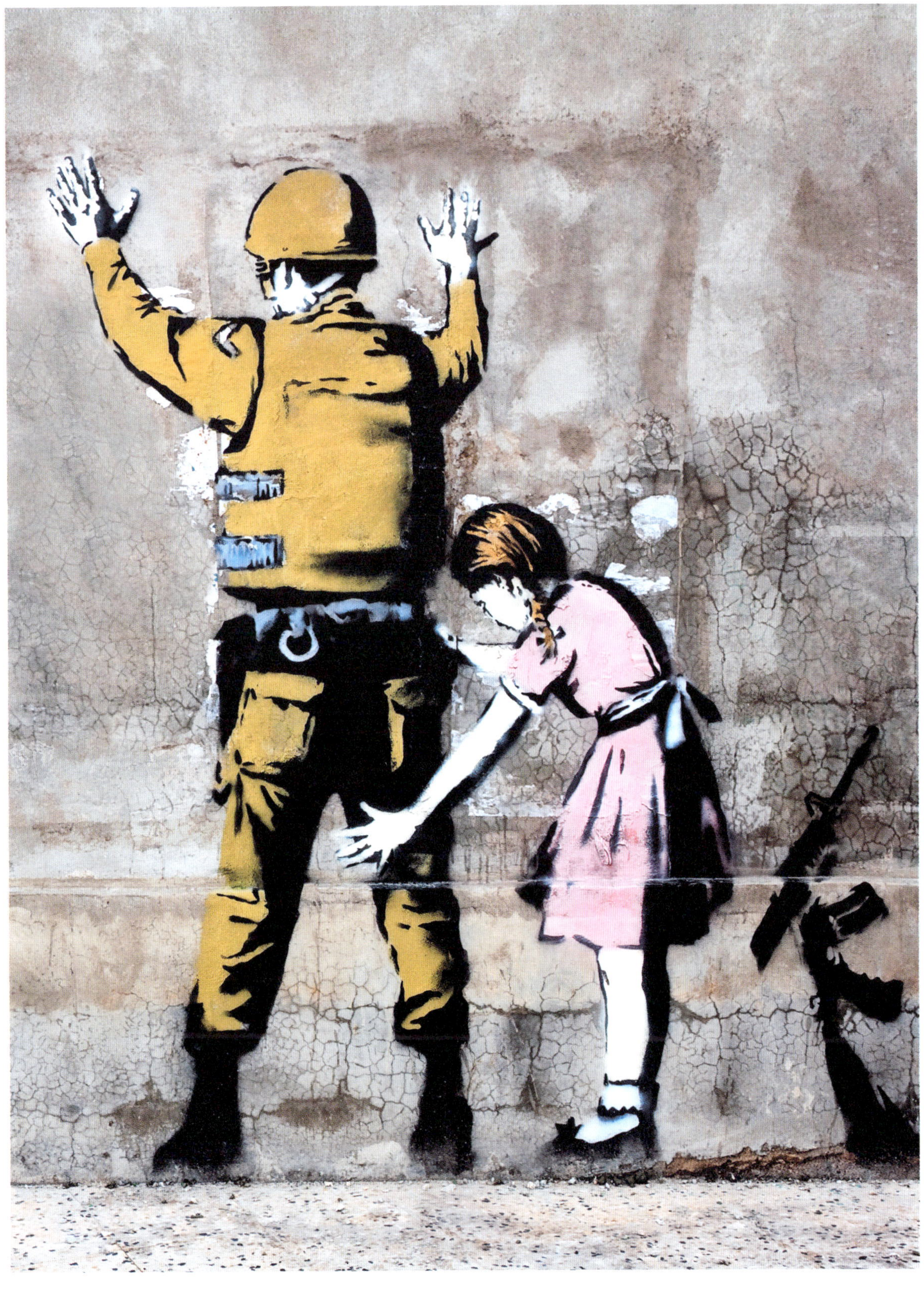

SEASIDE SHOWDOWN

⦿ BEACH PATROL BOAT HOUSE, WEST BEACH, CLACTON-ON-SEA CO15 1QX

Very few people have ever actually seen this Banksy in its original position, painted on the wall of a boat house in Clacton-on-Sea, because the local council was swift to scrub it off almost before the paint was dry. A pity, because it is a very good piece – a lonely tropical bird sitting on a telephone wire being shunned by our home-grown pigeons. *Guardian* art critic Jonathan Jones called it 'the best Banksy I have never seen.'

The seafront at Clacton is a jolly place. Apart from the windfarms out to sea, it is very much a scene from the 1950s or 60s, with Union Jacks flying from the turrets on the pier and holidaymakers looking at the sky, trying to decide if it is beach or choo-choo train weather.

When I was there a beach patroller told me, 'The Banksy was very different from most of the graffiti we see at the seafront.' But the local council, dismally, failed to recognize that fact. For years local councils had been treating Banksy like any other graffiti artist and painting over anything he put up, but by 2014, when this was painted, councils had begun to recognize him as someone to be welcomed rather than obliterated. Not, however, Tendring District Council who, very soon after the piece went up, received a complaint that the graffiti was 'offensive and racist.' Council staff decided that pigeons holding signs reading 'Keep Off Our Worms' and 'Go Back to Africa' could indeed be considered offensive. It was

all chemically removed within 48 hours of the complaint being made – job done.

The *New York Times* reported in a deadpan way: 'why the mural was interpreted as racist rather than satirical is unclear.' Particularly unclear given that the town was in the middle of a by-election after its MP, Douglas Carswell, defected from the Conservative Party to UKIP (a party with an anti-immigration policy at the heart of its appeal).

The BBC went to the trouble of filing a Freedom of Information request to see what complaints the council received once the removal had become public. One woman wrote from the USA: 'I absolutely applaud those that removed this painting,' she said. 'Banksy, whoever he is, is nothing but a cult artist who thinks he has the privilege of imposing his social comments on all of us. Well done Clacton.' But among about 40 messages hers was the only one of support. The others were much more disgruntled: 'Congratulations on making yourselves internationally famous as a bunch of pusillanimous morons,' one person wrote.

But what mystifies me about the original statement from the council's communications manager when he explained why the birds had been painted over was the hope that Banksy might come back. 'We would obviously welcome an appropriate Banksy original on any of our seafronts,' he said, 'and would be delighted if he returned in the future.' Some hope.

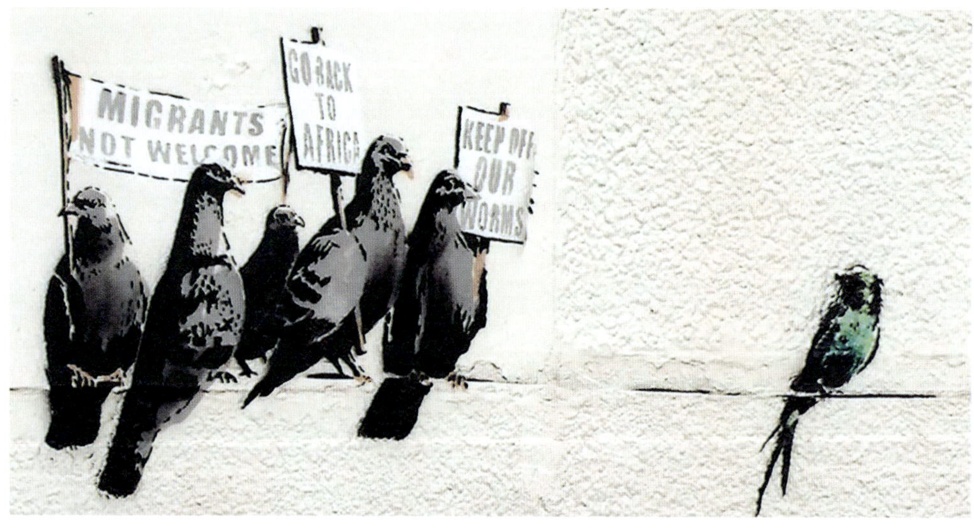

THE BARTERED WIFE

◉ PARK PLACE, MARGATE CT9 1LE

I am somewhat embarrassed to say that I own a fractional share of a Banksy.

The cost was £128 (including fees) and it was my assumption that my one share was – and always will be – worthless. But I wanted to see exactly how the system worked, what control I had over it (none so far) and I hoped for a nice certificate of a minuscule part-ownership to hang on my wall.

The Banksy in question, *Valentine's Day Mascara*, was painted early in 2023 on the end wall of a terraced house on a scrappy back street of Margate about five minutes' walk from the seafront. It is an extraordinarily good piece – it might even be called an installation since it also encompassed an old chest freezer and a broken, plastic chair. Here was a 1950s housewife wearing a pinny and her washing-up gloves, looking all very traditional apart from a missing front tooth and a black eye, which were ruining her attempt at a smile. All that could be seen of her bully-boy husband was his feet sticking out of the freezer – he had got what he deserved.

On Valentine's Day Banksy acknowledged that it was his. Although photographers were swiftly on the spot, they had already been beaten to it. The month beforehand Banksy, showing considerable attention to detail, had asked plein-air artist Pete Brown to be ready to record the scene once the housewife had been put up. So Brown was already there, capturing in a very enjoyable series of oil paintings what happens when Banksy arrives in town.

By the end of April the wall plus freezer and broken chair had all gone. At a cost of about £205,000, it had been taken down and, after a visit to a restorer, had found a temporary home in Margate's Dreamland on the seafront, where it resided quite impressively in the 'retro roller room'.

Julian Usher of Red Eight Gallery, who was advising the owner of the house, announced that the piece had been valued at what seemed an absurd £6 million and was to be sold in fractions to the public. The last time I looked only 2,216 fractions had sold, amounting to about £265,000, somewhat removed from £6 million. Soon afterwards these sales were suspended. As for the battered housewife, when the summer ended she was shipped off to London, first to add lustre to an unofficial Banksy exhibition on Regent Street, where she looked an afterthought, and then on to Yamaha's 'flagship' music store in Soho, where she was displayed amid the pianos – bizarre, but certainly impossible to miss.

Mr Usher says, 'Ultimately we have now saved this piece. Loathe it or love it, it will be around forever.' But he certainly will not get any thanks for this from Banksy.

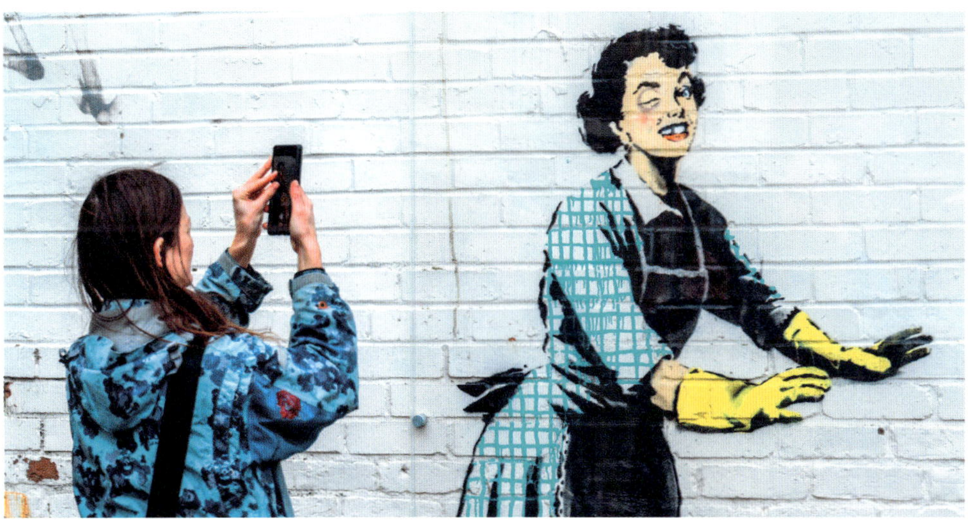

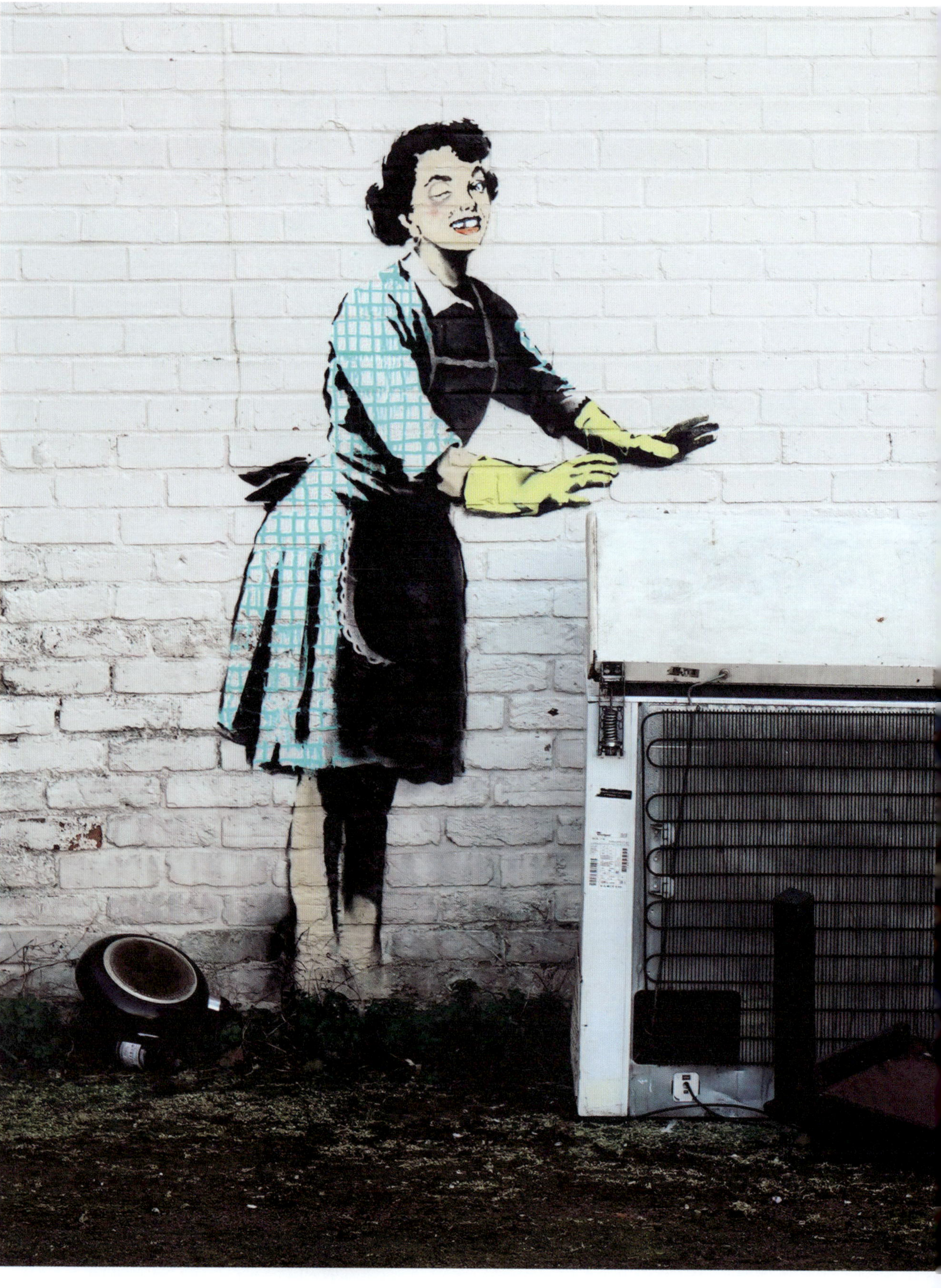

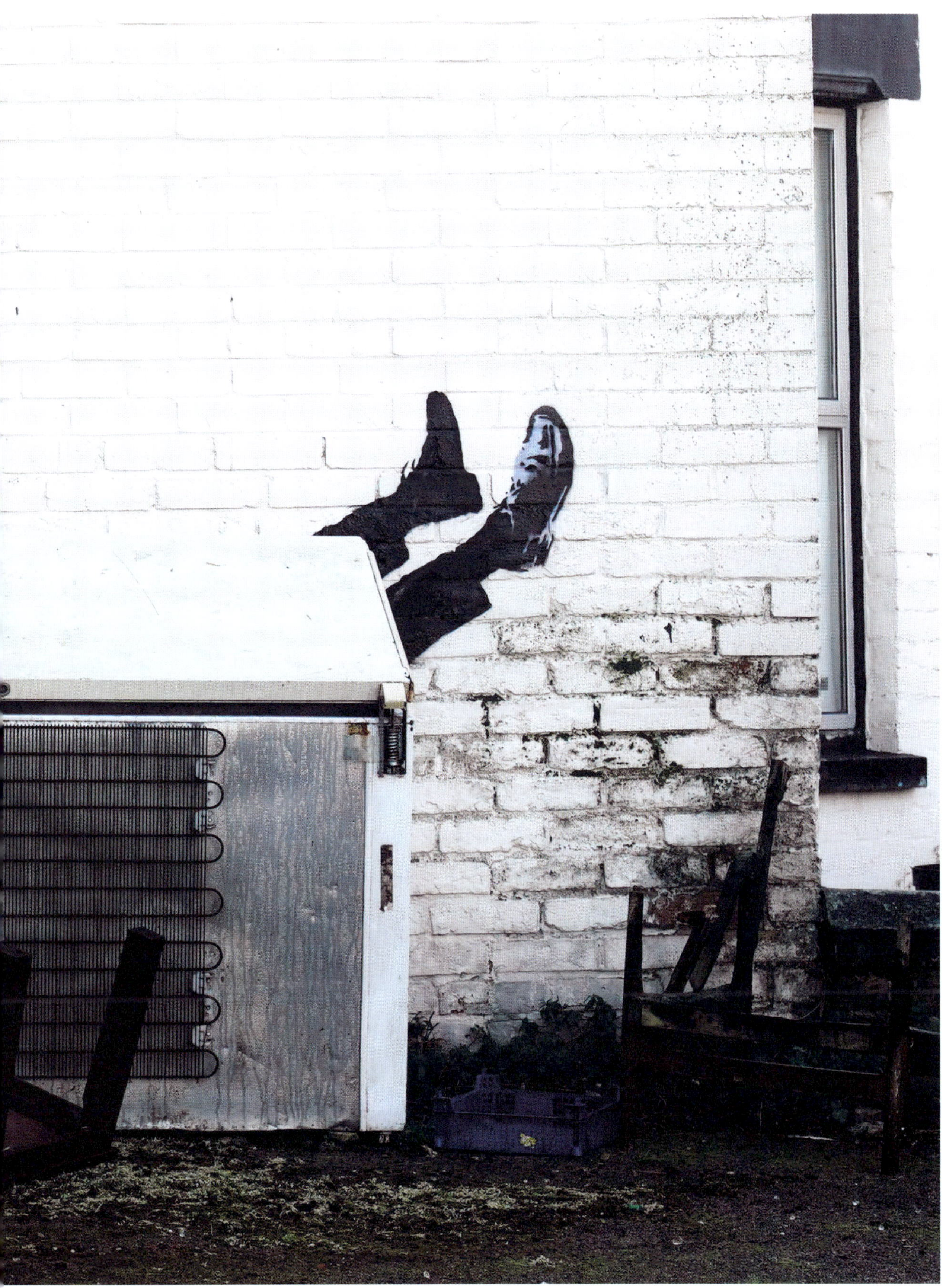

11

THE DISAPPEARING DIAMOND

⦿ VAN DYKE, BETWEEN MILTON AND PALMETTO, DETROIT MI 48234

There is only one Banksy where I think the people trying to take it from the wall actually made it into a better piece than the original – however briefly – and it is this one, *Diamond Girl*. Banksy painted it in Detroit when he was jumping across America, publicizing his film.

His original looks sweet enough but she is almost overwhelmed by the other graffiti surrounding her. But when all the bricks around her have been chiselled out and she is left stark and all alone, she is very striking.

The area where Banksy painted was all dilapidated buildings and crack houses at the time – it is very different now. On the web there were hints that Banksy had hit town and Shane McMurphy, only a few years out of high school, went hunting with his friends Terry and Libby, in Terry's '73 Cutlass, until they found it. 'We had this Wild West mentality in Detroit in those days,' he says now. 'We had to go do this. I don't know what we thought we were ever going to do with it. We just didn't want rich people to buy it.'

It was about two in the morning when they started prising out the bricks until they reached the point where they realized it was too unstable and they needed packaging film to stretch across the front to keep the piece together. So off they went to the hardware store.

By now it was about 6am. Enter Pete Senteris, a fan who was up early Banksy hunting on his way to work. He found it with all the bricks missing, 'but I couldn't understand why they had done all that work and not actually taken the piece!' He contemplated taking it himself but 'in the end I just didn't think it was right.' At one point, though, he was tempted enough to hold one of the bricks near the top, 'but I could tell it was separating the paint, so I left it.' He went off to work and, as the sun came up, Shane McMurphy and friends returned from the hardware store. The piece was gone. There was just a hole in the wall. 'I was mind blown,' Shane says. 'Everything in Detroit at that time was a cash grab ... We never went up to the wall, we all went, "Let's just go home now."'

He says the wall must have either crumbled to the ground or 'someone got it out in a safer way than we had planned.' He did not remember seeing any rubble, but it is very hard to imagine that someone came across *Diamond Girl* and extracted it safely all within a two-hour time slot.

So what did happen? Shane said to me, 'I was kind of hoping there would be some sort of weird closure where you might have figured out where it was.' I had hoped for the same from him. So no one knows for sure, but my bet is on the pile of rubble.

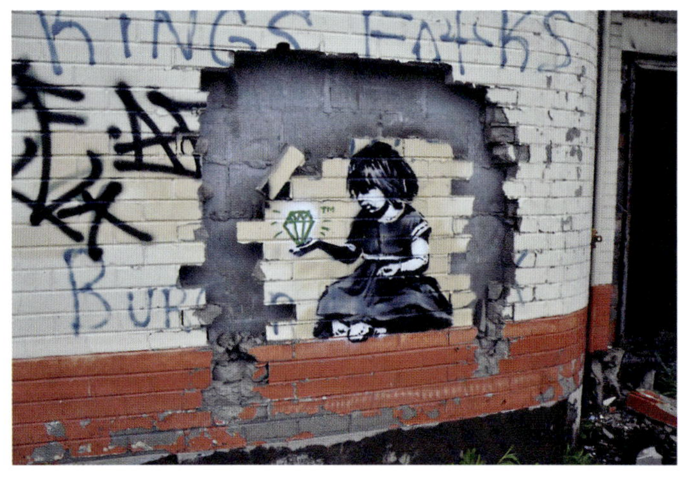

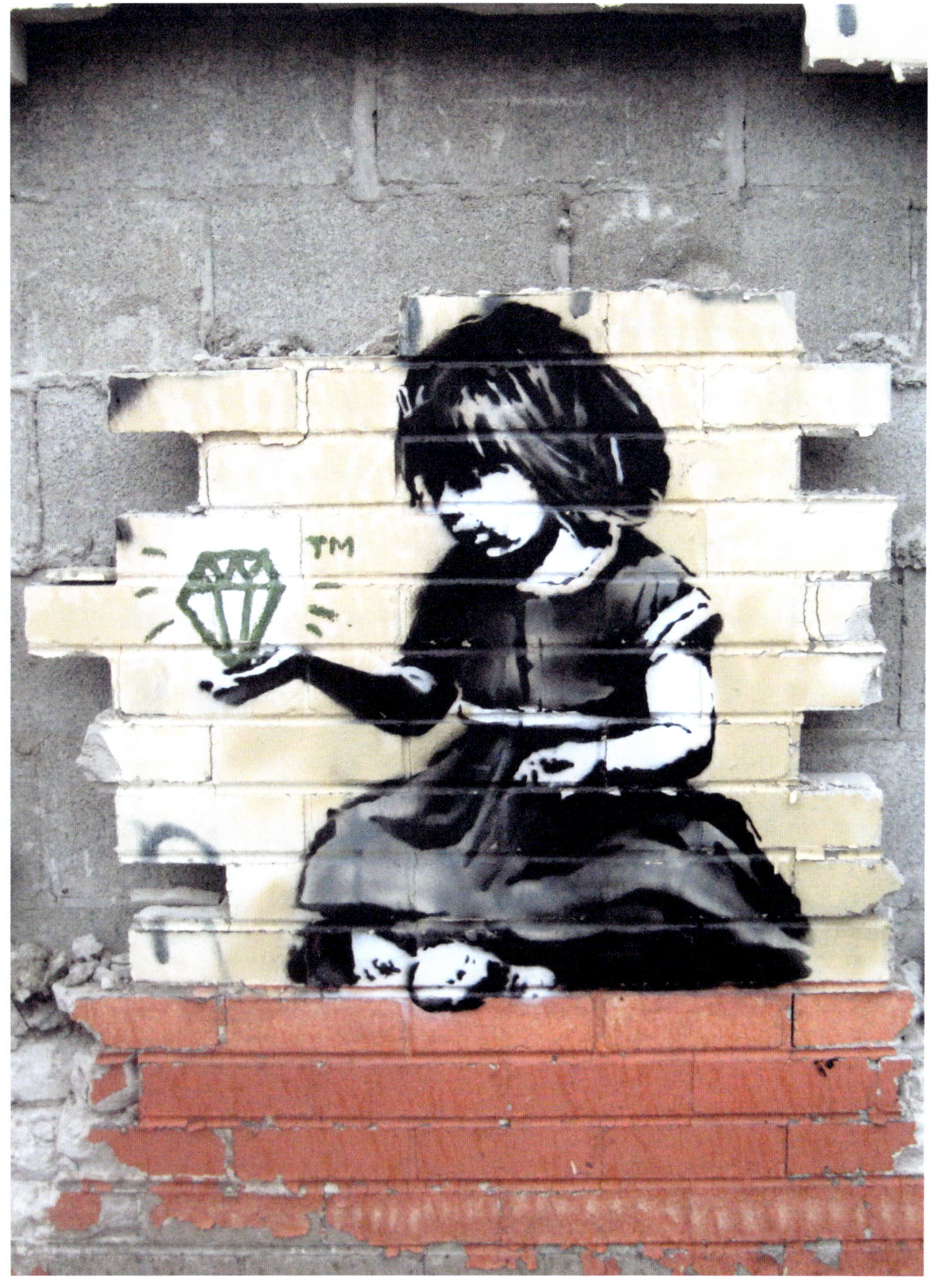

12

LOVED TO DISTRACTION

◉ CLEMENT STREET, ST PHILIP'S, BRISTOL BS2 9ES

Although Banksy almost never authenticates work taken off the street, he has made a couple of exceptions for charitable causes and this is one of them.

The work that Banksy painted on a plywood board nailed to a door close to the Broad Plain Boys' Club in Bristol is a wonderfully shrewd piece of graffiti where two lovers are more engrossed in their mobiles than with each other. It is also quite complicated; just look for a moment at the shading on the two lovers' faces lit up by the glow of their phones. In fact, it was so well executed it may well have been painted in his studio and brought to the doorway, rather than being painted in a hurry on the street.

Dennis Stinchcombe, who ran the club, was alerted to the piece by the TV crews who suddenly appeared there to film the latest Banksy. An artist friend of Banksy's told him, 'You need to take that, Dennis, get it into the club, it's what it is meant for.' With the help of a crowbar and a fellow worker from the club, he did just that.

So that was another Banksy gone from the street where it had sat only very briefly. But before Mr Stinchcombe could even think about selling it, the city council stepped in. The council said the work was painted on a doorway owned by the council and it was therefore their property. While the club and the council argued, the painting was removed from the Boys' Club and put on show at the Bristol City Museum and Art Gallery, where Banksy had held an extraordinarily successful exhibition back in 2009.

Thankfully this was a dispute that did not end up in the law courts. In an ending almost too good to be true, a note was posted under the entrance door of the youth club from Banksy – yes, Banksy – himself. 'I don't normally admit to committing criminal damage but seeing as it looks as though charges won't be brought any time soon, you have my blessing to do what you think is right with the piece. I'm a great admirer of the work done at the club and would be chuffed if this could help in some way.'

Game over. Bristol's mayor withdrew gracefully and the board, plus Banksy's letter, was sold to a private collector for £403,000. *Mobile Lovers* was lost to the rest of the world but enough money had been made to save the youth club. 'I think the guy is an absolute diamond,' said Mr Stinchcombe.

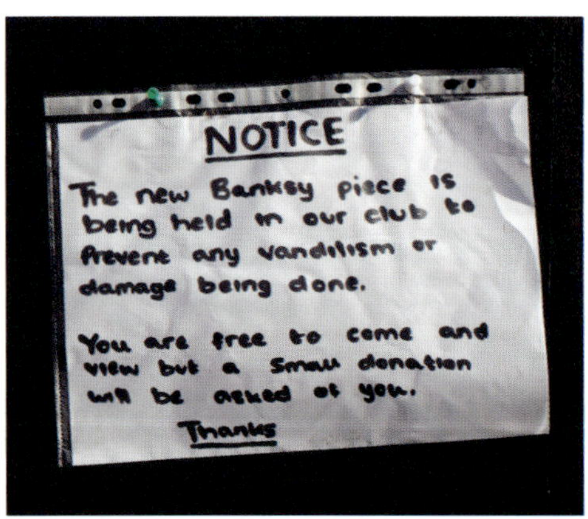

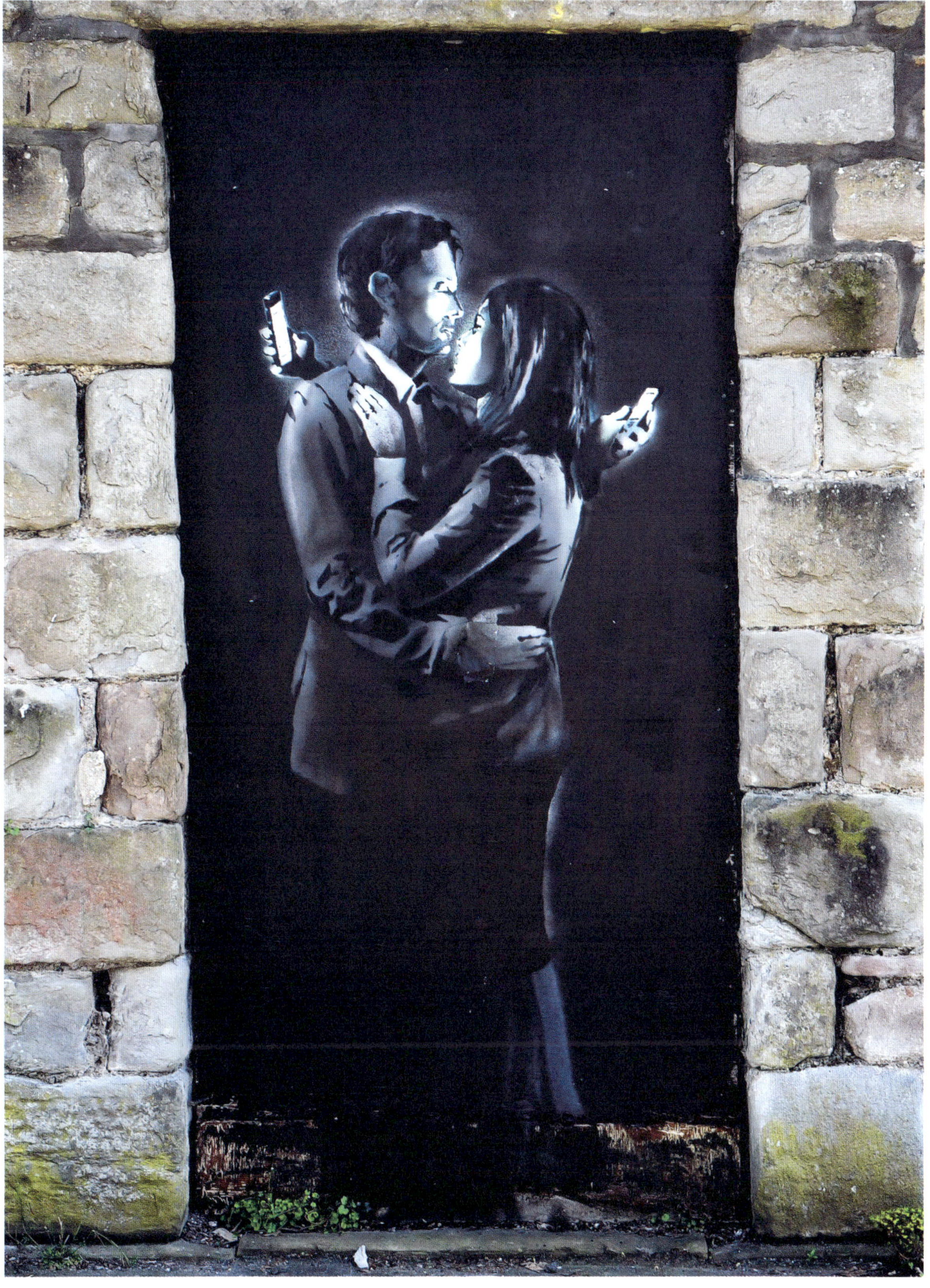

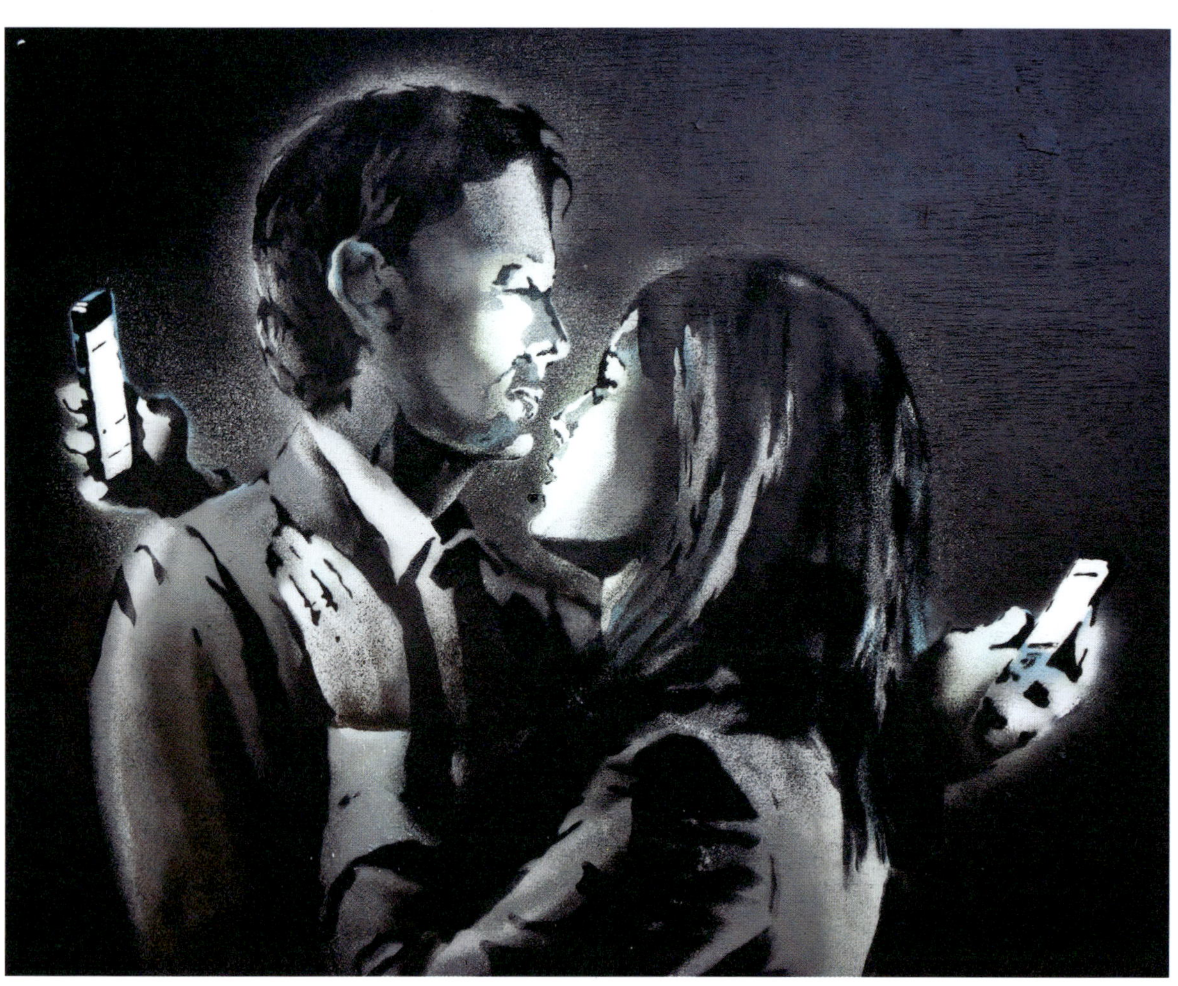

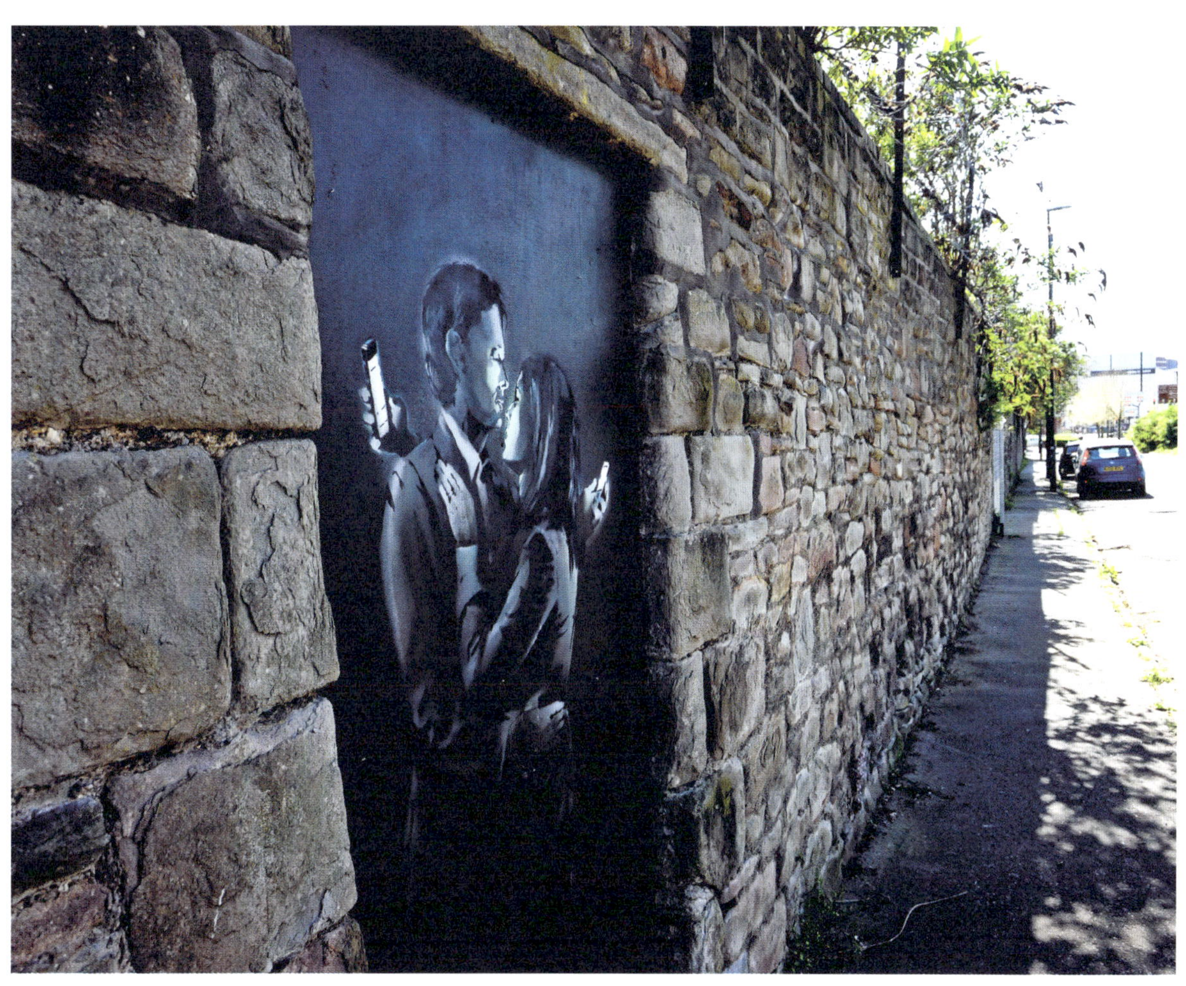

13

CRAZY CAR DOOR

159 LUDLOW STREET, NEW YORK NY 10002

This car door once belonged to a late-1990s Mazda Protégé which ended up on the streets of New York as part of a complicated installation by Banksy called *Crazy Horse*. It would have been too much to steal the whole car, but the door disappeared very quickly, reappearing three years later at an auction in California.

In the background of the installation, painted on the side of a lorry, were three terrifying horses, rearing up in night-vision goggles. In the foreground, painted on the car door, a young man looks up at them – duly terrified. What made this work easy to understand, and gave it its title, *Crazy Horse,* was a toll-free phone number painted on an oil drum. If you called it you heard a recording (released by WikiLeaks in 2010) of two US Apache helicopters, one with the call sign Crazy Horse 18, attacking a group of people on the streets of Baghdad who were mainly civilians.

The door (and the traffic cone that went with it) was bought at auction for $87,500 by Steve Spina, who owned a removal firm in Malibu California. Had he seen the original piece in New York? No. So why did he buy it?

'Because I liked it. It was a kind of unique piece. Something that reminded me of some of the problems we had during the Vietnam War and the wars of today, when innocent civilians get killed because they are just caught in the middle of it all.' (From making and selling surfboards, Mr Spina was drafted into the Vietnam War. After he left the army he was diagnosed with post-traumatic stress disorder.)

Not only did he like the piece but he also liked Banksy. 'I feel for him and I can understand his anonymity. I don't think the monetary aspect of what he does has any meaning to him. He's a pure artist.'

He did try to trade the piece back to Banksy in return for an authenticated piece, but unsurprisingly he heard nothing from the Banksy camp. It was in his office for about six months but he eventually decided it was unsafe there and moved it to his firm's warehouse. Eventually, seven years after he bought it, he sent it back to the same auction house. This time it sold for almost twice the price, $162,500.

Why did he sell it? 'I couldn't display it, so nobody could see it, and I thought that the piece should be out there for people to view... Now who knows who has it. It's kind of sad that it went underground. Maybe Banksy bought it back...'

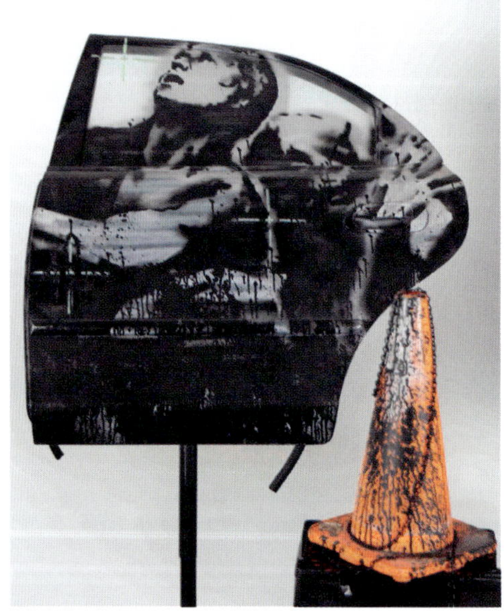

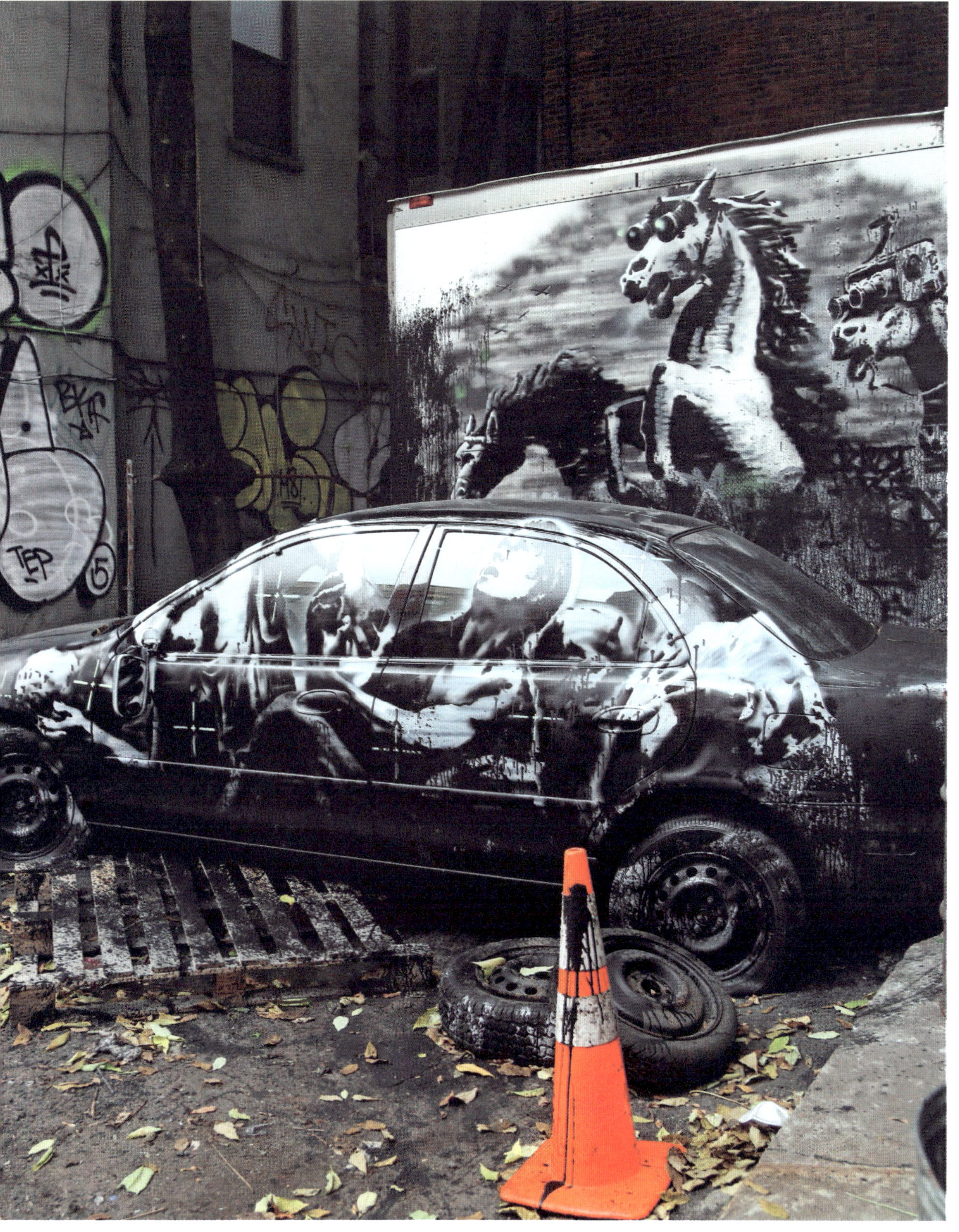

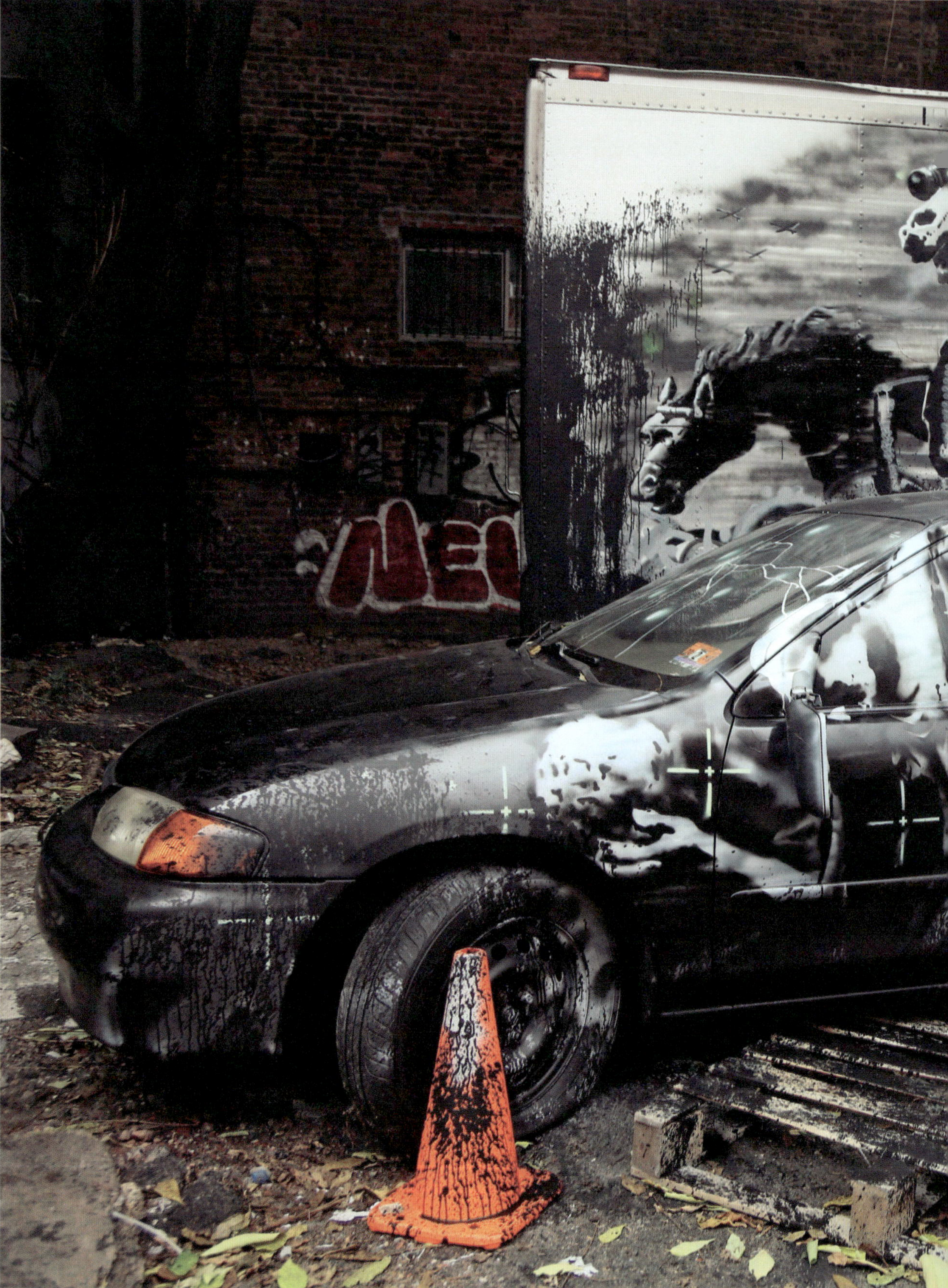

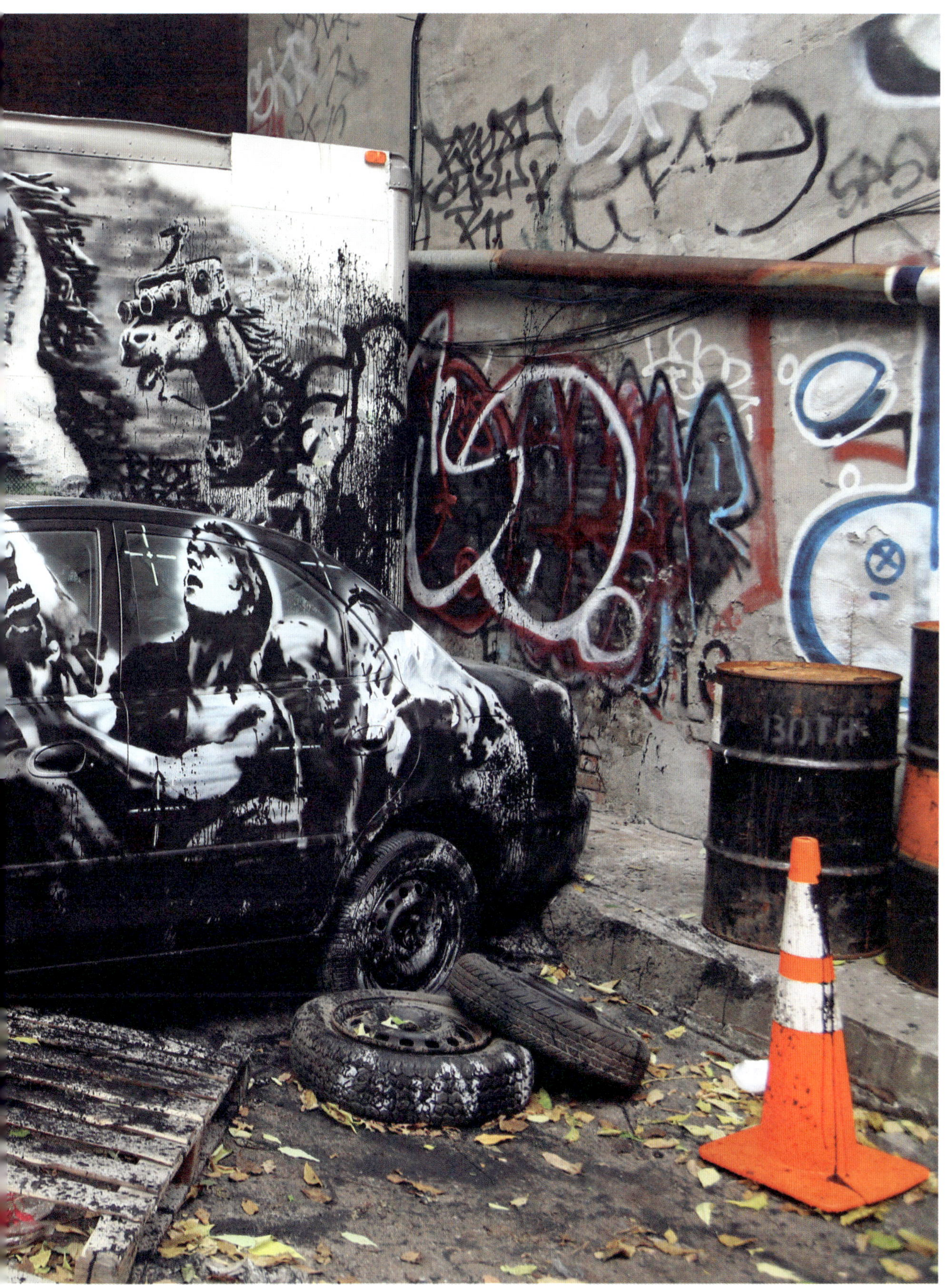

14

DODGING THE MINEFIELDS

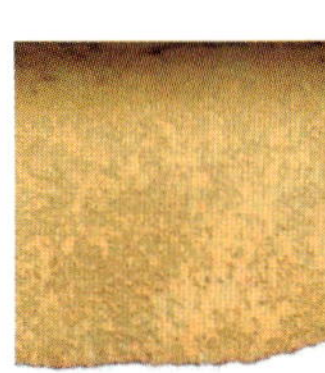

The first day Banksy arrived in Ukraine in November 2022, he was scouting for locations where he could paint when he absent-mindedly walked past a sign warning of landmines. His fixer, who was helping him find the locations, 'lost it with me'. In his defence Banksy said he thought any warning of a landmine would have the traditional skull on it instead of the simple Ukrainian 'МІНИ'.

But minefields or not, he still managed to paint a series of seven pieces on partially destroyed buildings around Kyiv at a moment when Ukraine needed all the help it could get.

In Hostomel, a town about 15 miles from Kyiv which had been occupied briefly by the Russians after a fierce battle in the early stages of the war, Banksy painted a woman standing in her dressing gown, hair up in old-fashioned curlers, wearing a gas mask. Her only weapon was a fire extinguisher. She gave an eerie sense of one lonely woman against the might of Russia. Less than a month after being painted, she had vanished.

However, it was not Russians who had anything to do with her disappearance.

Serhiy Dovhyi, a fixer for foreign journalists, who spotted the work on an abandoned apartment block even before Banksy acknowledged it was his, put together a team of eight men to steal it. Because it was painted on a layer of insulation, it was a relatively easy piece to take off the wall and, armed with just a saw, it took them an hour to do the job. They had just finished wrapping it in stretch film when the police arrived.

Mr Dovhyi said he wanted to put the piece up for auction. The money was not for himself, he claimed, but for the army. 'Street art, in contrast to a piece of art in the Louvre, doesn't belong to anyone,' he told the *New York Times*.

However, the actual owner of the flat, Tetiana Semenova, who fled abroad after the Russians invaded, did not see it his way: 'Some subhumans decided to steal the painting. Orcs [Russian invaders] mutilated it inside and subhumans finished it off.' (Mr Dovhyi eventually pleaded guilty and was given a five-year suspended sentence and put on probation for three years.)

One of Banksy's works in Ukraine has already been turned into a postage stamp and, rather than allow his works to be demolished along with the buildings they were painted on, they will be saved. But their job has already been done. They were a rallying cry for Ukraine, a call for support for the underdog, way beyond anything that a government department could ever dream up.

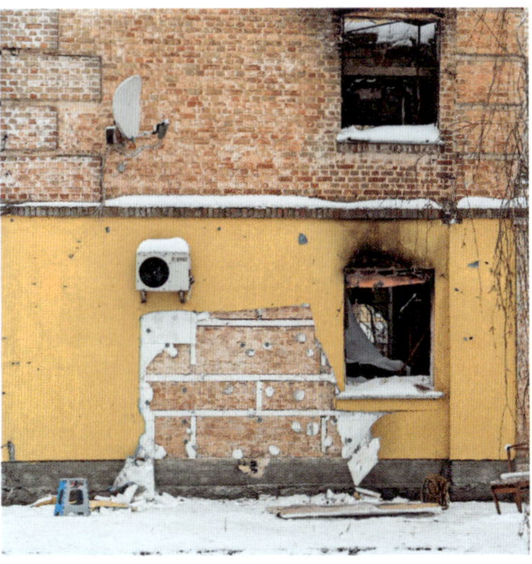

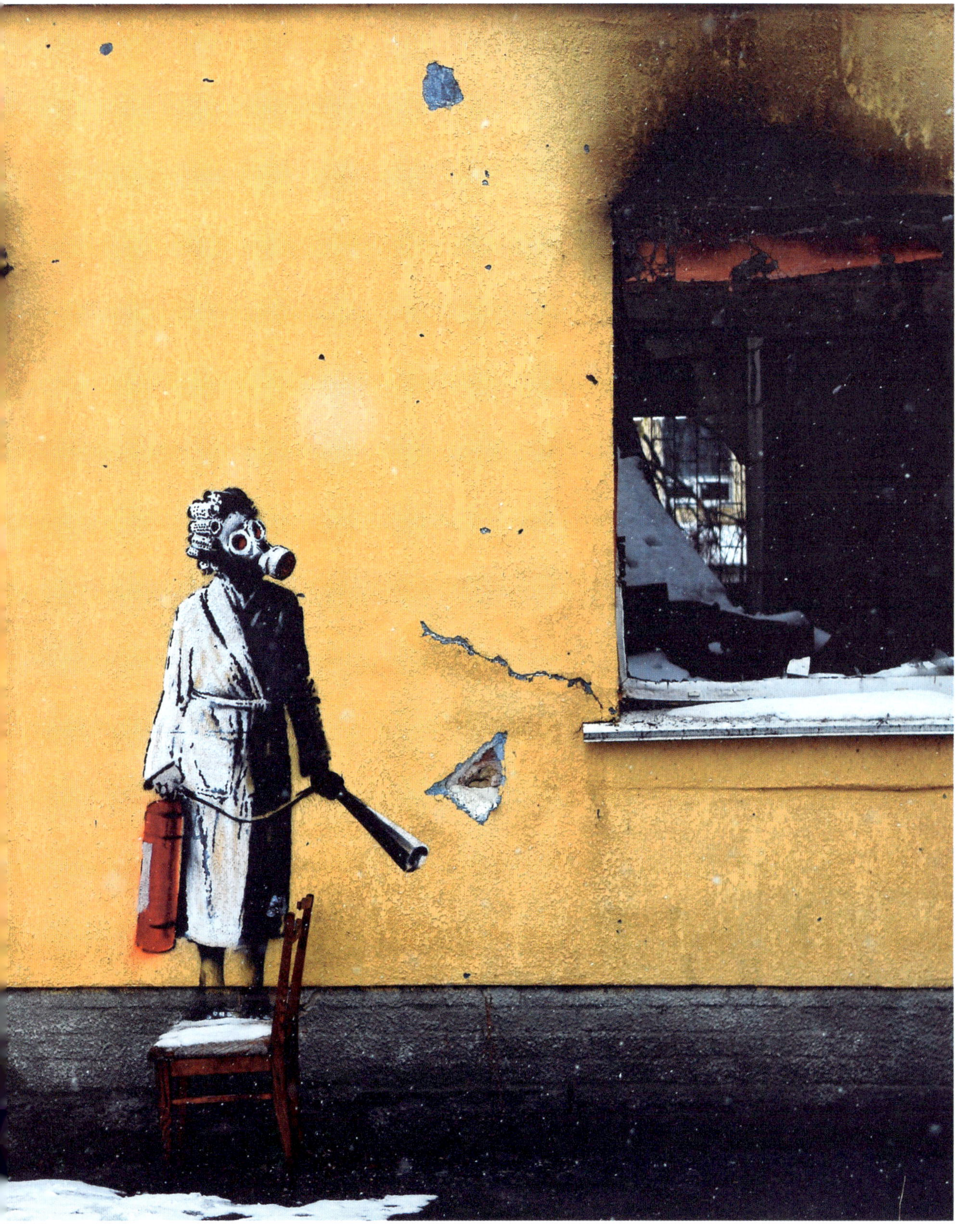

15

CRABS
IN PERIL

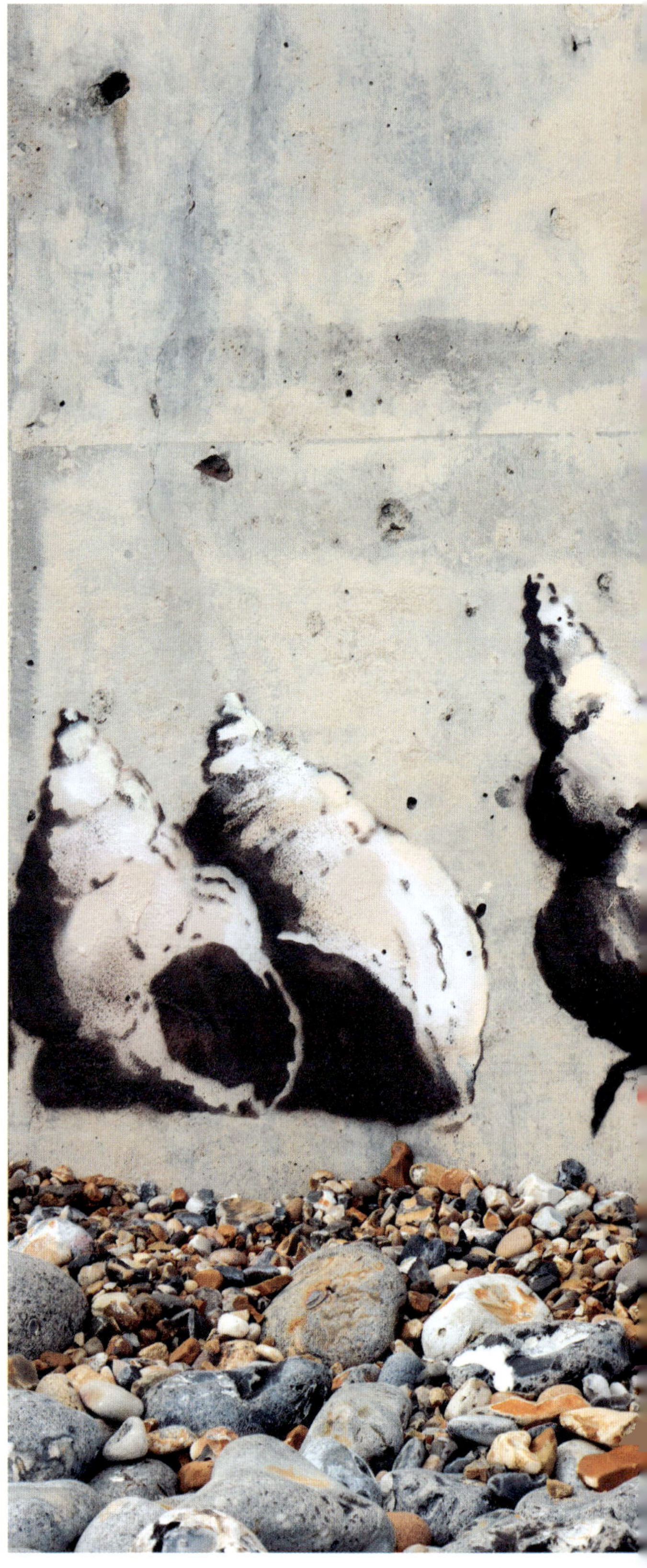

Walking along the beach at Cromer, looking for a Banksy, reminded me of childhood scavenger hunts in Cornwall. Excitement, frustration and ultimate satisfaction. On a grey July day there were few people on the beach and very few who were interested in Banksy.

When I eventually found the right breakwater, the hermit crabs that Banksy painted there seemed quite gentle, unassuming, making a point about second homes while still having a bit of fun. Very much worth the effort, like finding just the right stone with a hole in it.

The crabs were painted in August 2021 and, perhaps because Cromer is a bit off the graffiti writers' track and the breakwater even more so, they have never been seriously attacked. The sea has been a much greater enemy than any rival graffiti writers.

The only note of anger came from a writer on Margate's Crab Museum website who argued that Cromer was not famous for hermit crabs but for *Cancer pagurus*, and anyway Banksy's work represents an 'anatomically inaccurate hermit crab'. But for once a local council seemed to get how to handle a Banksy just right.

A coat of resin was applied to give the work some protection, but that was that. Tim Adams, leader of the North Norfolk Council, told the local paper, 'We made a conscious decision not to remove it. It would have been a challenging job as it is on a very big piece of concrete, but we thought the artist's intention was for it to be left.'

He added, 'It will be lost to the sea eventually,' and he would be 'surprised if it survives through the winter.' This was in September 2023 and how right he was. By January 2024 the crabs were completely covered by stones and shells washed up by gales on the high tide. Maybe they will be dug out in the summer, but their end is nigh, and it seems somehow just the right way for this Banksy to go.

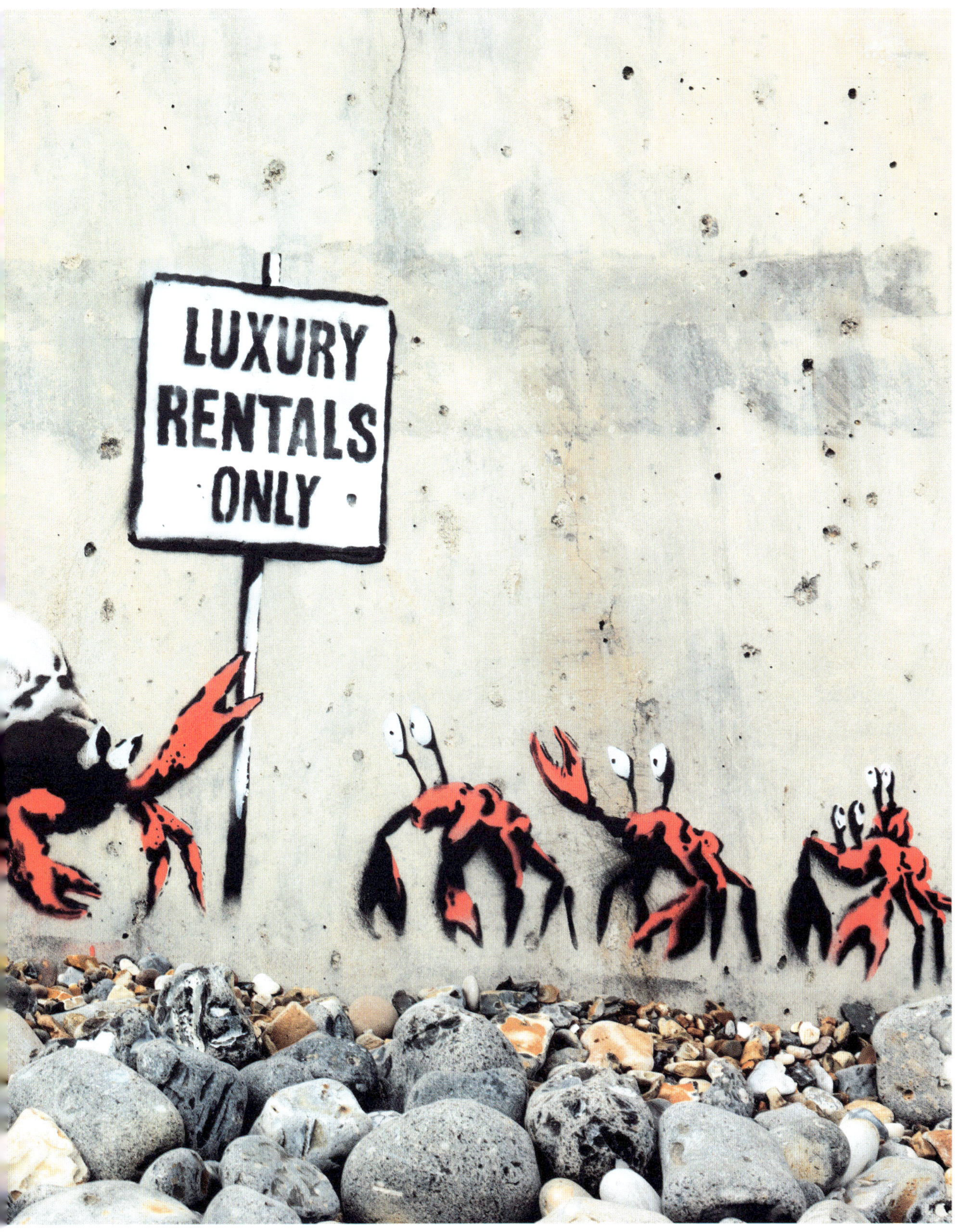
LUXURY
RENTALS
ONLY

16

RAT NEEDS GOOD HOME

📍 1665 HAIGHT STREET, SAN FRANCISCO CA 94117

When Banksy's uncomfortably large and angry rat was taken from high off a wall in San Francisco, it was assumed it was another of his works which would soon be off to the market. Reading about it I certainly thought so too. But many years later Brian Greif, the former television executive who captured the rat, convinced me that his aim had always been to save it, not sell it.

Banksy painted the rat on the side of a sort of hippy B&B, the Red Vic in the Haight-Ashbury district, back in 2010. It took five months for Mr Greif to negotiate a very San Francisco deal with Sami Sunchild, the owner of the Red Vic – the final part of their contract required him to attend the two-hour World Peace Conversations that Sunchild held for her guests every Sunday morning.

Once the deal was signed, the painting was relatively easy to take down since it could be sawn off into 11 neat pieces of redwood cedar cladding. For the next two years the rat remained wrapped up cosily in Mr Greif's cupboard. He had hoped that the San Francisco Museum of Modern Art would provide an obvious home, but John Zarobell, an assistant curator at the museum, said, 'Some artists make work to be destroyed. They don't want the art to survive and if that's the case it is not the museum's business to preserve it.' In addition, of course, the work was not authenticated.

So the rat, now put together as one piece, is on permanent tour between galleries, who are permitted to take the rat on condition that they organize a free street-art show to go with him. From New York to Kokomo, Indiana, from Windsor, Ontario, to Los Angeles, the rat has been there.

Mr Greif says, 'Every time I ship it out I am a nervous wreck until it arrives safely.'

He argues that 'street art and graffiti are incredibly important art movements. We can't save everything but there are some pieces that need to be taken off the wall and preserved for posterity, where the public can enjoy it forever.' But what if Banksy disagrees? 'That's the difficult part,' he admits, 'but to this point he hasn't said anything negative about it.'

The offers for the piece started at about $500,000 and are now in the millions. But he is not interested. So what does he think will happen to the rat? 'I don't know. I figure at some point fate or karma will kick in and it will be obvious where it is going to go. But it is safe and in good condition and it looks just like it did when it came off the wall.'

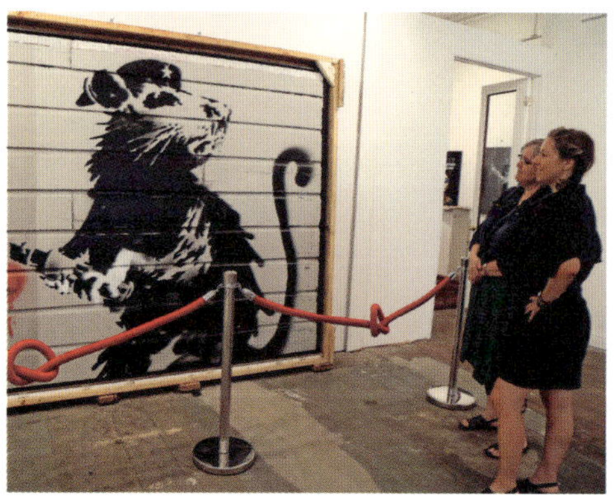

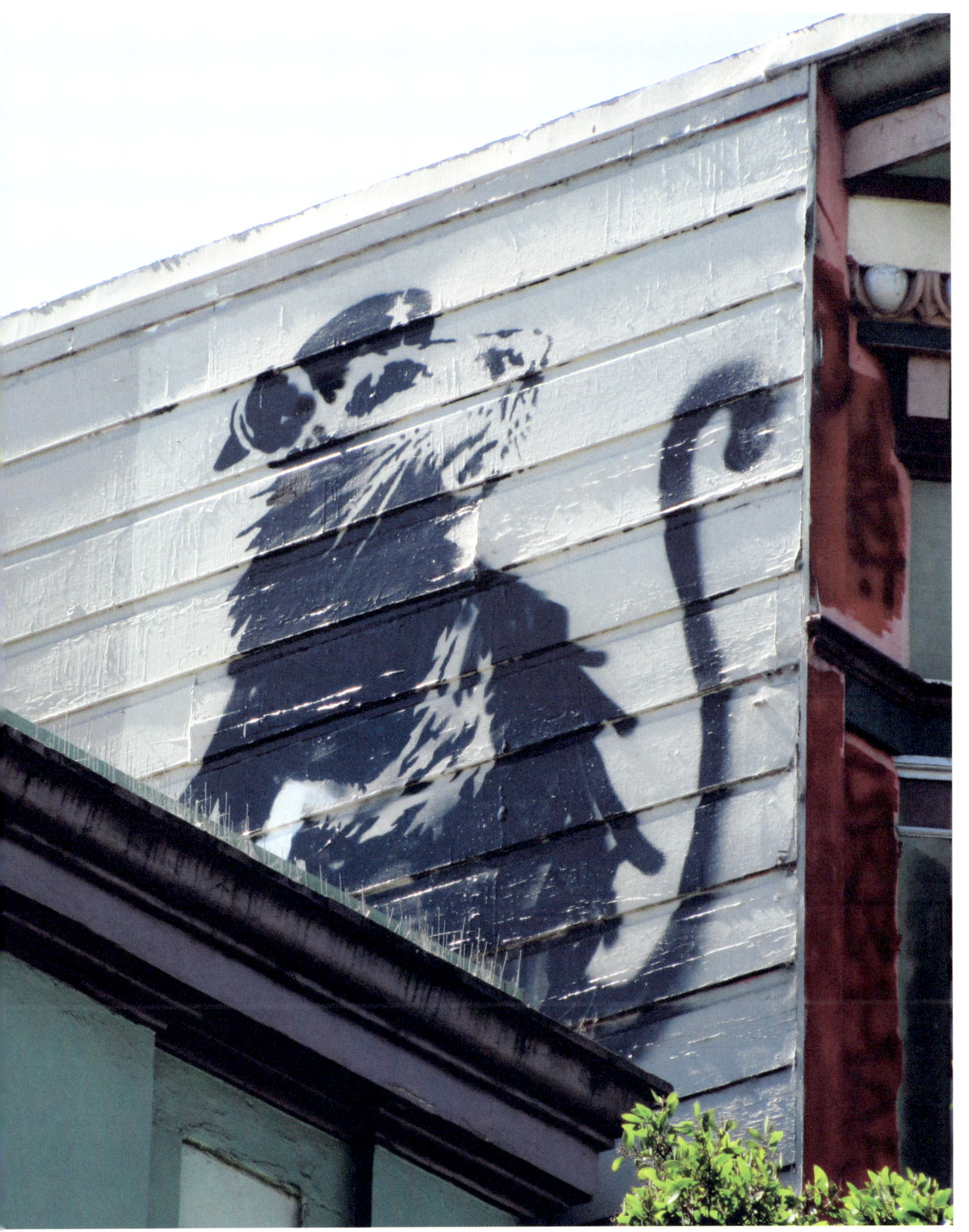

NO BEATING ABOUT THE BUSH

◉ CANONBURY SQUARE, LONDON N1 2AL

It only took a few nicely drawn lines to give a clump of unloved ivy straggling down a white wall off Canonbury Square in North London its 15 minutes of fame.

Nudity has never had much of a role in Banksy's art but here the strong black curves which he had added to the pure white wall were undoubtedly a woman's thighs and there in the middle was the ivy, magically transformed into her pubic hair. It was a little bit unkempt but it was unmistakable.

It was painted in 2012, and 11 years later when I visited the area, one of the residents of the house whose wall had been Banksy's canvas remembers it fondly. 'We were happy, we really enjoyed it. Cab drivers dropping someone off said they didn't want a tip; they just said, "It's cheered my days up, made me laugh so much." It was just before the London Olympics started and the council was tidying everything up round here, so they sent someone in a high-vis jacket to trim it into better shape.'

The work lasted about three months before an agent managing one of the houses in this particularly smart part of Islington complained to the council and the curves were whitewashed away and the ivy disappeared.

It was only when I got on the bus on the way home after talking to this resident that I realized we had both been Banksyed. The idea of any council sending a man to trim Banksy's bush before the Olympics was absurd. Banksy has always believed in the power of the high-vis yellow jacket to convince onlookers that whatever he was doing to a wall was official. So, soon after he finished his lines around the ivy, he must have sent one of his team along with a hedge-cutter and high-vis jacket to finish the work. It was just neatly trimmed – certainly not a Brazilian.

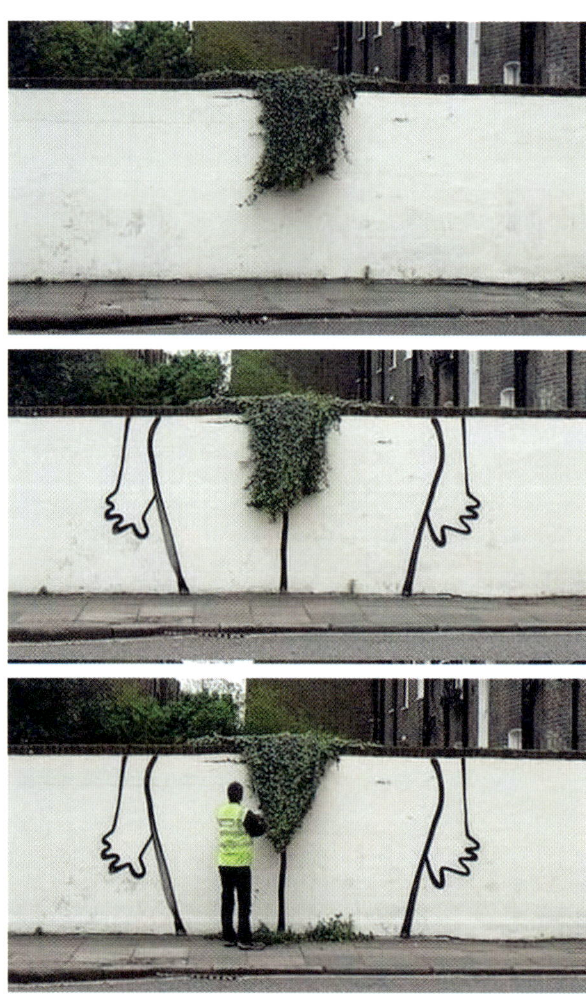

PEEL AND STICK

For most Banksy hunters the easiest way to get their prize is to take the wall down – or at least the chunk where he painted. But there is another way, although whether they end up with a 'real' Banksy is debatable.

On the wall of an abandoned petrol station in Clerkenwell, London, Banksy painted a piece called *OLD Skool* featuring four old-age pensioners complete with shopping trolley and Zimmer frame looking like teenage yobs – all bling and boomboxes. It was not only a good piece but, in a funny way, it was an encouraging piece – old age does not necessarily mean pipe and slippers by the fire.

Painted in 2006, it lasted for about two years and then suddenly it was gone. In its place was one word: 'COLLECTED', enclosed in a neat rectangle of broken lines – a satisfying reference to an earlier work by Banksy with the same broken lines marked 'Cut Out and Collect'.

What had happened was that Tom Organ, a man accustomed to conserving Byzantine mosaics in Istanbul or ancient Egyptian wall paintings in Luxor, had been called in to work his magic. At a cost of about £30,000 he took six weeks to do the job. Using mural transfer techniques developed following the disastrous floods in Florence of 1966 and updated since then, the paint layer was first supported from the front using a strong flexible film with a reversible adhesive. Mr Organ then carefully separated the paint layer from the plaster

support onto this adhesive. Finally, the paint was remounted onto three 2.4x1.2m (8x4ft) aluminium honeycomb panels, and the figures were reunited with the central ghetto blaster which, being on a rough concrete infill to an old fireplace, had been removed complete with the render.

At the time, it was reported that a German who worked in advertising had bought the wall, or rather the painting, for £1,000. In 2014 it had a price tag of £350,000 when it was shown at an exhibition in London. Whether it ever achieved that price is unknown. But can a Banksy painted on one surface and transferred to another be the real thing, or is it more some sort of Banksy tribute?

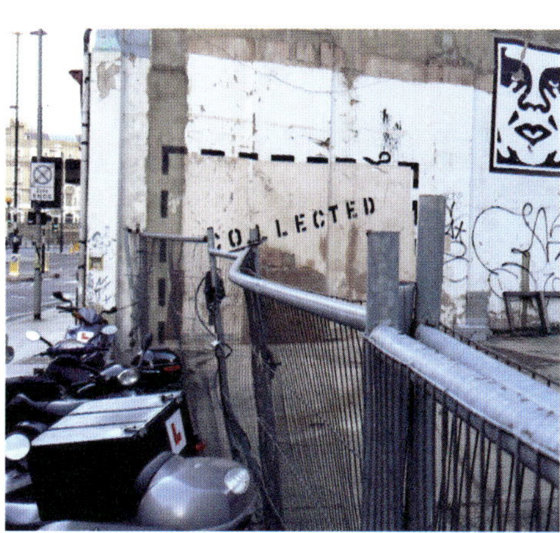

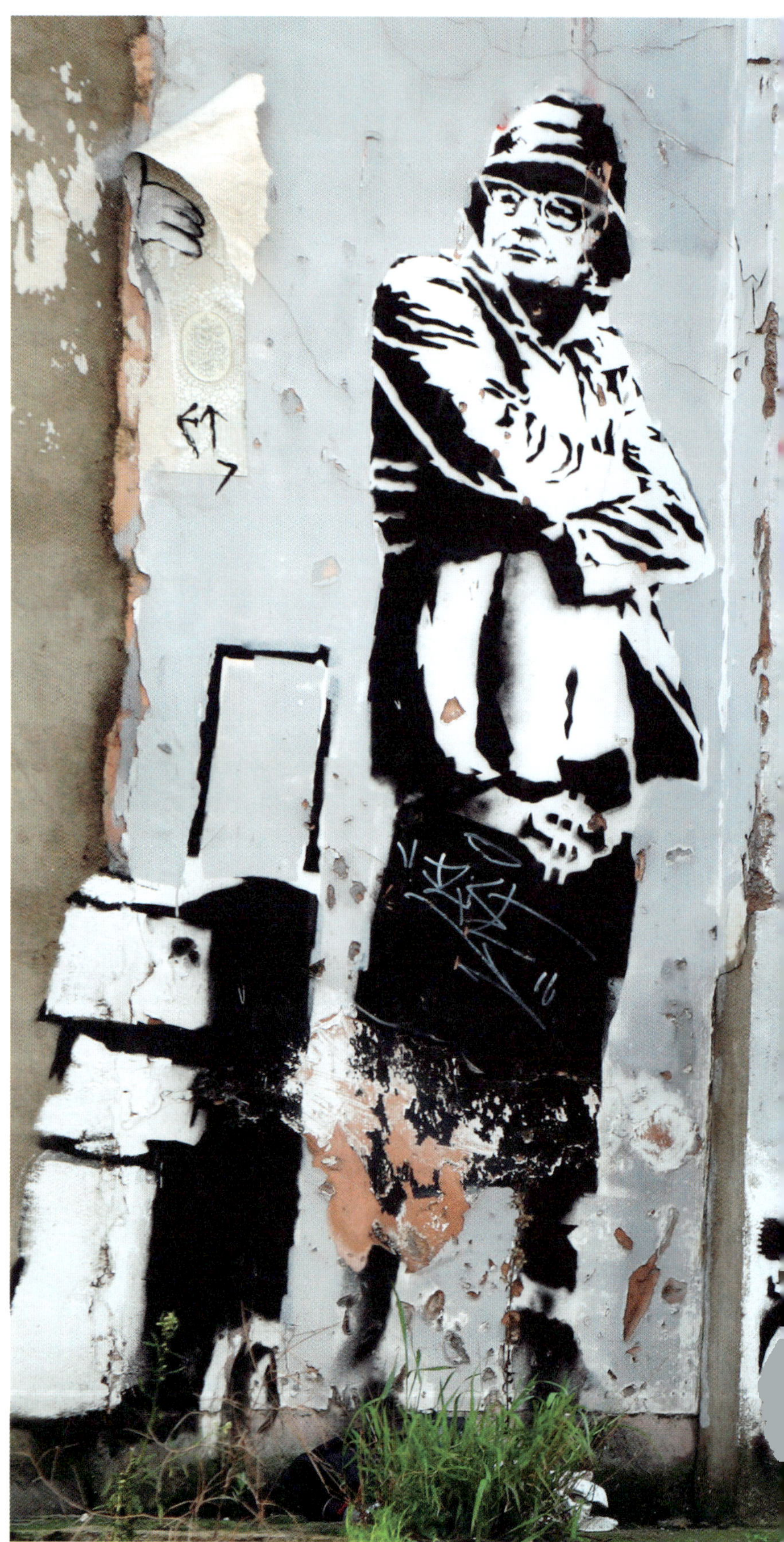

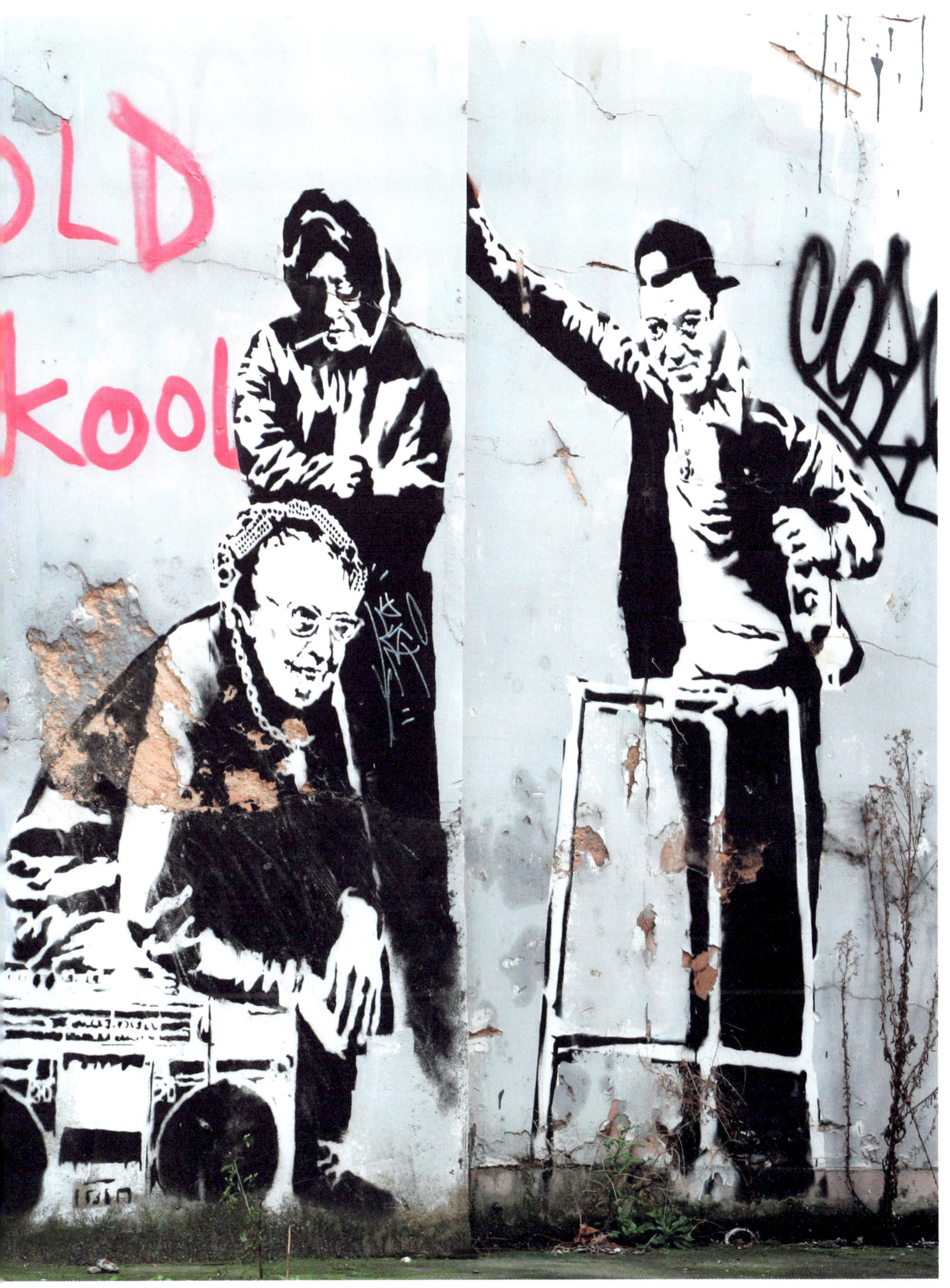
OLD
KOOL

19

BLINK AND IT'S GONE

How long does it take for a Banksy to disappear? There are those very few Banksys, almost all in Bristol, that last for years; but usually the lifespan of a Banksy piece can be measured in weeks, days or even hours. It can come down to a race between those who want to steal the Banksy, write over it or whitewash it out of existence.

Take this strolling brass band playing their instruments through gas masks in New Orleans. In his book *Cut & Run* Banksy says, 'I can never tell which paintings are going to last but it was bizarre that out of all of them, this one should be the shortest period. It was on the most run-down building I could find in the most run-down part of New Orleans. Three hours after I finished it, me and my fixer rolled past to find an old dude dressed only in speedos and sandals painting it out.

'He explained that a TV news truck had just been filming so it had to go. I'd painted the side of a brothel.'

Banksy, it has to be said, likes to gently tweak his stories on occasions and the photographer who took this picture, Anthony Turducken, says that to call it a brothel 'sounds too nice... it was more like a crack house, although there might have been some hookers staying there.' He thinks too that 'only three hours' might be a bit of an exaggeration if the time stamp on his photograph is correct, unless it was painted at midday in broad daylight, which of course with Banksy is perfectly possible.

But even if Banksy is correct and it did last only three hours, then this is considerably longer than his piece in Peckham, south London, which was gone less than an hour after it had been put up. Just over two months after the war in Gaza escalated in October 2023, Banksy stuck three military drones flying in menacing formation across a STOP sign. Once he confirmed that it was his on Instagram, two men set about stealing the sign, together with its drones, amid a gaggle of spectators who seemed so bemused by the spectacle they were witnessing, all they could do was film it. One of the men even had time to run off to collect a pair of bolt cutters so he could finish the job. (Two men were subsequently arrested on suspicion of theft and criminal damage.)

But here is Banksy's dilemma: is it worth claiming his own work? Confirming that the piece is his on Instagram keeps his art in the public eye – he has no gallery to exhibit in. But equally this now means that it may disappear just hours after being put up.

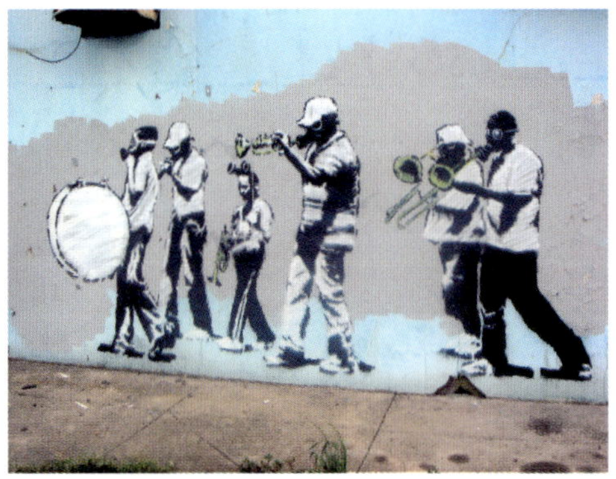

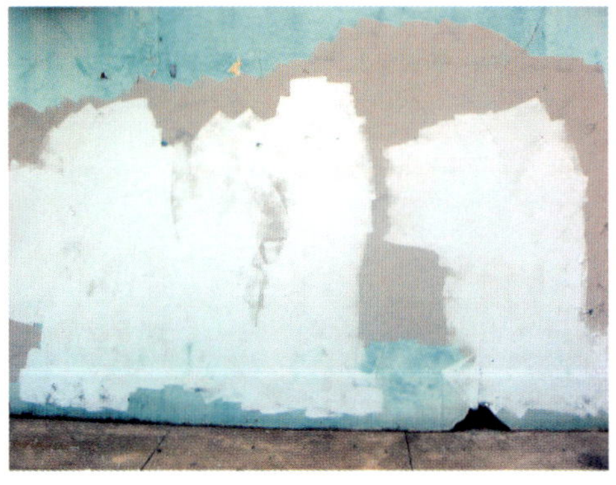

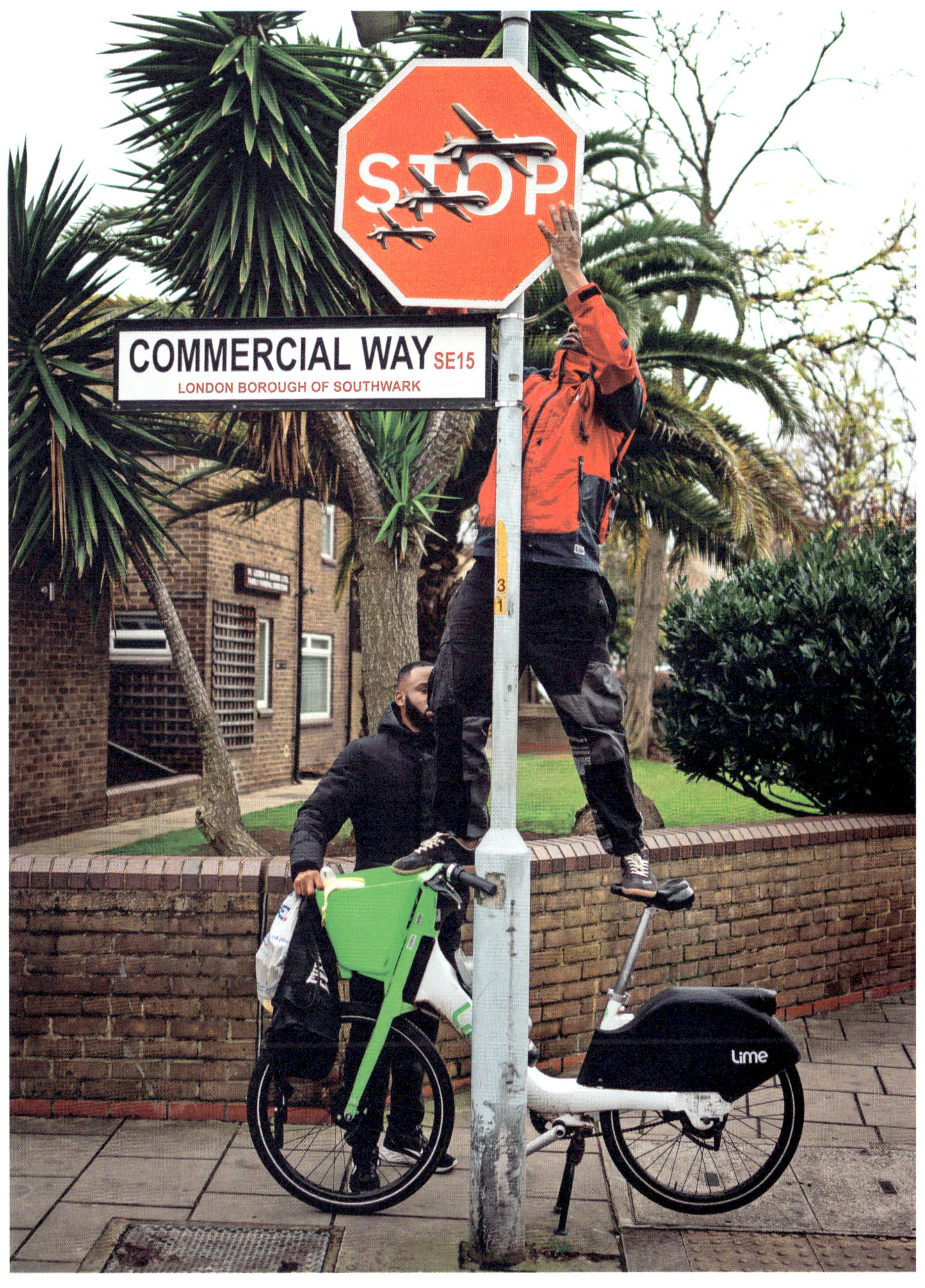
STOP
COMMERCIAL WAY SE15
LONDON BOROUGH OF SOUTHWARK
Lime

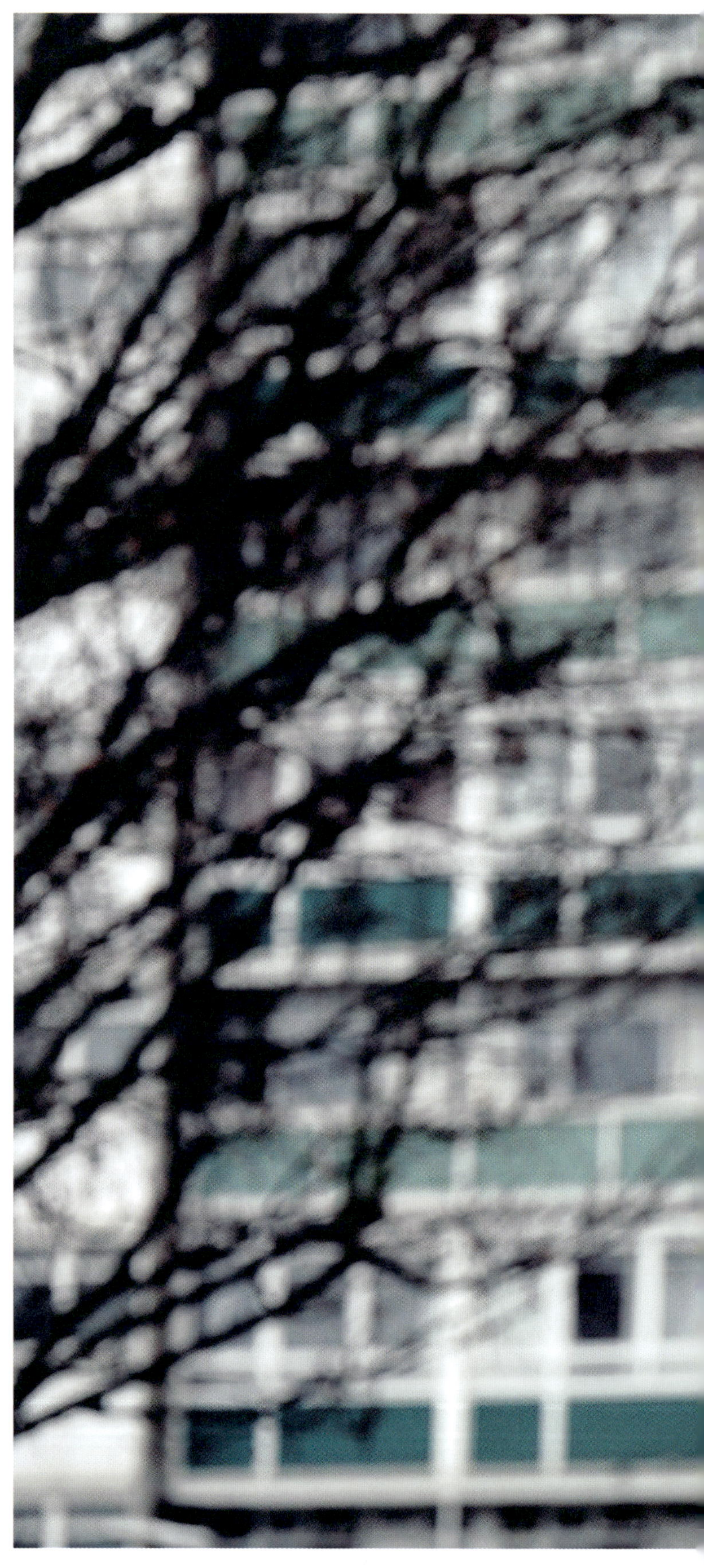

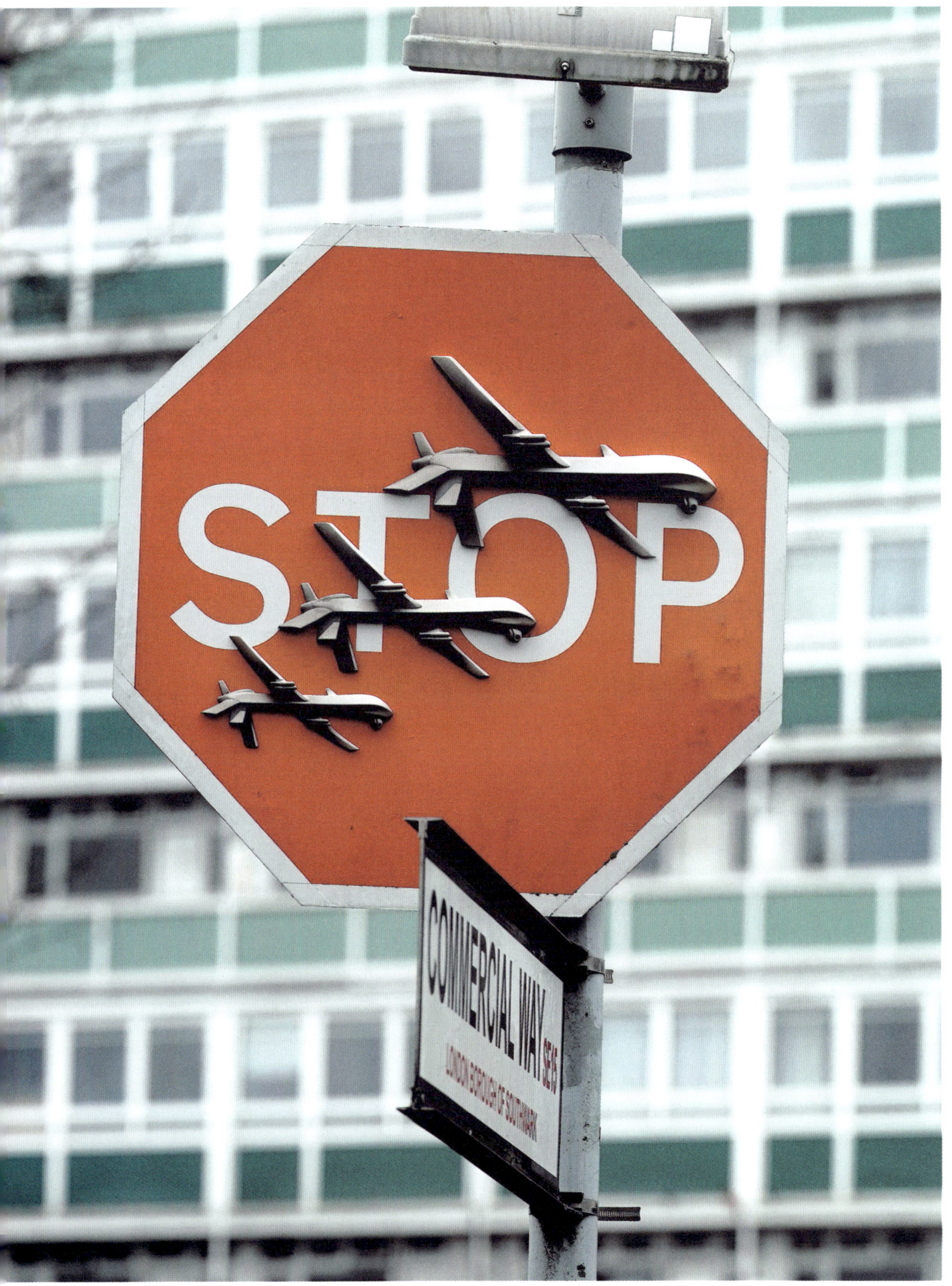

STOP
COMMERCIAL WAY SE15
LONDON BOROUGH OF SOUTHWARK

20

THE £800,000 STABLE

📍 MERRIVALE MODEL VILLAGE, MARINE PARADE,
GREAT YARMOUTH NR30 3JG

Banksy has always been good at distraction. When he infiltrated the Metropolitan Museum of Art in New York in 2005, he was helped by an accomplice who pointed to an entirely innocent visitor and shouted, 'Guards, guards, he just stuck his finger up my arse, get the dirty bastard.' The guards came running but, in the meantime, Banksy managed to put up one of his pictures on the museum's wall.

Distraction was a key part of the plan when Team Banksy, some of them wearing Covid masks, infiltrated the Merrivale Model Village on the seafront at Great Yarmouth in August 2021. In one of their cool boxes they were carrying not a Banksy painting but a Banksy model stable. Colin Darlow, the village's gardener, was there that morning and, as we sit beside the spot where Banksy struck, he tells me the extraordinary story of what happened next.

'One of the women asked the model maker about how all the models were made and he took her into the workshop to show her. While he was doing this they was out here putting up a drone. So he came out of the workshop and they've got a drone flying around. It was ever so low so he grabbed a fishing net and tried to catch it.'

It must have been a moment of high farce set amid this miniature perfect world. They had done their job perfectly, for what Colin calls this 'little bit of commotion' gave Banksy the chance to add his own model to the village, a pretty little thatched stable, complete with graffiti on the walls.

Mr Darlow did notice the new stable early the next day, 'but I thought it might have been just Matt the model maker having a joke as he did sometimes.' It took 48 hours before a visitor told the then owner of the village, Frank Newsome, that

he had a Banksy on his hands, and, it was part of Banksy's 'Spraycation' – making his mark across the seaside towns of East Anglia.

A nightmare or a dream come true? The village had had a dismal two years because of Covid and the Banksy name quickly drove up visitors by almost 50 per cent. But Mr Newsome found the whole thing 'a bit scary.' He had to hide the stable away from the village every night for fear of it being stolen. So it was not long before the stable was sent off to auction, where it fetched an extraordinary £800,000 or £1,000,000 once all the fees were included.

Mr Newsome had a heart attack shortly before the auction and, although he recovered, he and his wife decided to sell the village a few months later. The village now has a replica stable, complete with graffiti. It is protected by a hard plastic case, but it is difficult to imagine that anyone would want to deface a replica, let alone steal it.

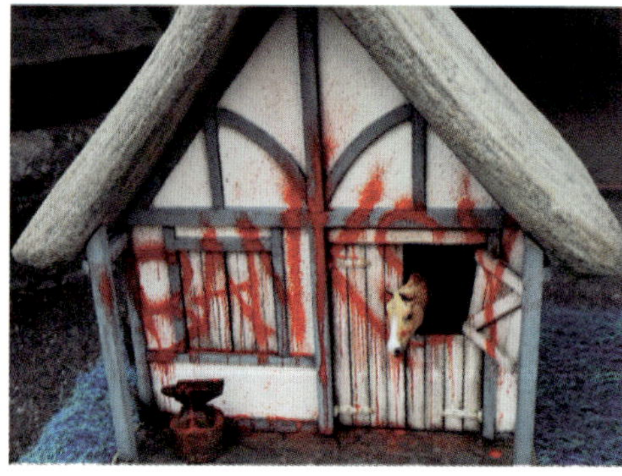

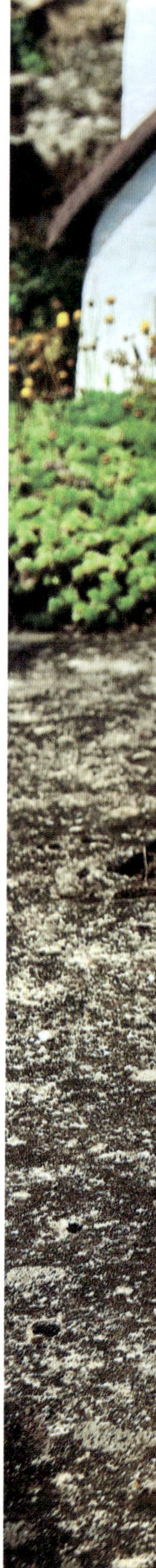

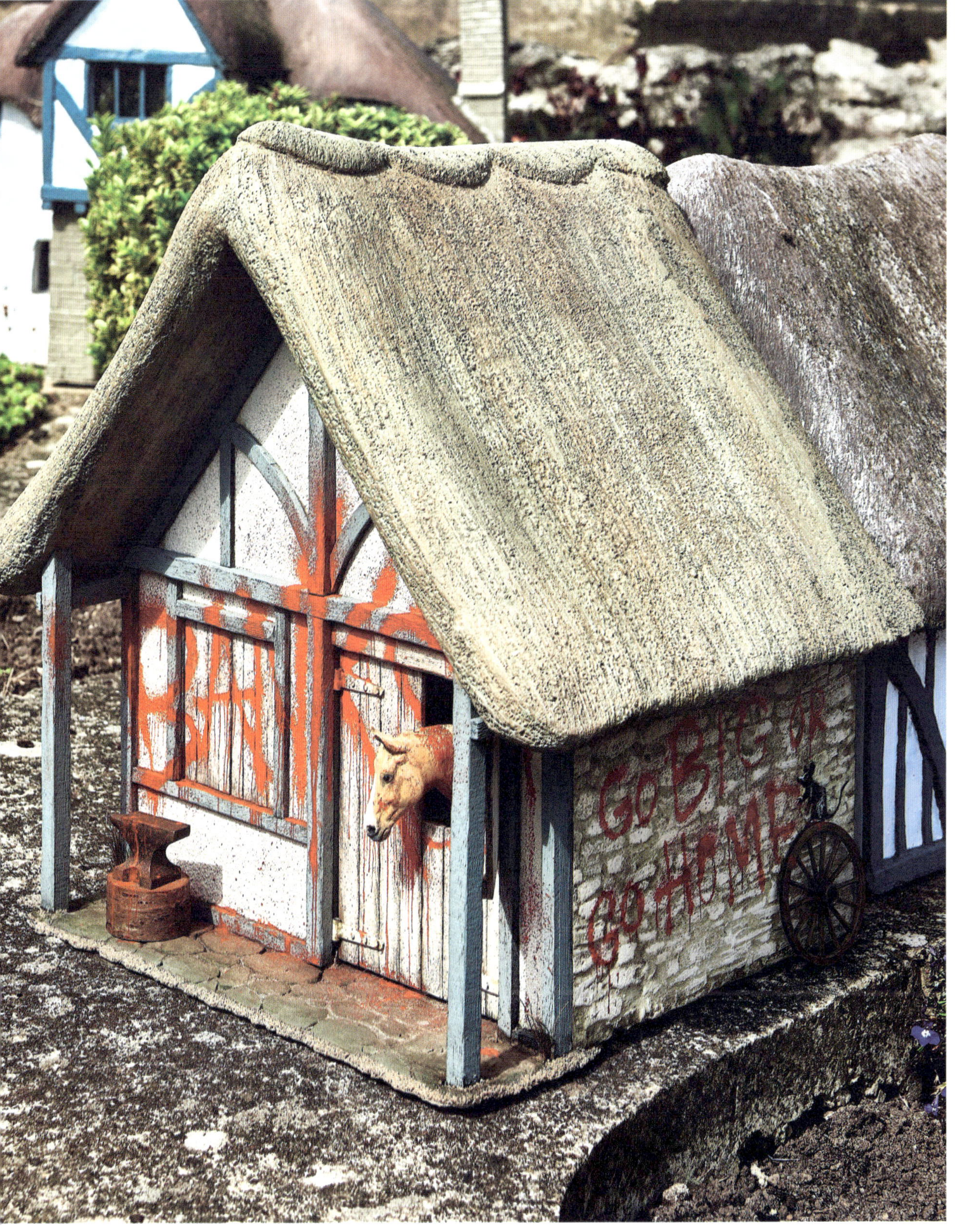

Go BIG or
Go HOME

21

VANDALIZING THE VANDAL

9901 SANTA MONICA BLVD CA 90212 (*PEEING DOG*);
908–910 S. BROADWAY, LOS ANGELES CA 90015 (*GIRL ON A SWING*);
537 MAIN STREET, PARK CITY, UTAH 84060 (*ANGEL BOY*)

When Banksy and Robbo started painting over each other's work, it was headlined a graffiti war and compared to the rivalry between Picasso and Matisse. However, when an unknown artist tried to paint over four of Banksy's pieces in Utah and California he was simply called a vandal and at one point faced five years in prison.

David Noll, 35 at the time, an unsuccessful artist having to deal with what he called a 'bi-polar problem', was on a crusade. On his LinkedIn profile he wrote: 'My lifelong goal is to NOT stop battling until mODERN aRT as we know it is destroyed.' At the end of 2013 Noll defaced two Banksy pieces in Los Angeles: *Peeing Dog* he painted over with black paint, and for *Girl on a Swing* he chose blue. But there was more to come. He travelled from his home in California to Park City, Utah, where Banksy had painted seven works to coincide with the premiere of his film at the Sundance Festival. There he attacked two more Banksys, with mixed results. On one piece he got no further than the bulletproof glass, but on the other he managed to crack the cover and spray over *Angel Boy*, this time choosing brown paint.
He shot ill-lit YouTube videos of himself doing all this, which made him easy enough to catch.

It appeared as though the three works were lost forever, but while *Peeing Dog* never resurfaced, both *Girl on a Swing* and Park City's *Angel Boy* were restored, although *Angel Boy* needed some radical work.

But if David Noll was to be charged with vandalism, why not Banksy too? The district attorney in Los Angeles explained that while the owners of the buildings had complained about Mr Noll, no one had complained about Banksy, a simple enough explanation if not exactly a fair one.

Eventually, faced with five years in jail, Mr Noll accepted plea bargains in both California and Utah with probation for five years and community service. In Los Angeles a restraining order prevented him coming within 100 metres of a Banksy, which might have forced him to dodge and weave ridiculously down the street if Banksy was in town, and in Utah he, or rather his parents, had to pay $13,000 restoration costs. All this was certainly not Banksy's fault but it was hardly surprising that one 'ImNotGrimey' wrote on the web: 'Dear Banksy, Please do the right thing and offer to pay this poor man's restitution. Street art is made to be temporary, painted over, erased, and stolen.'

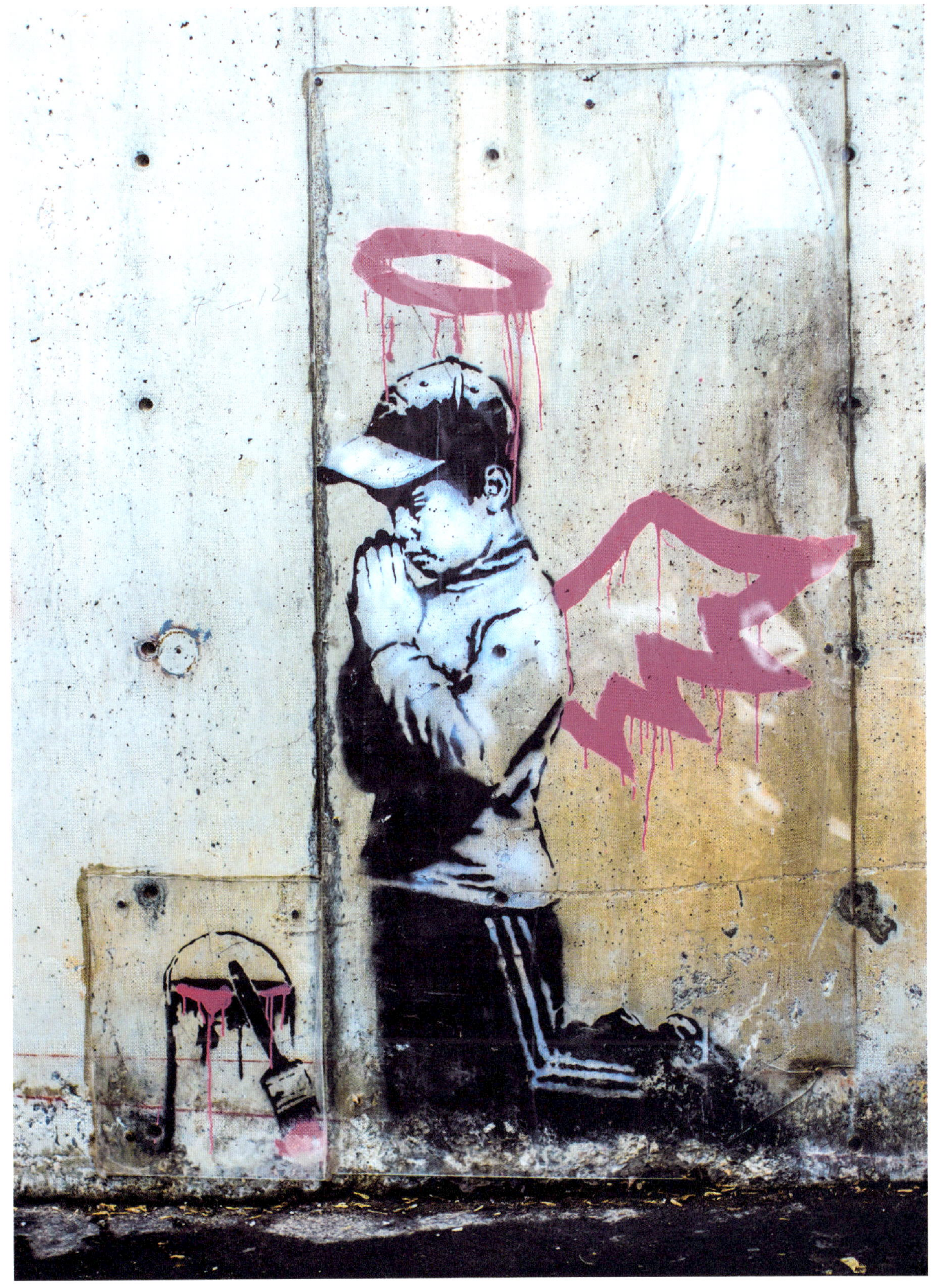

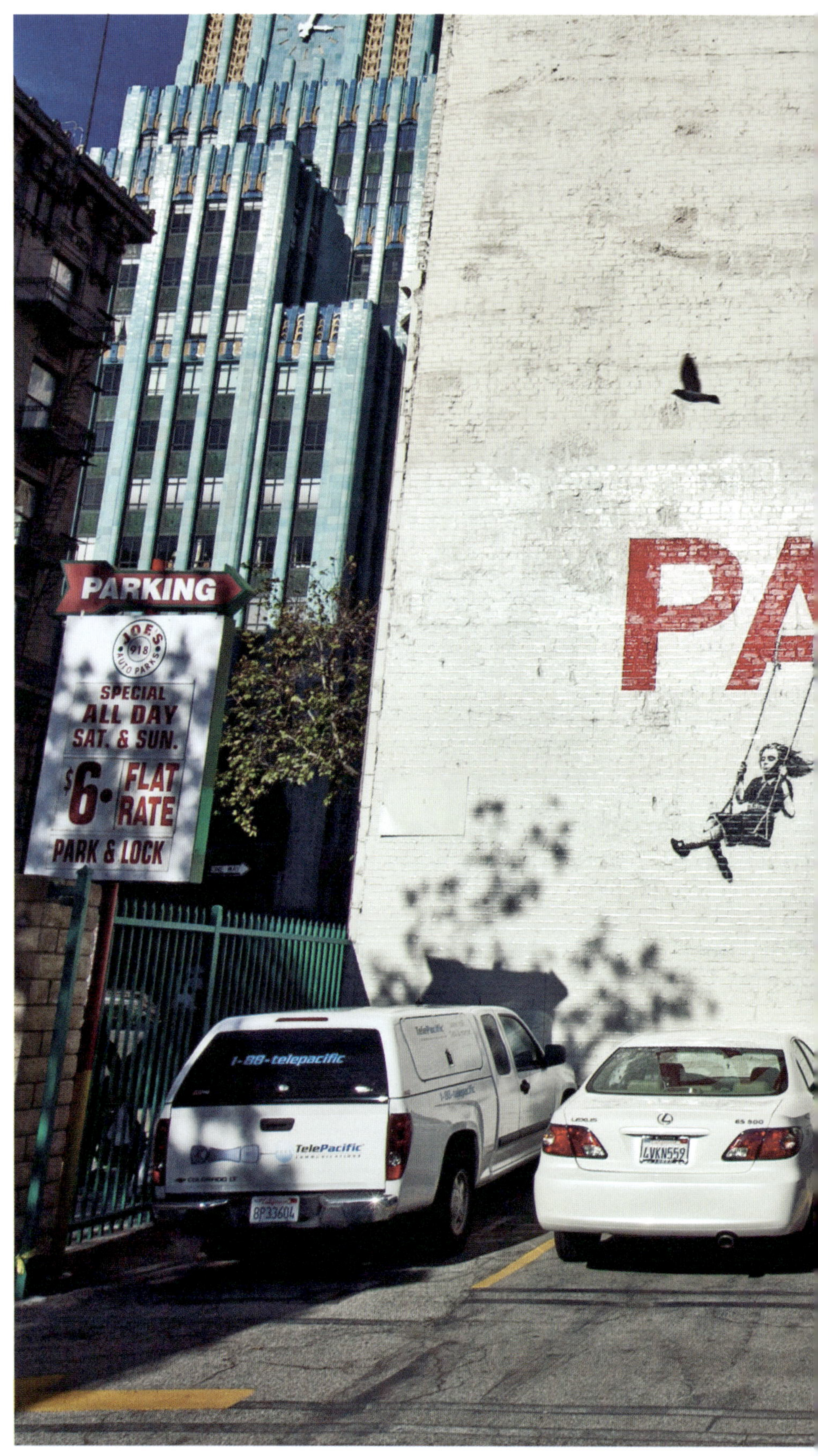

PARKING
JOE'S
918
AUTO PARKS
SPECIAL
ALL DAY
SAT. & SUN.
$6• FLAT
RATE
PARK & LOCK
1-88-telepacific
TelePacific
PA

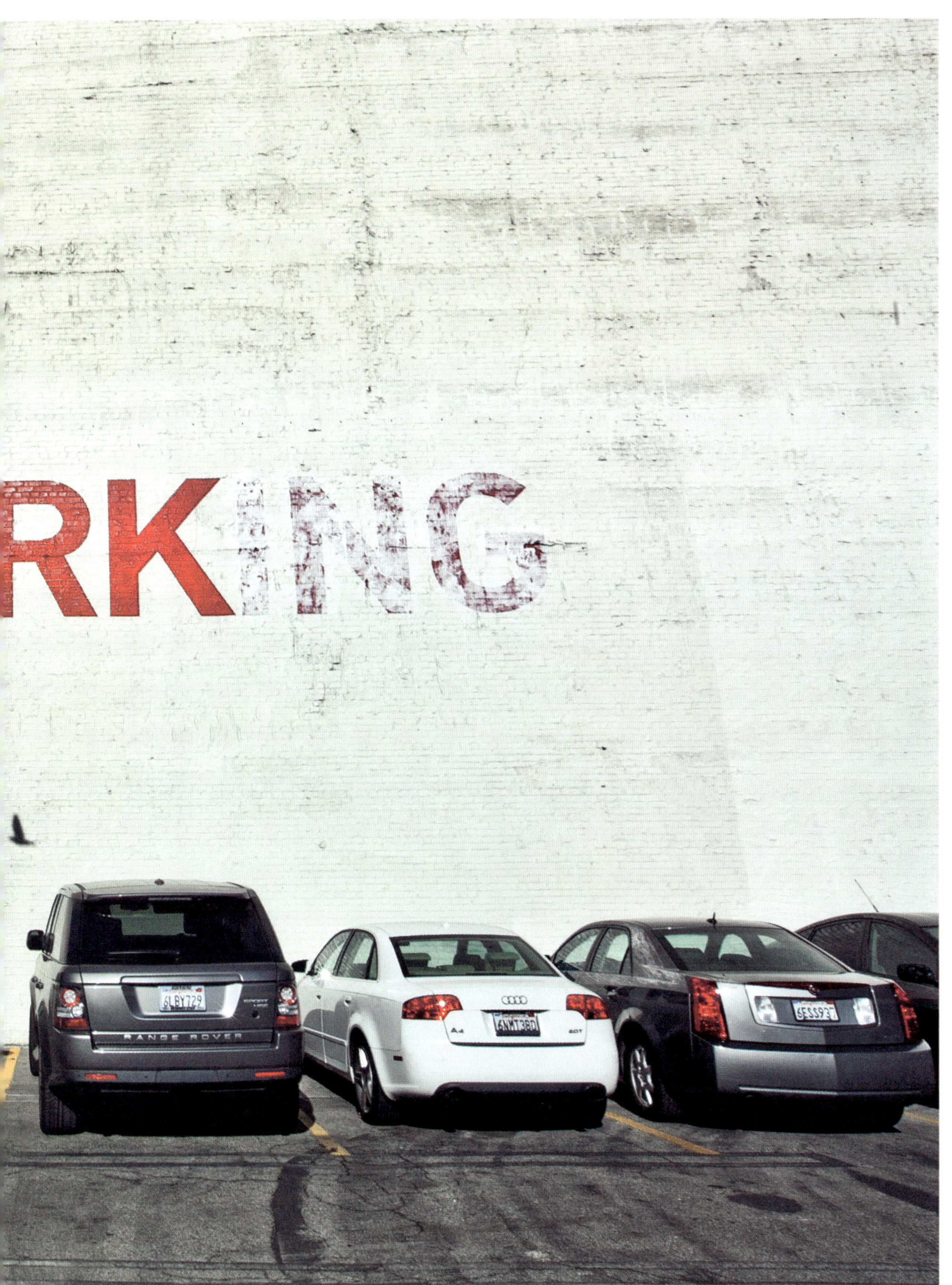
RKING

22

THE DEMOLITION JOB

◊ BLACKSOLE FARM, HERNE BAY CT6 6LA

When Banksy organized the self-destruction of *Girl with Balloon* in front of a disbelieving audience at Sotheby's in 2018, it seemed he had proved his point about the ephemeral nature of his art. But five years later he stage-managed the destruction of not just a painting but a whole building with one of his works on it.

He has never admitted this but it does not take much detective work to work out that when Banksy painted *Morning is Broken* on the plywood protecting a window of a derelict farmhouse, he knew the young boy joyously opening his corrugated-iron curtains only had days to live.

The farmhouse on the outskirts of Herne Bay, Kent, was quite close to a main road but completely shielded by undergrowth and bushes. Almost five hundred years old, it had spent its last years empty and forlorn, and in December 2022 the owner, Kitewood Estates, won permission to demolish it and build 67 homes there. Goody Demolition served the local council with a demolition notice in January 2023, so everyone owning property nearby was officially informed and the council gave Goody the go-ahead. Everything was done by the book; it was no secret that the building was going to come down.

The demolition team started fencing off the site in March 2023. Although they did not realize it, the Banksy was already there, but it had only been there for a short time. Quite how short is unclear, but the footpath running right by the farmhouse was used by shoppers on their way to a new Sainsbury's superstore. If the boy had been there for any length of time, word would have got out beyond a few shoppers.

What convinced me that Banksy wanted it destroyed before anyone could get their hands on it was the fact that he did not claim ownership of it on Instagram until the day after it had been demolished. Two of the three pictures he put up were of the boy, but the third showed the demolition men at work and the wall gone. So Team Banksy had been there on the spot waiting to capture this moment.

But like *Girl with Balloon*, where the shredder concealed in its picture frame stopped, allowing half the picture to survive, *Morning is Broken* did not entirely disappear. When the demolition team discovered what they had done, they rummaged in their skip and found much of the boy still intact, although the two major pieces of plywood needed marrying together. (The boy's cat had not fared so well – with not much more than his ears left.)

The plywood was given to the site's owners, although it is unclear what happened to the corrugated-iron 'curtains'. It is reasonable to assume that the boy will be restored and one day will appear on the market with or without the curtains. So Banksy's attempt to spray a work on a wall and have it disappear before anyone else could profit from it will surely end ultimately with someone making a lot of money.

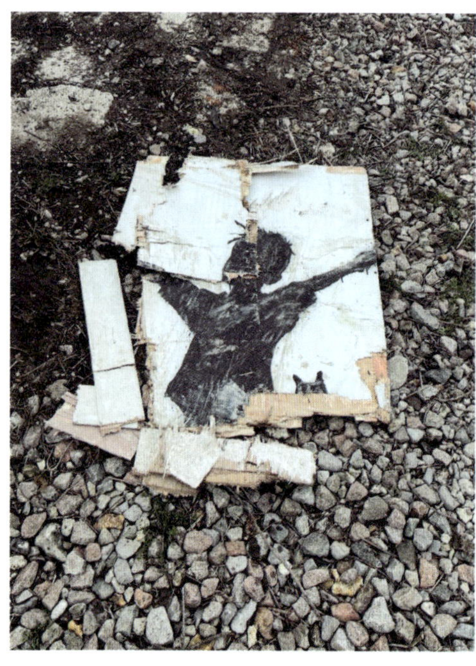

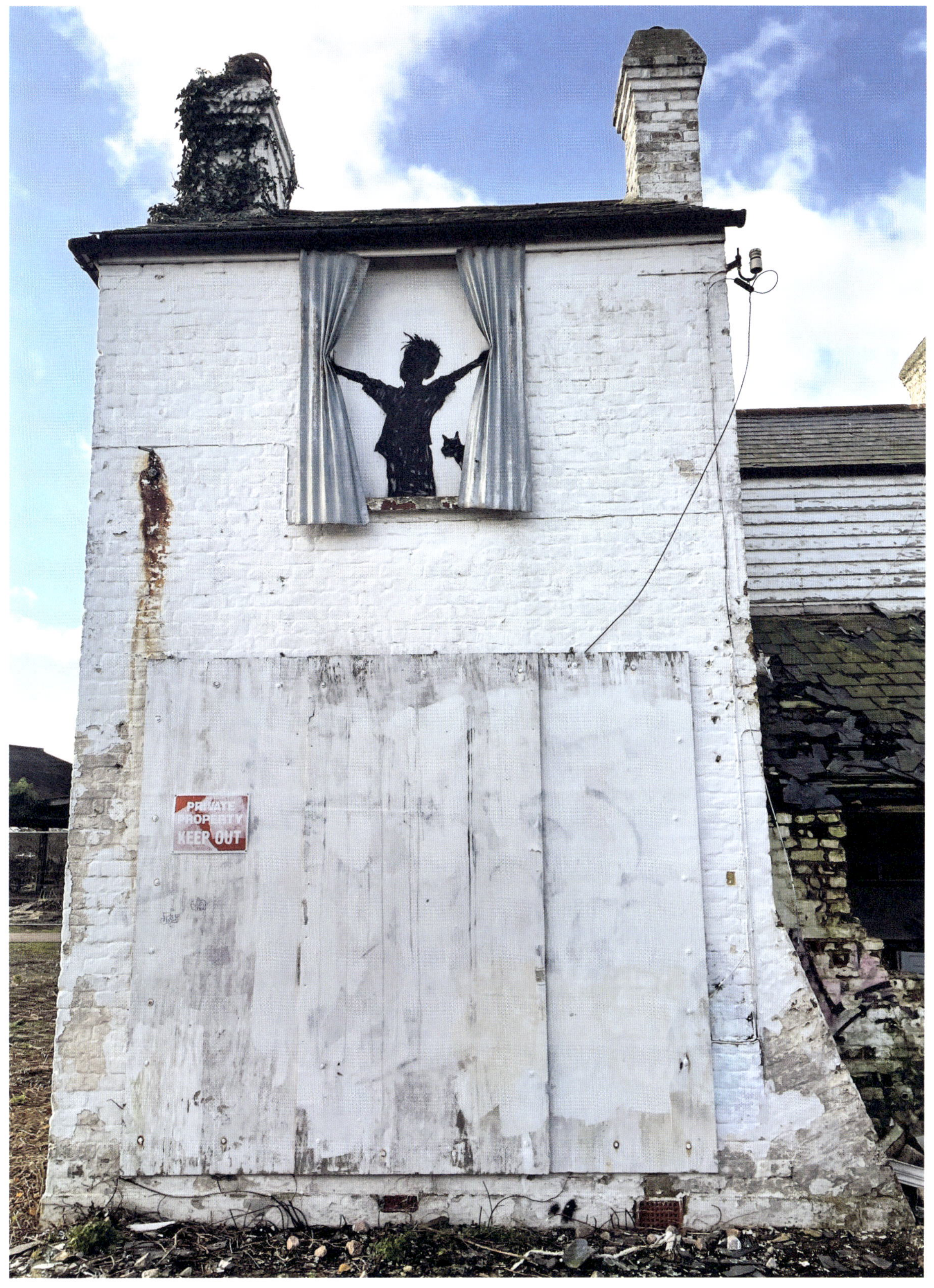
PRIVATE
PROPERTY
KEEP OUT

23

MEDDLING WITH MICKEY

◊ SUNSET BOULEVARD AND NORTH LAUREL AVE, LOS ANGELES CA 90046

Banksy has subverted a few ads, but only a few. Perhaps the fact that the only time he has been arrested was when he was hard at work subverting a Marc Jacobs poster on the rooftop of a building in New York's Meatpacking District has made him cautious about doing many more.

But in Los Angeles in 2011, when he was looking for publicity just before the Academy Awards, he found a billboard just waiting to be subverted right in front of the Directors Guild of America headquarters on Sunset Boulevard.

It was a strange ad in its original form – one scantily dressed woman, with too many words around her, promoting the 'perfect lifestyle' in Las Vegas. Indeed one suggestion on the web, without any evidence to back this up, was that it was actually put up there specifically for Banksy to subvert. Whether or not he had a helping hand, it certainly became much more interesting once Banksy had finished with it. He inserted a lascivious Mickey Mouse, his tongue hanging out, his hands very full, a cocktail in one and the woman's breast in the other. Minnie looked on gleefully.

However, within 72 hours the billboard company decided it did not meet their standards and had to be taken down. The piece, painted on a plastic drape that covered the fixed billboard, was lowered down on ropes and then rolled up rather humiliatingly. By 2011 people were beginning to realize there was money to be made from Banksy, and it is still possible to see on the web a short but fierce row developing over ownership as this enormous roll of Banksy is squashed into a van.

But that was not the end of this particular work. The company that paid for the ad, The Light Group of Las Vegas, succeeded in claiming that it was theirs to take. 'We were flattered Banksy tagged on our ad – it was epic,' said their spokeswoman.

Quite what happened to the poster remains a mystery. Beth Bartolini, speaking for the company, said at the time it would be taken back to Las Vegas and the founder of the company, Andrew Sasson, would find a space to display it. But while the company did display a large Banksy, *Smiley Coppers Panel I*, when it opened a new restaurant on the strip, I have yet to see a drunken Mickey and Minnie appear anywhere in public again.

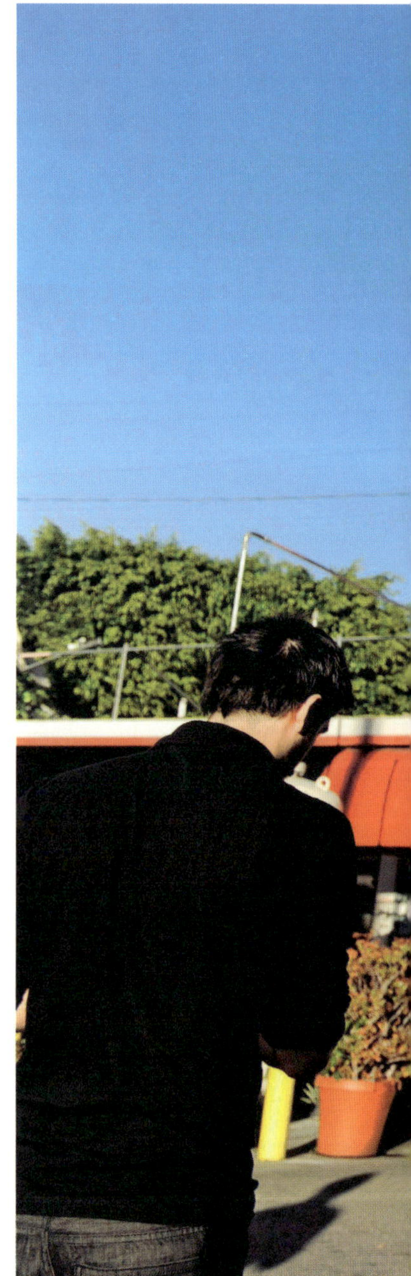

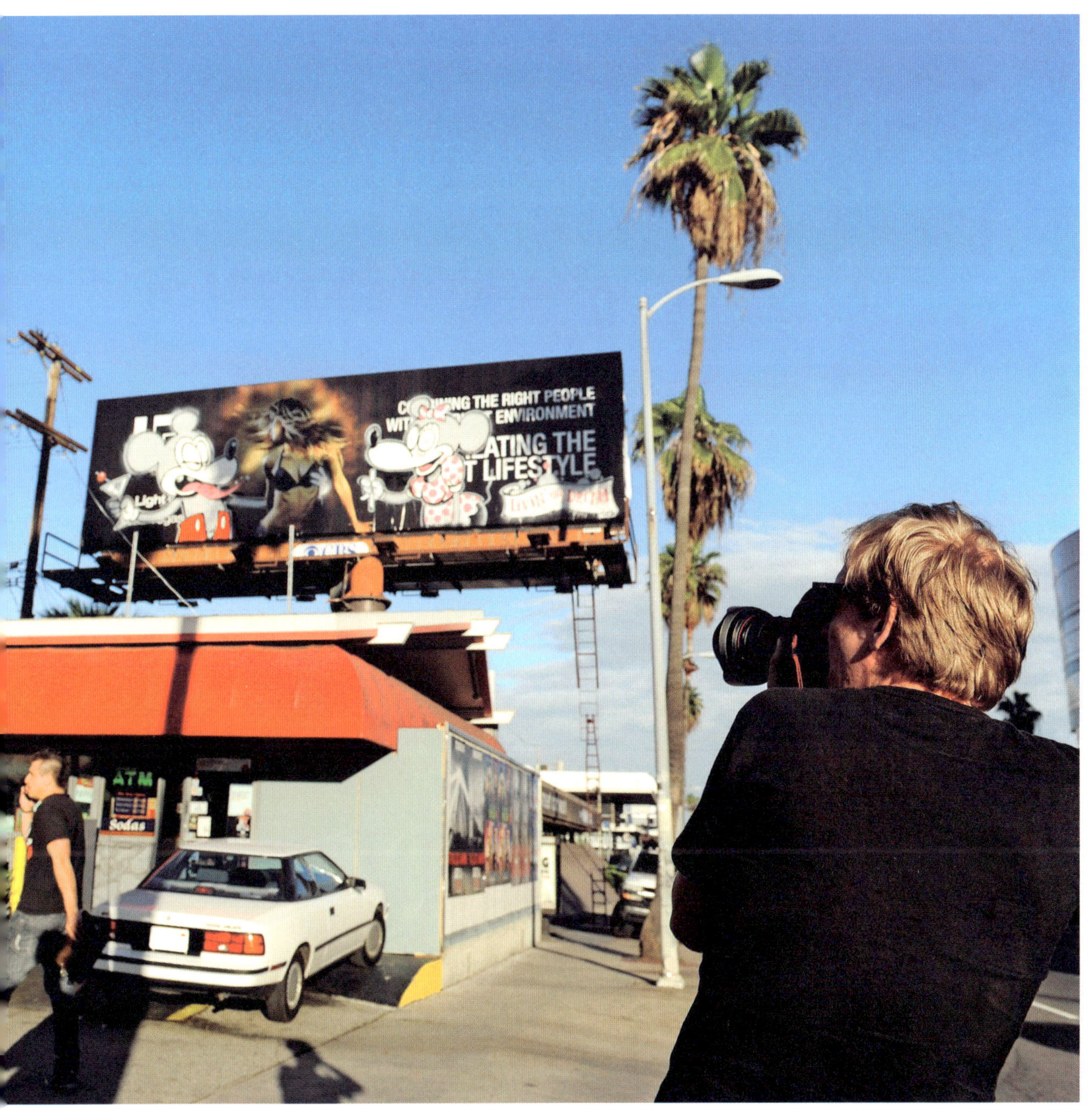
COMBINING THE RIGHT PEOPLE
WITH THE RIGHT ENVIRONMENT
CREATING THE
RIGHT LIFESTYLE
Light
ATM
Sodas

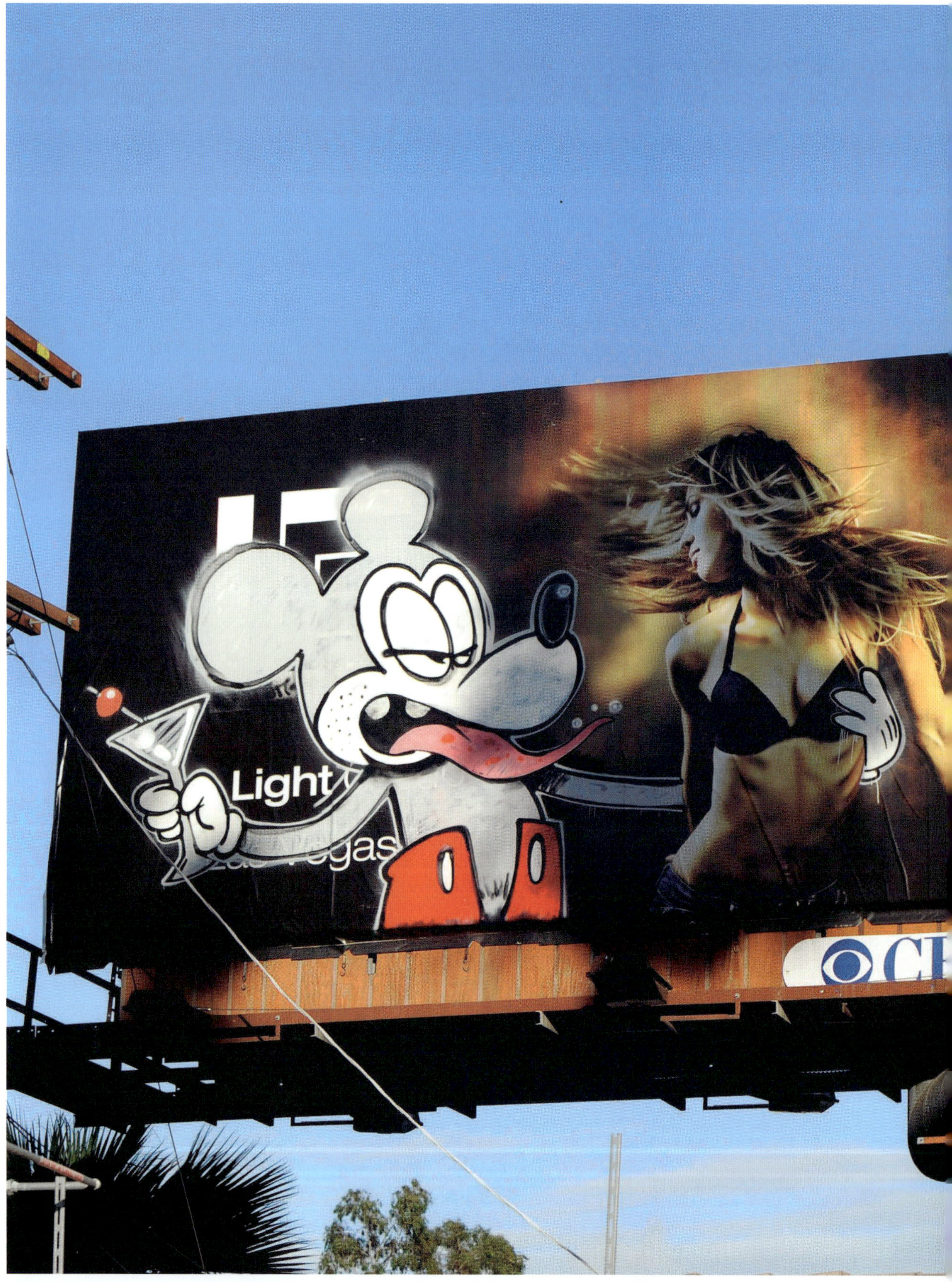
Light
Las Vegas

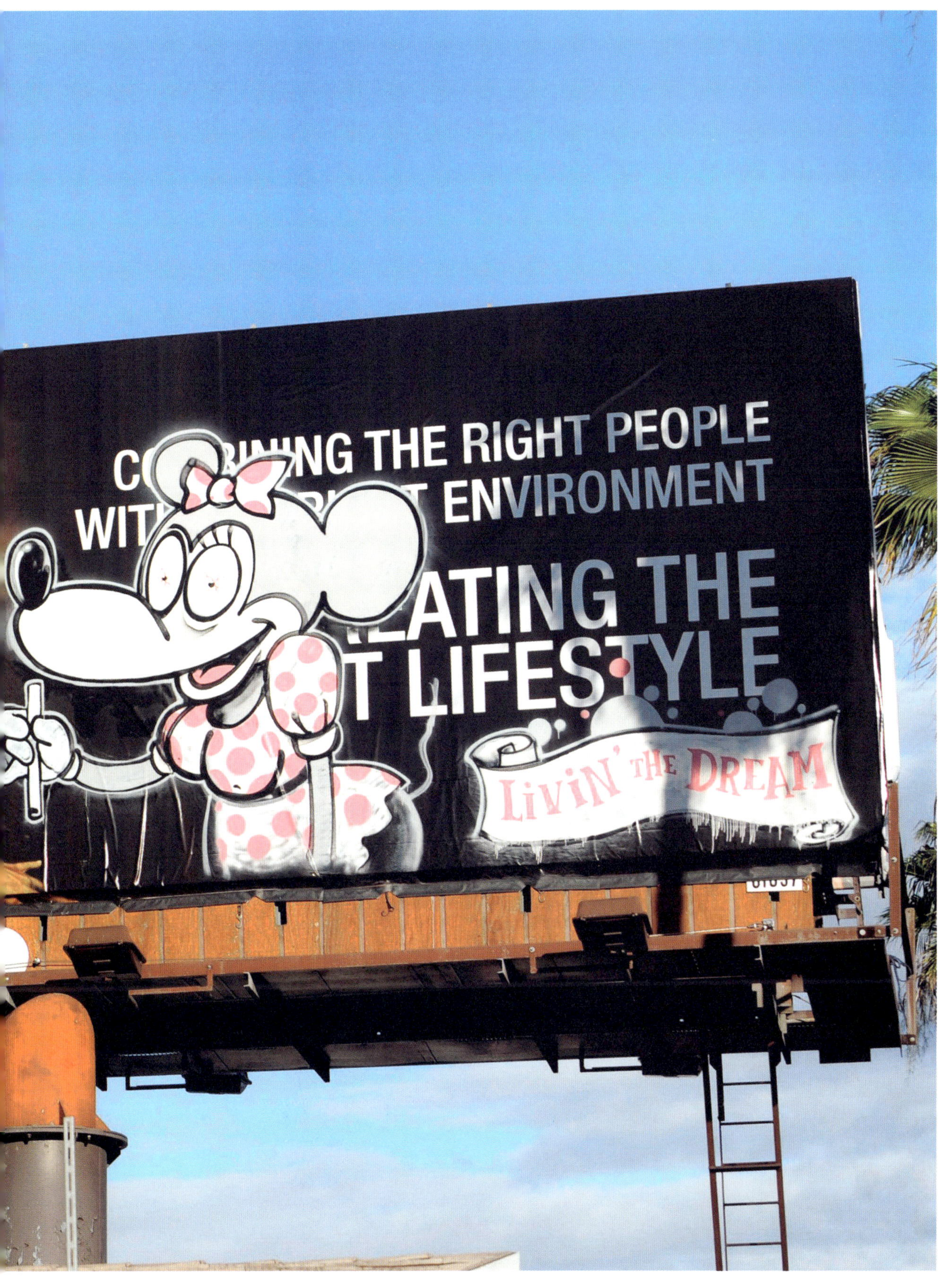
COMBINING THE RIGHT PEOPLE
WITH THE RIGHT ENVIRONMENT
CREATING THE
RIGHT LIFESTYLE
LiviN' THE DREAM

THE LOST BOY

◉ 1560 E. GRAND BOULEVARD, DETROIT MI 48211

In many ways this story is the ultimate test of whether a Banksy should be taken from its surroundings, its context, or left to die and be demolished.

In 2010, Banksy painted a touching piece on a wall of a long-abandoned Packard car factory in Detroit. A slightly haunted-looking boy stood there, paint pot and paint brush in hand, beside the words he had just written on the wall: 'I remember when all this was trees'. It lasted just three days before it was cut out and taken away.

For Carl Goines, a sculptor and co-founder of the 555 non-profit art space in inner-city Detroit, this was an easy test – the Banksy had to be preserved. After 50 years of total neglect, part of the factory was being pulled down and he had to stop the Banksy being pulled down with it.

Mr Goines had known nothing about Banksy or his work until a photographer friend called asking for his help in trying to save the piece. With his father and three friends he went to inspect it. A foreman on the site said they could take the wall, which he mistakenly thought was worthless, as long as they did not take any scrap metal. So they went to work – it took just 24 hours to cut it out.

But instead of being hailed as saviours, they were very soon being cast as villains. The piece went on display for just ten days before it was put into storage for a year because there was so much anger swirling around about the ethics of 'saving' it.

One critic wrote on the website dETROITfUNK: 'The point of "street art" is for it to exist in its natural environment, it is by nature temporary. Disappointing when a good piece fades away? Yes. But that's life. More meaning in that than some art f*gs cutting it out and sticking it in a gallery shortly after it's appeared. The power of that piece was in its environment... I just can't fathom how someone could miss the point to such a degree that they'd remove it and boast that they were "SAVING!" it.'

At that point it was easy enough to sympathize with Mr Goines. But five years later, having claimed originally that 'we are not selling it, we are protecting it', the gallery announced that it was to be auctioned off. The proceeds would help to pay for converting an empty warehouse into a new art space.

The piece sold for $110,000, which, although a lot of money, was considerably lower than predicted. The buyer was Steven Dunn, founder and chairman of Munchkin, a very successful California baby-products company. Physically destroyed? No. But lost? Certainly.

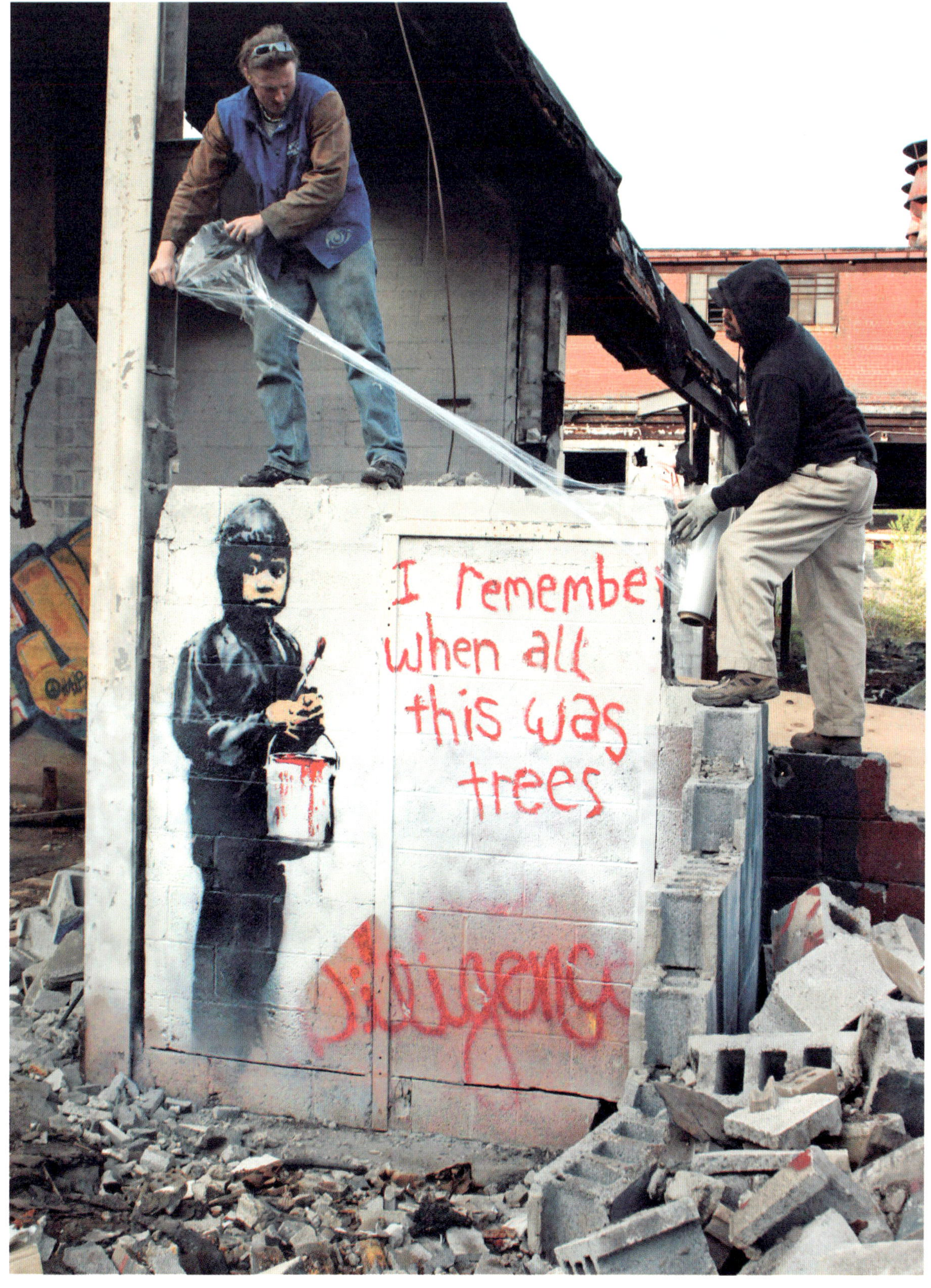

I remember when all this was trees

25

TREE SURGERY

◉ HORNSEY ROAD, LONDON N19 4HS

When I first saw a picture of Banksy's 'tree' – great splashes of green across a wall cleverly providing the foliage for a naked cherry tree that looked badly in need of it – it never occurred to me that the tree was in any way lost. But that was before I went to see it. (Finding it up the Hornsey Road in Islington was relatively easy; such is the power of Banksy that three weeks after being painted it was already on Google Maps.)

The tree was not lost; it was actually worse than lost. The owner of the building put up what was the most heavily engineered protection of any piece of street art I have ever seen. Islington council followed, first with a protective metal fence and then an elaborate wall, where painted wooden columns held up Perspex viewing windows. So we were seeing, or rather attempting to see, Banksy's green foliage through not one but two layers of Perspex. A cyclist stopped to ask me what was going on; he had been going past there for several days and just could not work out what it was all about. No wonder.

The owner of the building, Alex Georgiou, who runs a family estate agency on the same road, said the first he knew of it was when he got a text from his tenant there. Then what? 'Obviously I have never been in this situation. I thought, what the bloody hell am I going to do with this?' He was still thinking when, within 24 hours, someone 'threw a load of white paint on it.' It was then he decided Perspex was needed. Protecting it, including security, cost him 'about fifteen grand.' While he wanted it to stay on the wall – 'let people enjoy it, it's good for the area' – he had also been in touch with Julian Usher, the art dealer who masterminded taking Banksy's battered housewife off the wall in Margate. He says Mr Usher is advising him on 'how to protect it long-term by taking it off the wall.'

But the cost of doing this, said Mr Georgiou, 'is within the hundreds of thousands. And if I spend all that money, will I get my money back? Nobody knows.' And what about the tree? Mr Georgiou said that 'whoever would buy it would just end up re-creating the tree, almost like a set designer.'

Reappearing in a museum or a massive private home as an expensive installation with a fake tree in front of it; remaining partially obscured behind the Perspex; or sitting there with no protection, a target for other graffiti writers – Banksy left him with no easy answers. The irony, of course, is that shortly after all this the tree itself came into leaf as if nature was agreeing with Banksy that it needed some clothes on.

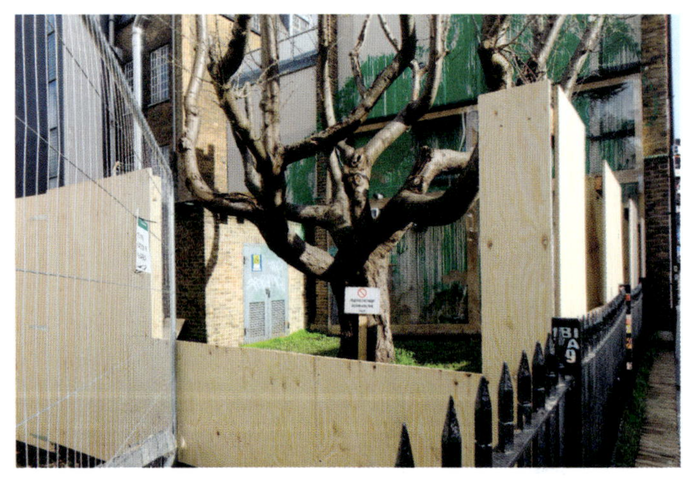

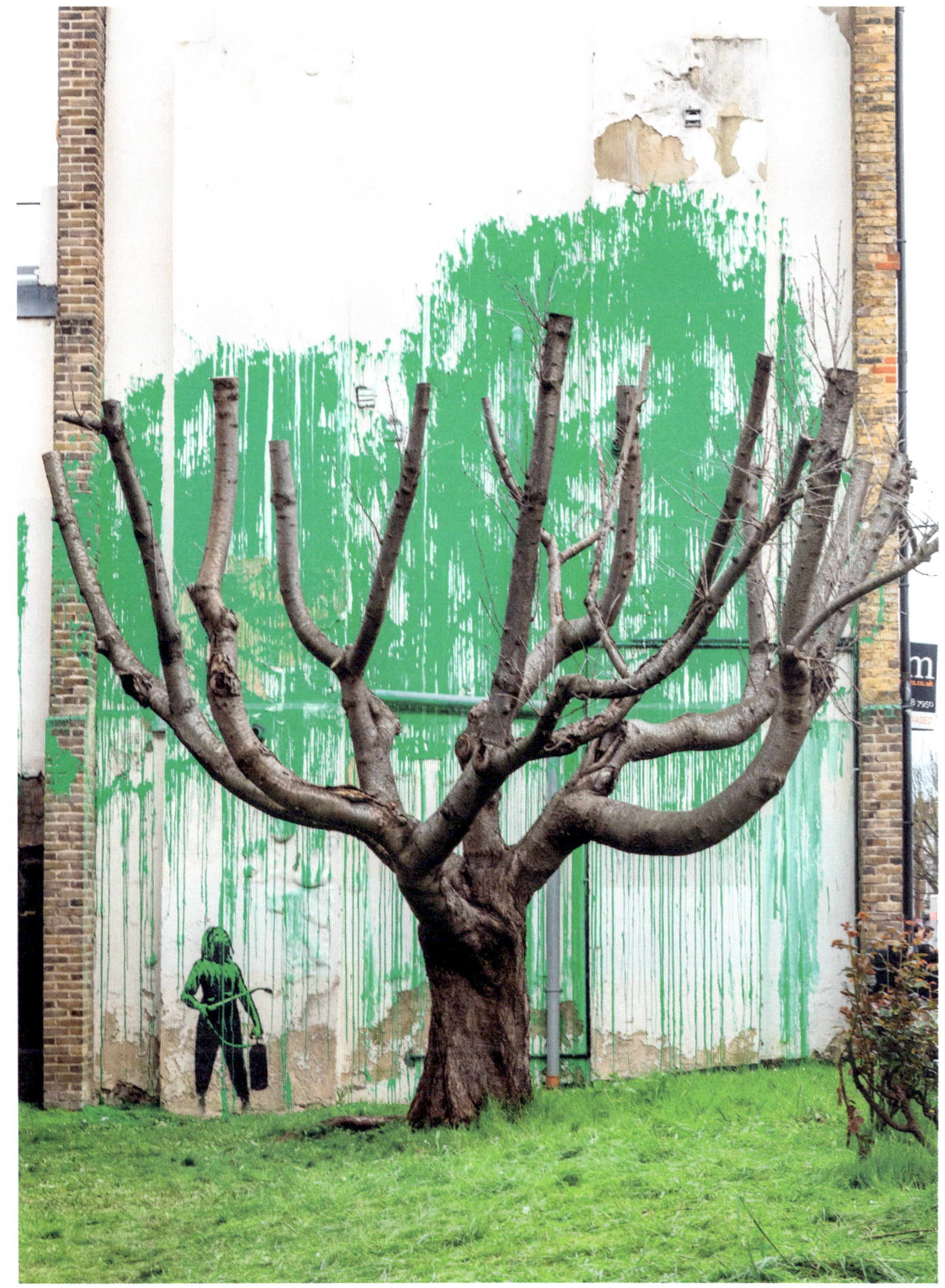

26

DOOR TO NOWHERE

◉ GAZA

In retrospect Banksy was light years ahead of much of the rest of the world in calling attention to the plight of Palestinians in Gaza. But his attempt to awaken the world ended not in any kind of victory but in a mean squabble over who owned a door he had painted on.

He entered Gaza in February 2015, following the war between Hamas and Israel the previous summer which had left more than 2,000 people dead and 18,000 homes destroyed. He came and went through one of the tunnels from Egypt. Once back home he released a powerful two-minute video entitled 'Welcome to Gaza', which painted a depressing picture of the strip while exhorting viewers, in true travel-agent style, to 'Make this the year YOU discover a new destination.'

One of the four pieces he painted while he was there was an image of the Greek goddess Niobe, weeping for her children. As his canvas he used an iron door, literally all that was left of a two-storey house in northern Gaza. It was hardly surprising, given Gaza's isolation, that Rabie Darduna, the owner of the house and thus the door, had no idea who Banksy was or what the painting might be worth. So when he was offered 700 shekels, just under $200, for his door he was happy to accept it. But then he discovered his painful mistake. 'I did not know that it was this valuable. I heard it can be sold for millions,' Mr Darduna told the Associated Press. 'Now I want the door back.'

He soon armed himself with a lawyer (Banksy has inadvertently provided work for a considerable number of lawyers over the years) who announced, 'I will seek to return the door to its true owner. My client was cheated.'

The new owner of the wall, Belal Khaled, an artist and freelance journalist, told the rival news agency Reuters, 'I am the true owner of the door now, and I will seek to establish this in court.' The Hamas police were not impressed. They arrived at Mr Khaled's home and told him they were confiscating the work until the legal dispute between the two men was settled.

I started researching the fate of Banksy's *Niobe* in the summer of 2023 before the latest war in Gaza started. It was impossible then to find out the fate of Banksy's goddess, even more impossible today. Soon after he bought the work, Mr Khaled told Reuters that he had no plans to sell the door 'at the present time.' Nevertheless, the London dealer Robin Barton has spent some $15,000 on a deposit and preliminary handling costs on the piece. But among the rubble of Gaza today, the chances of him or anyone else ever seeing the work again must be quite slim.

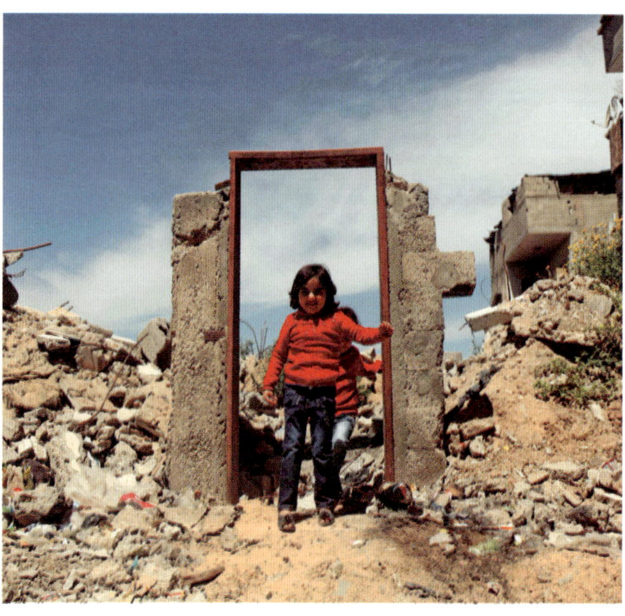

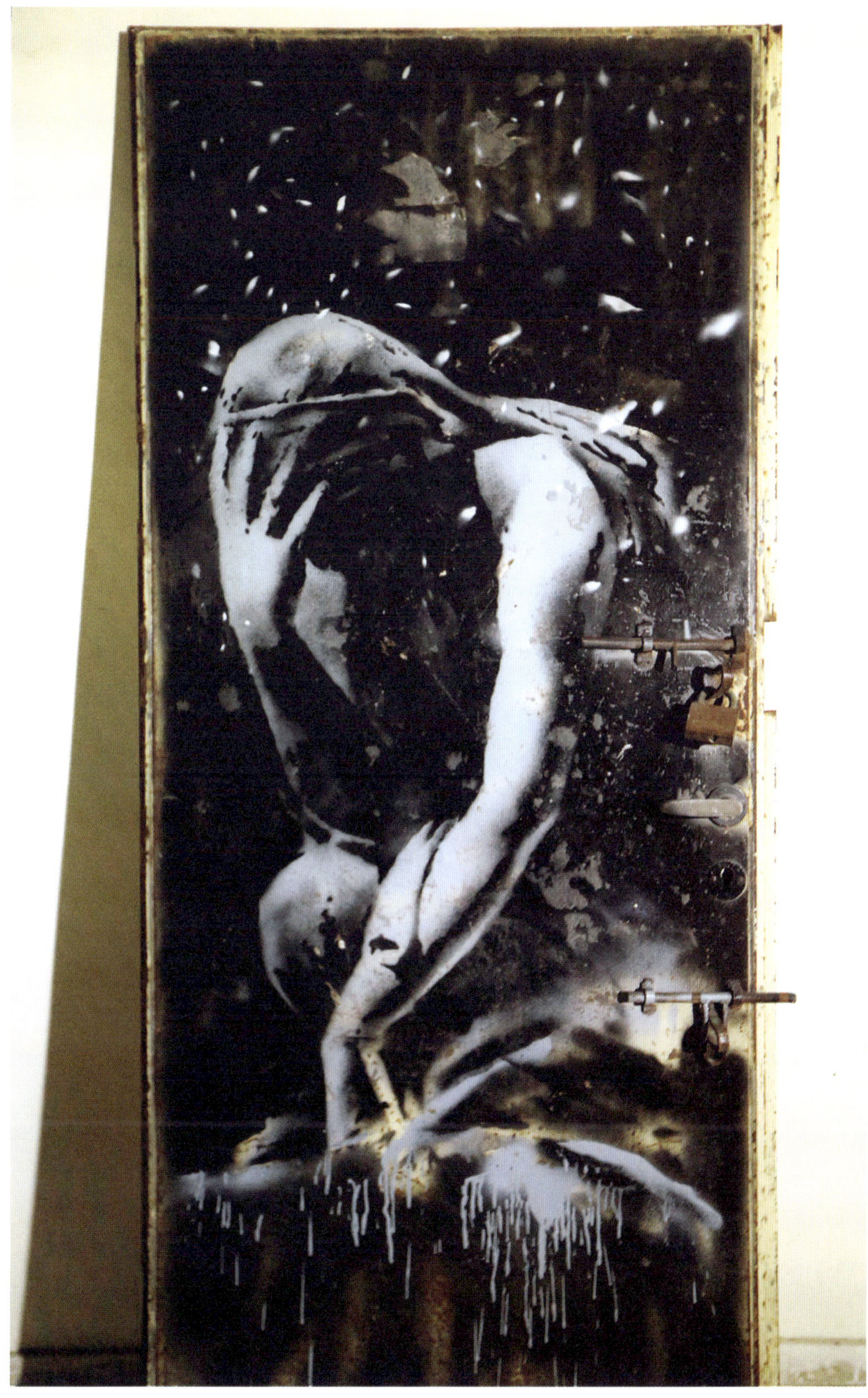

27

ESCAPE
OF THE RAT

⚲ JEFFREY'S STREET AT CAMDEN STREET, LONDON NW1 9PR (*TOX*);
⚲ THE STANDARD HOTEL, LONDON WC1H 8EG (*THE RAT*)

Once upon a time there were two Banksys in the London Borough of Camden. One, a rat, painted on council property (an extension to the town hall), the other painted on the side of a private block of flats. One survives, the other is lost.

The dilemma that local councils sometimes face with Banksy, especially now that he is so celebrated, is whether his work should be preserved or scrubbed out like any other graffiti artist. The council decided that their small rat near Kings Cross station should be protected by a Perspex screen. But what should the council do about a much better and bigger piece he painted a few years later on the end of a terrace in Jeffrey's Street in the centre of the borough?

To heighten the dilemma, this piece was a very obvious tribute to the graffiti artist Tox, with a boy blowing huge bubbles in the shape of the TOX tag. Tox had been jailed for 27 months for essentially doing the same thing as Banksy but doing it much more prolifically and much less interestingly.

The owner of the building put up a £600 Perspex shield to protect the Banksy and then added a £2,000 CCTV camera to the wall. But when I saw it some years ago someone had gone to great trouble to drill through the thick Perspex and dribble paint down the poor boy. The Perspex was covered with stickers and the whole thing looked a mess. Residents in the street complained and eventually the council issued an enforcement notice: there had been no planning permission for the screen nor the CCTV camera and both had to come down. It was the end of Tox. All that is left now is a sign saying, 'Warning: CCTV in operation' – but there is no camera and no Banksy.

The council, on the other hand, has successfully navigated itself out of a tricky position given they could hardly scrub out their own valuable rat. They sold their brutalist town hall extension to Crosstree Real Estate, who in turn have transformed it into The Standard hotel. The council originally asked Crosstree to take Banksy off the building and return it to them, but Crosstree refused. Their final agreement stipulates that if ever Crosstree removes the Banksy, they have to hand it back to Camden at their cost.

The rat is easy to miss, quite high up on the side of the hotel – you wonder how Banksy managed to create it in the first place. If you travel a distance to see it, you will almost certainly be somewhat disappointed: it is faded and covered in Perspex. The council's options were limited, but seeing both the rat and the blank wall in Jeffrey's Street on the same morning, I could not help feeling that the wrong work was saved and the best work lost.

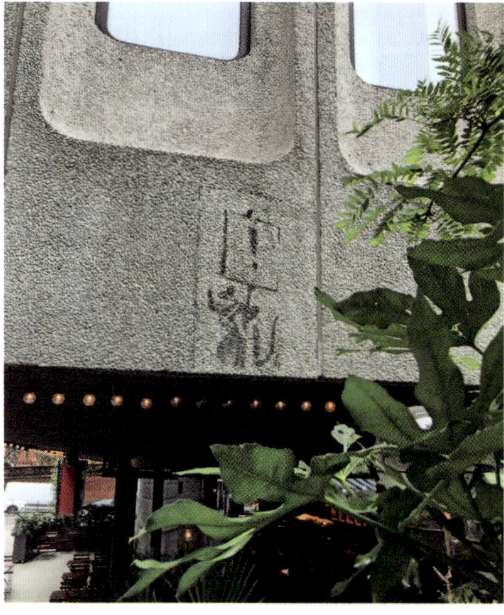

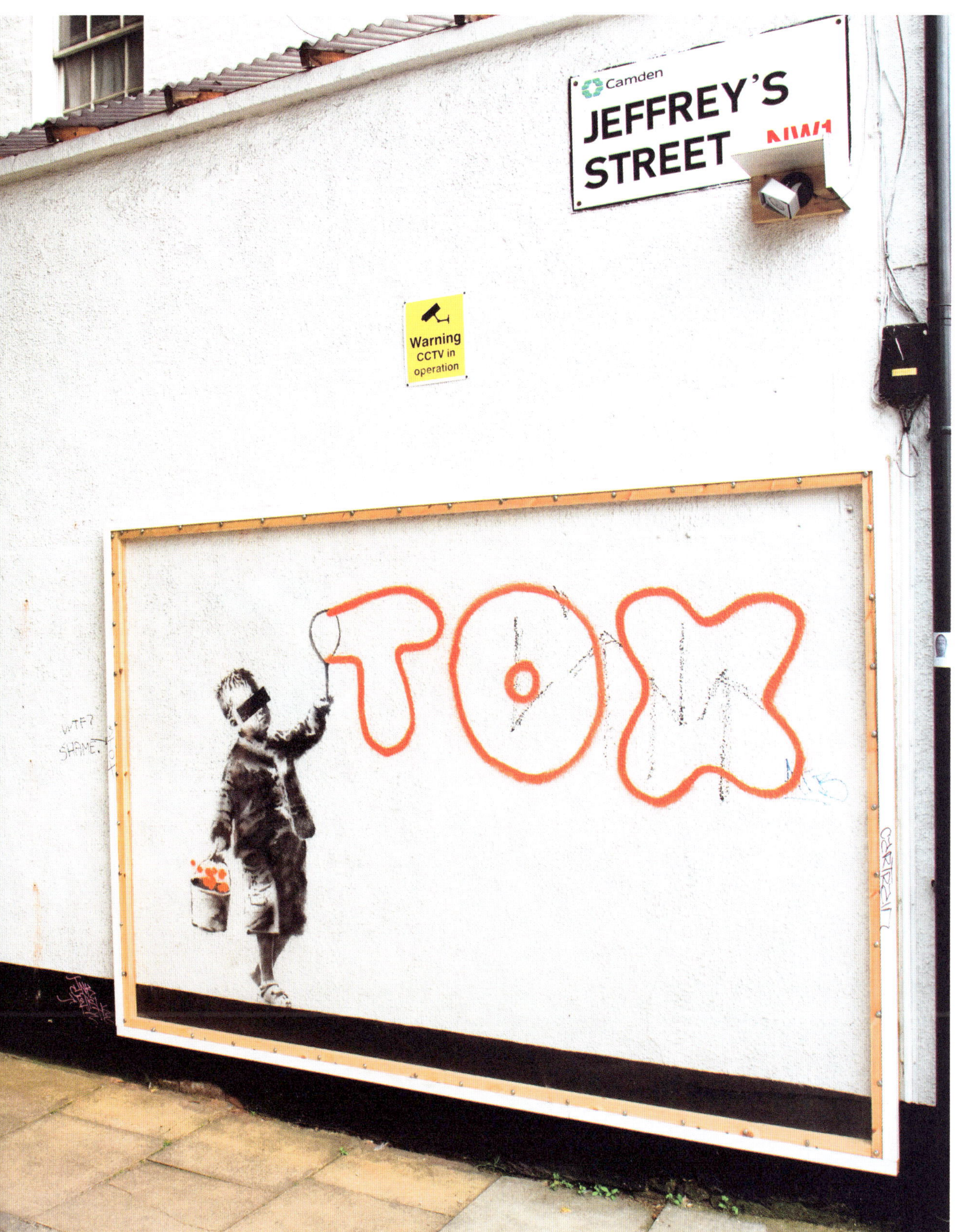

Camden
JEFFREY'S STREET
NW1
Warning
CCTV in operation
TOX

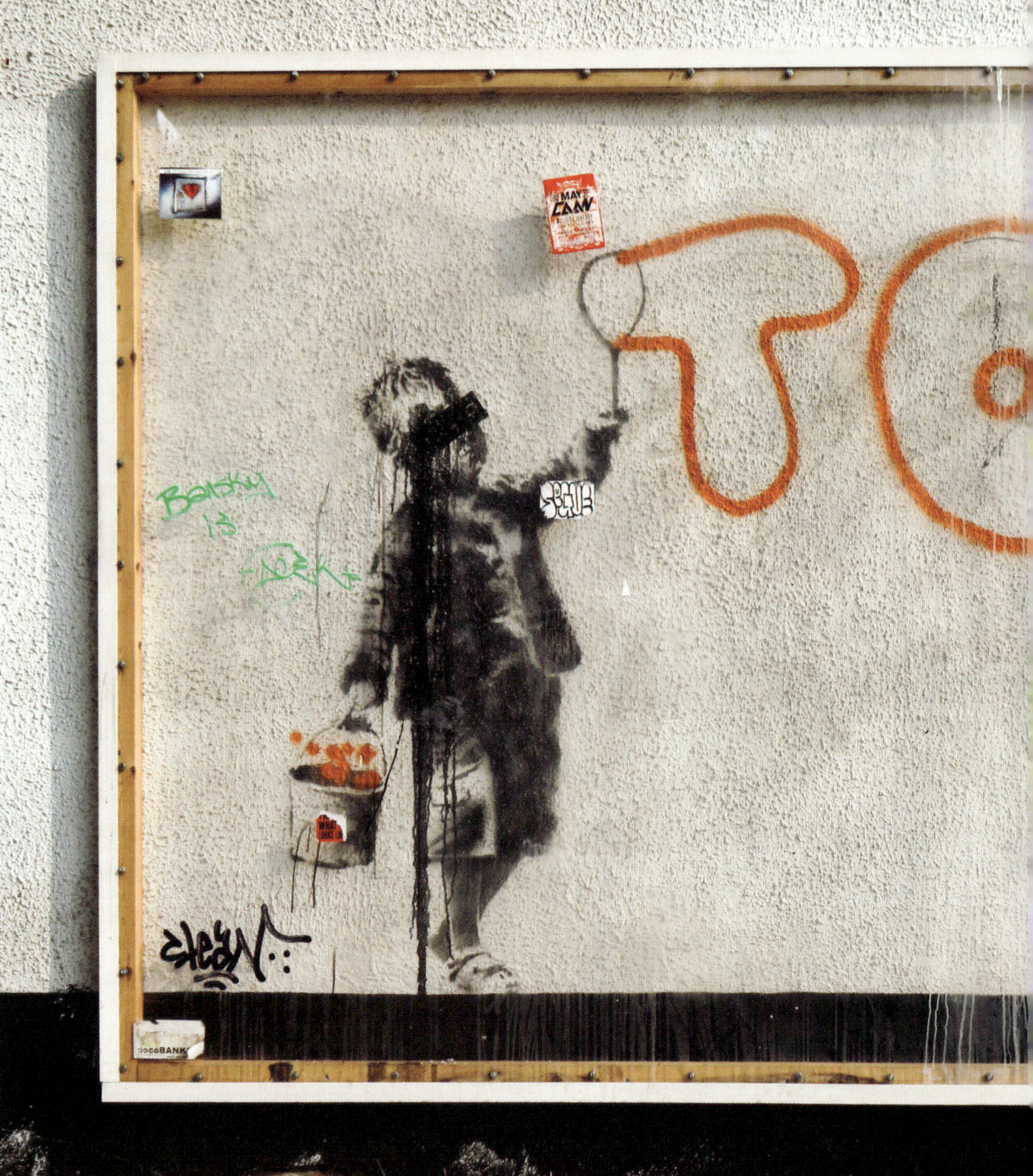

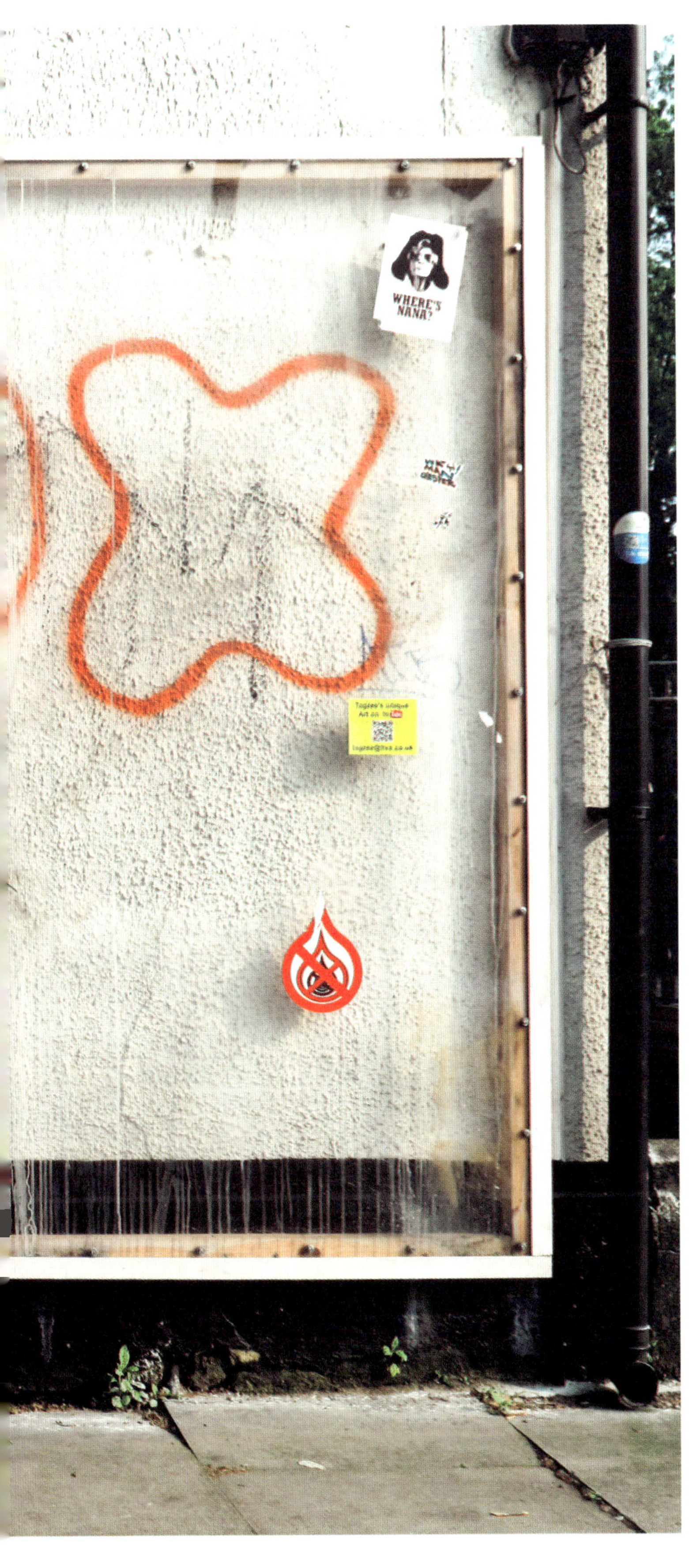

WHERE'S NANA?

28

THE OLD LADY OF FOLKESTONE

RENDEZVOUS STREET, FOLKESTONE CT20 1EZ (ORIGINALLY);
NOW AT 69 THE OLD HIGH STREET, FOLKESTONE CT20 1RN

When I finally found Banksy's *Art Buff* at the bottom of the imaginatively restored Old High Street in Folkestone, it was a bit of a disappointment. An extraordinary amount of effort had gone into rescuing it from Miami, where it had been sent to be auctioned off, but re-sited in a window of the Folklore Café, it was easy to miss.

Banksy painted this piece in 2014 on the wall of an amusement arcade during the Folkestone Triennial, a festival set up to bring art to a town badly in need of it. An old lady, with her back to us and headphones on, peers at a plinth where whatever was once on it had been 'buffed' out – hence *Art Buff*. Not the most successful Banksy, but a Banksy nevertheless.

Within six weeks workmen arrived on the scene armed with diamond-tipped drills and started their weekend task of drilling it out. At one point it needed a police cordon to separate the protestors trying to 'save' the Banksy from the workmen extracting it.

On Twitter a sad complaint from one resident read: 'We had a pier, switchback railway, thriving port and a Banksy artwork in Folkestone, now all gone.' In the House of Commons the Culture Minister Ed Vaizey, replying to a question by the town's Conservative MP, Damian Collins, delivered a remarkable riff transforming Banksy from graffiti artist into some sort of saint. 'Sometimes it makes one wonder about the motivation of one's fellow man when somebody as public-spirited as Banksy, who is prepared to create community artworks in public spaces for the benefit of the local population and has really been taken to the heart of many people, that somebody – because it happens to be on their private property – should seek to use that windfall.'

No matter, *Art Buff* was soon on its way to the Art Miami fair, but with a price tag of £470,000 it failed to sell. This gave the opportunity for the Creative Foundation, the charity set up to revitalize Folkestone, to go to the High Court – and they won. The victory was based not on authentication or copyright, but a prosaic case of property law. The tenant of the amusement arcade argued that in taking the Banksy off the wall it was abiding by the requirements of its lease to keep the building under good repair. Once off the wall, the bricks, mortar and paint – the Banksy – were all theirs to sell. But the judge was having none of it and the 'chattels' had to be returned to the landlord who had already assigned ownership of the wall to the Creative Foundation. *Art Buff* was on its way back across the Atlantic, and in 2020 the Foundation had it installed in the Folklore Café. A satisfying victory but still another Banksy lost, for *Art Buff* sitting protected in a café window is very different from a Banksy on a wall.

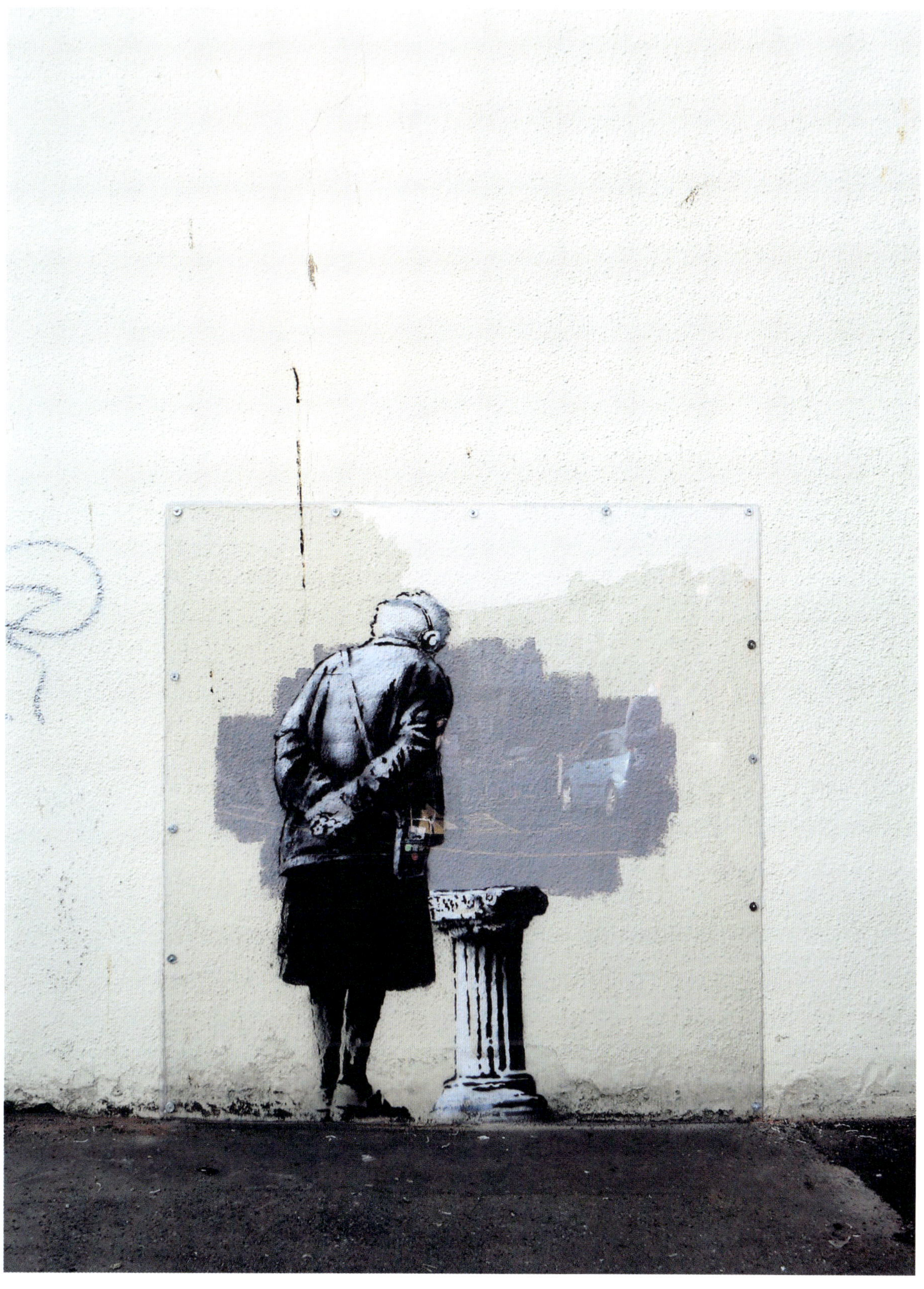

29

OFF TO THE JUNK YARD

◉ NORTHWOLD, NORFOLK IP26 5LQ

Before Banksy became famous, he painted two pieces on either side of an articulated trailer at Glastonbury and any festival goer who wanted to could watch him at work. Both pieces have now disappeared. One side was bought by an anonymous buyer over the telephone from a Paris auction house for £445,000. Intriguingly, the other side was bought back by Banksy himself, who disliked his own work so much he wanted it out of public view and possibly even destroyed.

Two travellers, Maeve Neale and Nathan Wellard, who had converted the trailer into a movable home for themselves and their four children, agreed to allow Banksy to use one side as a canvas for a piece of performance art in 1998 at Glastonbury, where they were regulars. He gave them two tickets and their diesel money to get there from their home in Norfolk. Over three days he and his fellow graffiti artist Inkie created *Fragile Silence* across a canvas measuring almost 10 metres long.

The next year he painted on the other side, but this time *they* paid *him*: 'Only a couple of hundred quid,' says Maeve, 'and I think we might still owe him fifty.' It was called *Fungle Junk*, an appropriate title since it was a bit of a mess, with monkeys on keyboard and drums central to the piece, and Sid Vicious and a pink vaguely *Playboy*-style bunny getting added later.

When the time came to enlarge their home, *Fungle Junk* was taken off so that a second trailer could be joined up. It was split into three pieces but luckily not destroyed. For when Banksy prices started to surge, Maeve and Nathan realized that their home might be worth very much more than the £1,000 they paid for it. There was, though, the usual problem: neither side had been authenticated by Banksy. Nevertheless, in June

2008 they sent two of the *Fungle Junk* pieces to auction in Scotland; while the bidding reached almost £100,000, the bids were conditional on authentication by Banksy. They tried again in London three months later, but again: no authentication, no sale.

Maeve was more than angry, for there was absolutely no doubt it was Banksy's work. Eventually she got on to Banksy himself and they had what she describes as a 'bit of a heated conversation.' In the end Banksy relented. Their deal was straightforward: he would authenticate *Fragile Silence* and he would give them a painting in return for them giving him *Fungle Junk.* They sold the painting, a version of *No Ball Games*, at auction for £30,000 and they drove *Fragile Silence* to a Paris auction in 2015 to massive success. As for *Fungle Junk*, one of Banksy's friends came with a van and picked it up.

'Banksy claimed to hate it quite a lot... he was embarrassed by it,' Maeve told me. 'They said they were going to destroy it, but it's hard to believe that that's what they did, just destroy it.' But if the likes of Claude Monet or Francis Bacon can exercise a bit of quality control and destroy their own paintings, then why not Banksy?

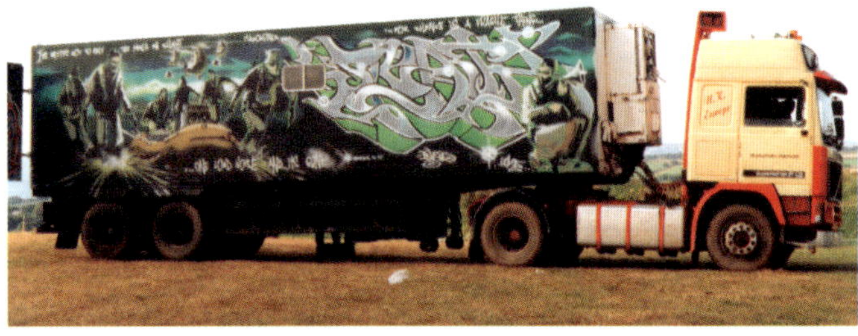

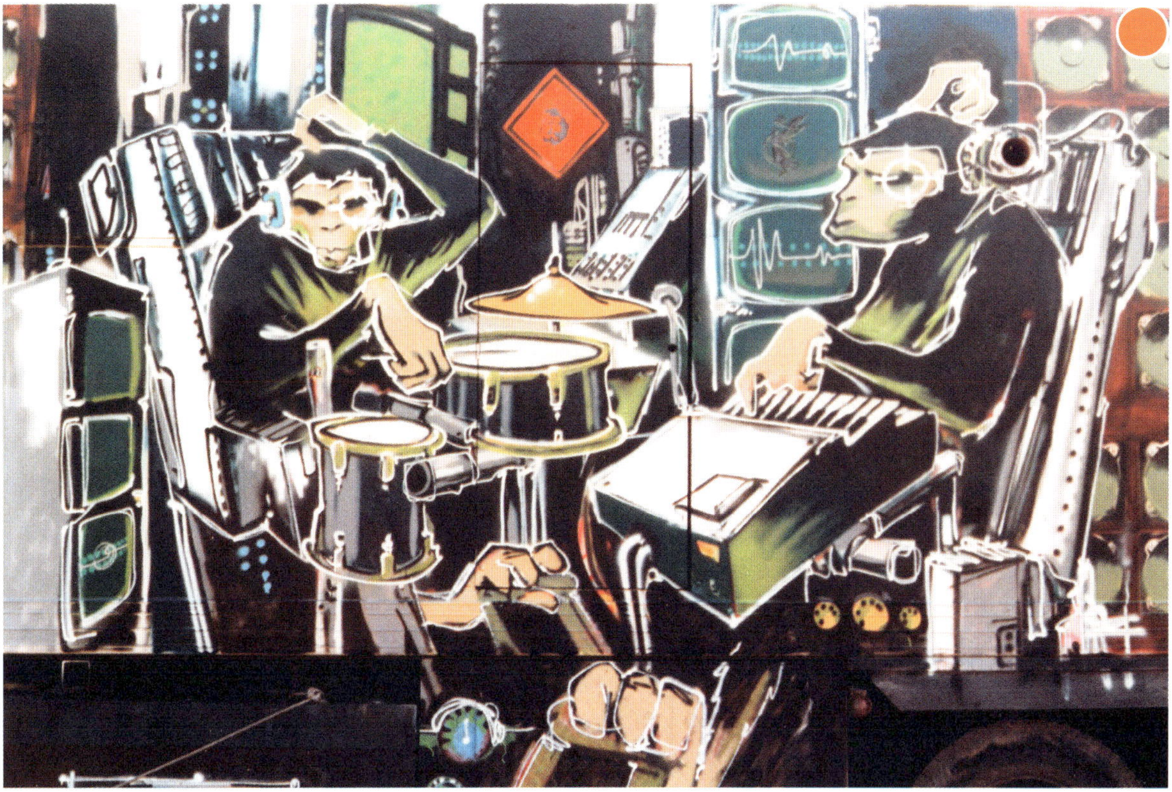

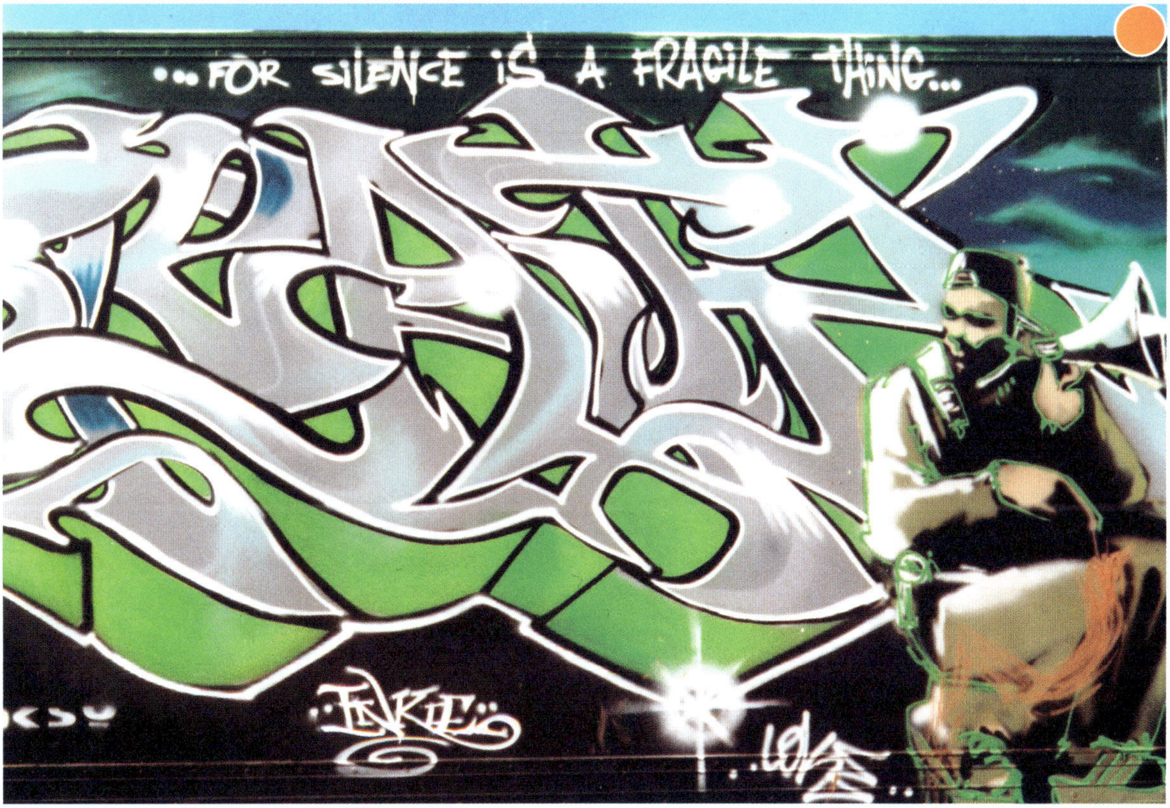

...FOR SILENCE IS A FRAGILE THING...

30

KISS THE COPPERS GOODBYE

⚲ THE PRINCE ALBERT, 48 TRAFALGAR STREET, BRIGHTON BN1 4ED

Chris Steward, the amiable owner of the Prince Albert pub near Brighton train station, was at the bar when a man came in asking for the landlord. 'I've got a mate who wants to paint a piece on your wall,' the man said. It was only after more questioning that it turned out the 'mate' was Banksy, a name which at the time – this was 2004 – meant very little to Chris.

The pub is certainly a colourful one and the wall already had a pink Buddha head on it as well as a tribute portrait of John Peel. Nevertheless, Chris told him he was not sure if he could allow it 'because it's a listed building and the council is a bit funny about it'. However, he was reassured by the man, who said, 'If they kick off about it you can just paint over it.'

So he agreed, never asking what the piece was going to be. A couple of weeks later he came to work and there on the wall were the kissing coppers. 'I was shitting myself when I saw it. I thought, we're going to get done for this, we'll get slaughtered.' An hour or so later about four or five police cars pulled up outside. 'I thought, oh Christ, here we go. But they all got out and stood around, some of them laughing, having photos taken beside it.'

There were two other versions of *Kissing Coppers* in London, which were soon painted over. But the Prince Albert coppers survived to become one of the key works in what auction houses now tend to call Banksy's 'oeuvre'. But its survival was precarious: two men, caught on CCTV, were fined £45 each for defacing the wall. They used black bitumen paint; others followed, choosing first red and then white paint. Every time it was cleaned the original faded a little.

Finally, another man walked into the pub looking for the landlord. It was Tom Organ, the wall-painting conservationist who, with a colleague, was working on St Nicholas' Church nearby. His proposal was to take the work *off* the wall and sell it, splitting the sale price. After a few days' work they invited Chris into the little shed they had erected and he watched them peel off what he says looked 'a bit like the Turin shroud' with the coppers stuck to it. The techniques they used were similar to the ones they used in *OLD Skool* (see page 59). The coppers were transferred to canvas and they stencilled a replica on the wall. When I was last there it was encased in Perspex and still untouched – Banksy's enemies are not too interested in replicas.

Chris hoped that having given him the pub wall Banksy would authenticate the canvas in return. 'It would have been nice if he had just said that's one of mine; it would have saved five or six years of f****** about with it.' But even without authentication it eventually sold at auction in Miami, with Chris putting his £125,000 back into the pub where it had all started.

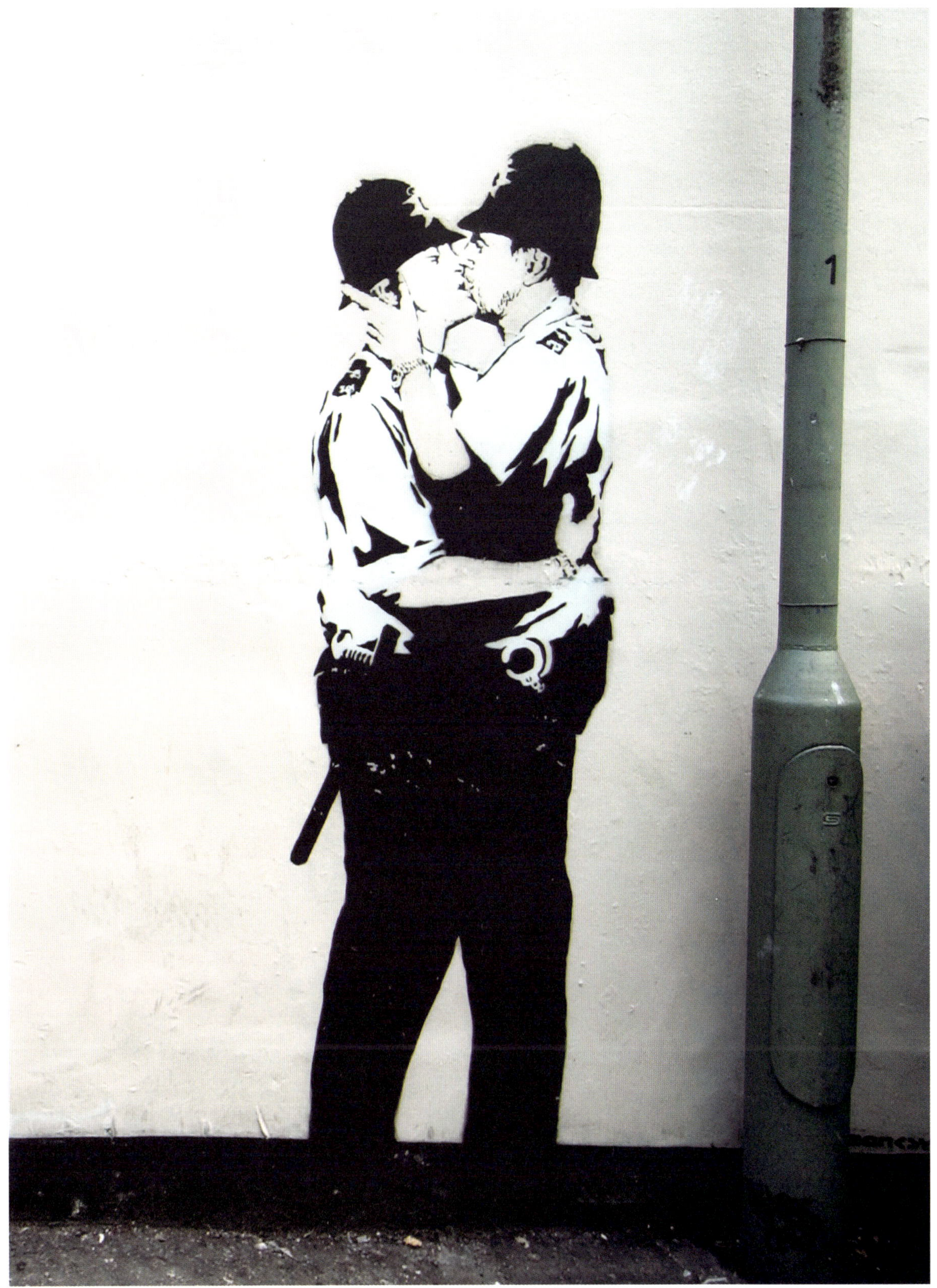

31

NO SAVING THE GORILLA

📍 147–149 FISHPONDS ROAD, EASTVILLE, BRISTOL, BS5 6PR

The gorilla in the pink mask was one of the few Banksy pieces in Bristol that stayed pretty much untouched over the years. But having survived ten years, disaster struck. In 2011 Saeed Ahmed, the new owner of the building with the gorilla on the outside, decided to smarten up the place and had the gorilla painted over before opening an Islamic cultural centre. He had never even heard of Banksy and when the error of his ways was pointed out, he was both embarrassed and apologetic. 'I thought it was worthless,' he said. 'I really am sorry if people are upset.' He gave the gorilla a jet wash but it was still quite faded.

Mr Ahmed called in a restoration expert, who said the gorilla could be fixed, although it would be time-consuming, finicky work to separate the layer of paint from the gorilla. So there it sat, all lonely and un-noticed, for another ten years until 2020, when suddenly instead of the gorilla on the side of the Jalalabad Islamic Centre, there was just a hole in the wall. The gorilla, it turned out, had been sold to a company new to the whole 'saving' Banksy scene, Exposed Walls, who planned to put it up for auction. Even though the gorilla looked decidedly less sprightly than the original, the online auction reached six figures when it was halted just before the deadline for final bids, the reason given being that Covid lockdown regulations meant potential buyers could not view it up close.

Instead the poor old gorilla was fractionalized into 10,000 non-fungible tokens (NFTs) that were put on sale for $750 each in January 2022, when the NFT market was still quite hot. By my maths, if the 10,000 all sold it would bring in an incredible $7,500,000. But there was no gold rush. When I last checked only 660 had been sold, and the last sale in the secondary market was for just $100 (although even 660 sales would still have raised about $500,000 – a healthy sum – for Exposed Walls).

The centre, which badly needed the money for repairs, had originally been paid £20,000 for the gorilla. There is disagreement between the centre and Exposed Walls over what extra money should be paid to them. There are murmurings of discontent, too, on the web from a few buyers of the NFTs who are unlikely to see their investment turn profitable. So all this nonsense – and surely fractionalizing a piece of faded, unremarkable graffiti really is nonsense – has left only a very few people happy.

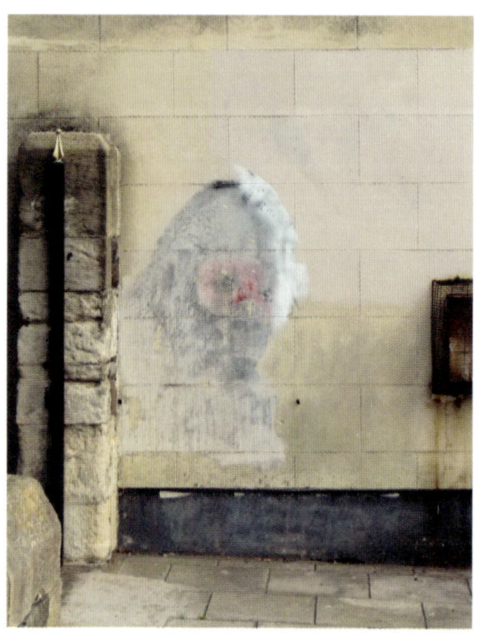

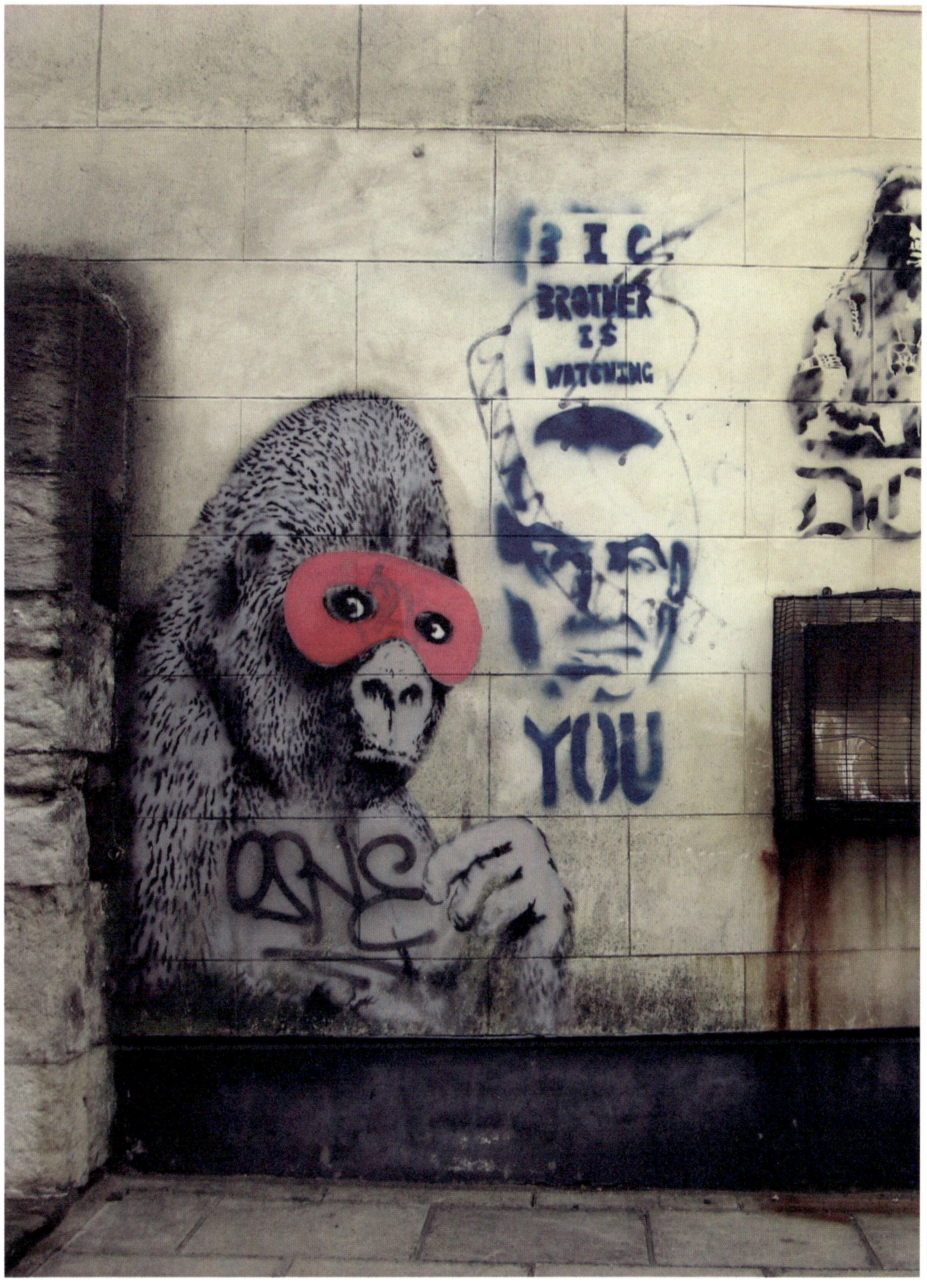

BIG
BROTHER
IS
WATCHING

YOU

32

A SHORT-LIVED VICTORY

📍 WOOD GREEN, LONDON N22 6BX

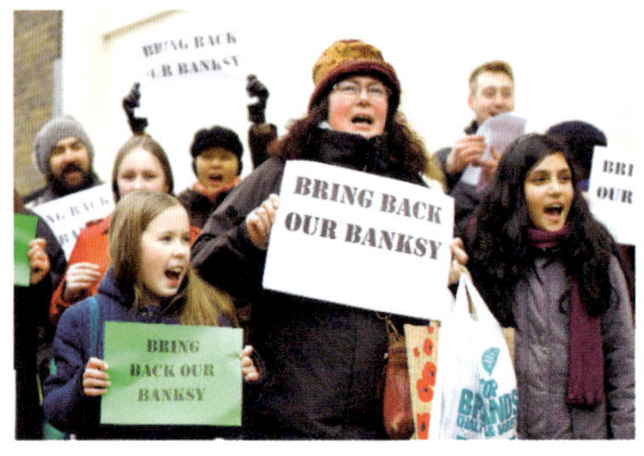

During the late Queen's Diamond Jubilee celebrations in 2012, Banksy painted a telling piece of a child crouched over a sewing machine turning out a line of bunting for the celebrations. The real bunting that had been strung up to go with the piece only lasted a couple of days before it was taken, and that was just the start of things. *Slave Labour* lasted nine months but eventually it too disappeared. But not without a fight.

The piece was painted on a Poundland store in Haringey in North London. When I went there to see the piece, it was like an open-air art gallery, with a crowd of locals standing on the pavement really enjoying 'their' Banksy (it is interesting how places claim ownership over 'their Banksys', which he has only put there because he found a convenient wall, not because he loves the neighbourhood).

By February of the following year the boy had gone, leaving a hole in the wall, and *Slave Labour* became Lot No. 6 at Fine Art Auctions Miami, with an estimated price of between $500,000 and $700,000.

However, the owners had not reckoned with a fierce 'Bring Back Our Banksy' campaign led by Haringey Council which, in the early days, was remarkably successful. The auctioneers felt under such international pressure that only hours before

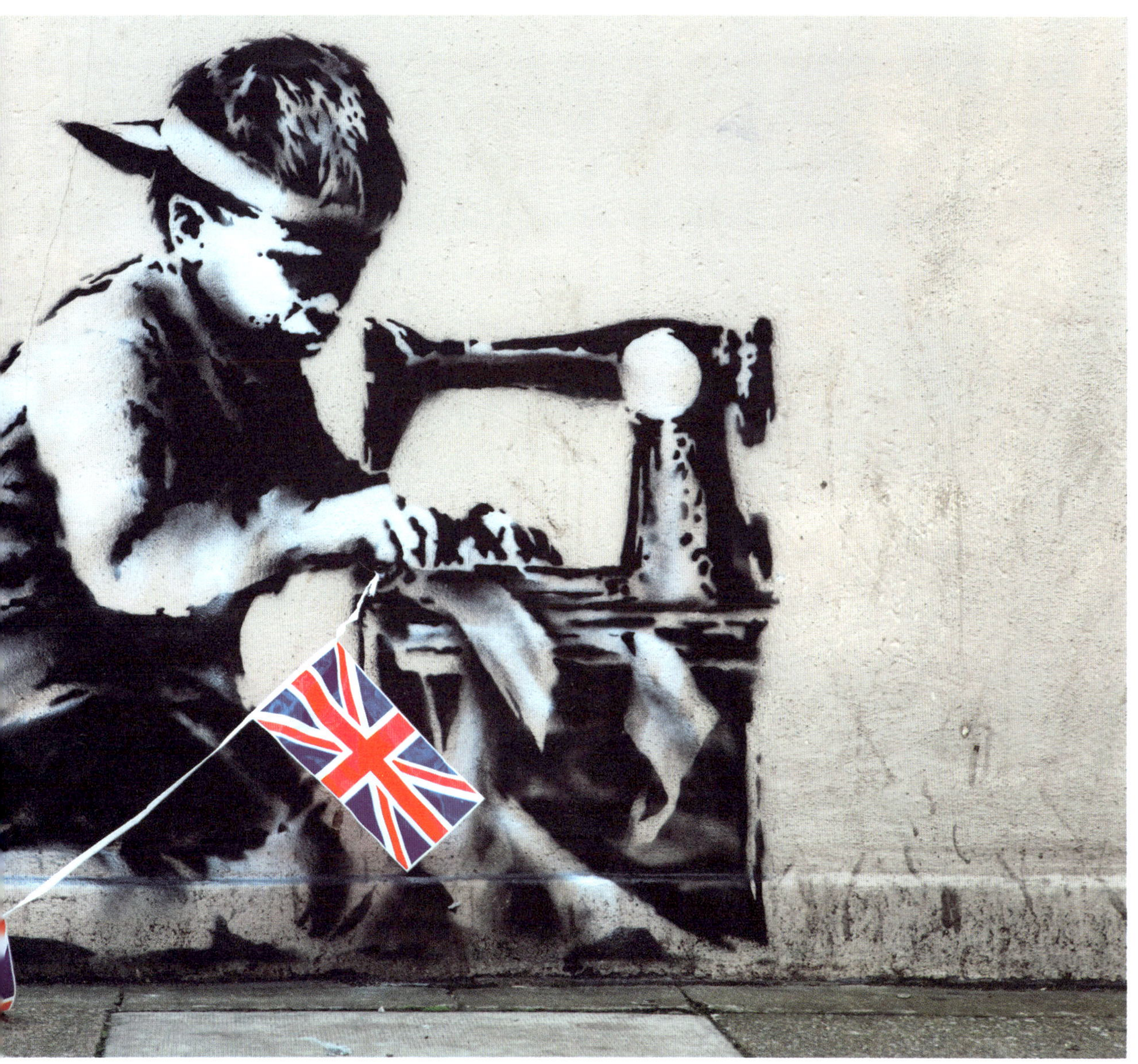

the auction was due to start, with an initial bid of $400,000 already placed, they pulled it.

Victory, but not for long. In the summer *Slave Labour* took pride of place at a silent auction, this time at the London Film Museum. The reserve was $1,000,000 and the auction was by sealed bids. It was a somewhat chaotic evening and right until the end of the evening there were no bids for it. Finally, Robin Barton, who represented the owners, was in the gents' washroom of the museum when he was given a sealed envelope by a fellow dealer. When he opened the envelope, there was a note that read: 'My client is prepared to offer $1,000,050 to secure the work known as *Slave Labour*.'

This time it really was sold and the story should have ended there. But no, five years later *Slave Labour* was on sale again, this time at Julien's Auctions in Los Angeles. The bidding only reached $730,000, but the buyer was an unlikely one, another very successful street artist, Ron English. 'I am going to paint it white,' he said. 'This is a blow for street art. It shouldn't be bought and sold.' Nevertheless, he still planned to sell his whitewashed version – 'I'm crazy, but not stupid' – and give any profit to charity. However, the *Whitewashed Banksy* has yet to hit the market.

33

HELP! THERE'S A
BANKSY ON MY WALL

⦿ GRAHAM AVENUE, EAST WILLIAMSBURG (CORNER OF GRAHAM AND COOK), NEW YORK

'Are you going to be rich?' was the first question people asked Cara Tabachnick when they learned that Banksy had been at work on a building her family owned in New York City. And after an exhausting day talking to lawyers, security companies, art experts and reporters her answer was: 'I have no idea. There is no rule book when one of the most famous artists in the world decides to drop his work into your life.'

On Day 17 of Banksy's month-long residency in the city in October 2013, he painted a piece on the Tabachnick family's East Williamsburg building, using a bricked-up basement window as his canvas. It has no significance, political or otherwise, that I can see, but it is charming and it demonstrates just how much location matters to him. For here he managed to turn a small piece of brickwork into a bridge with two geishas strolling on top of it and a bonsai tree growing beside it.

The first thing Ms Tabachnick learned was that for 'all the people that love and appreciate Banksy, there's another cohort of people that are out there to destroy him.' On the very the day the piece was 'unveiled' someone arrived with a backpack-load of spray paint to attack it. He had hardly started work when he was attacked by Banksy admirers, thrown to the ground and sent packing. Two of the defenders then used alcohol swabs to clean off the wet paint.

When interviewed on National Public Radio, she said her family was left in a 'very sticky place. He's put artwork on our wall and now we're expected either to protect it or let it be destroyed, and we can't sell it.' She said they had been approached by a gallerist: 'They could come, take down the wall, put it up for auction, and that could be the route that we go. It puts us in a conundrum. I mean, we believe – I think we truly believe that this art is for the public. But we're also not equipped to serve the public's needs.'

They hired a security guard to protect the work while they decided what to do. The guard was soon replaced by a $2,000 roll-down shutter, which has kept their Banksy safe but invisible over the years, although if you come in peace and ask nicely the optometrist on the ground floor might well roll up the shutter and let you have a look.

'It was a bit of a pain when it happened,' Ms Tabachnick says now, 'but it wasn't anything that was so disruptive that it ruined any of our lives or anything like that. In the moment it was something exciting.'

As for the question that her friends asked her 12 years before: has Banksy made her rich? No, and her family still has the problem of deciding what to do with it.

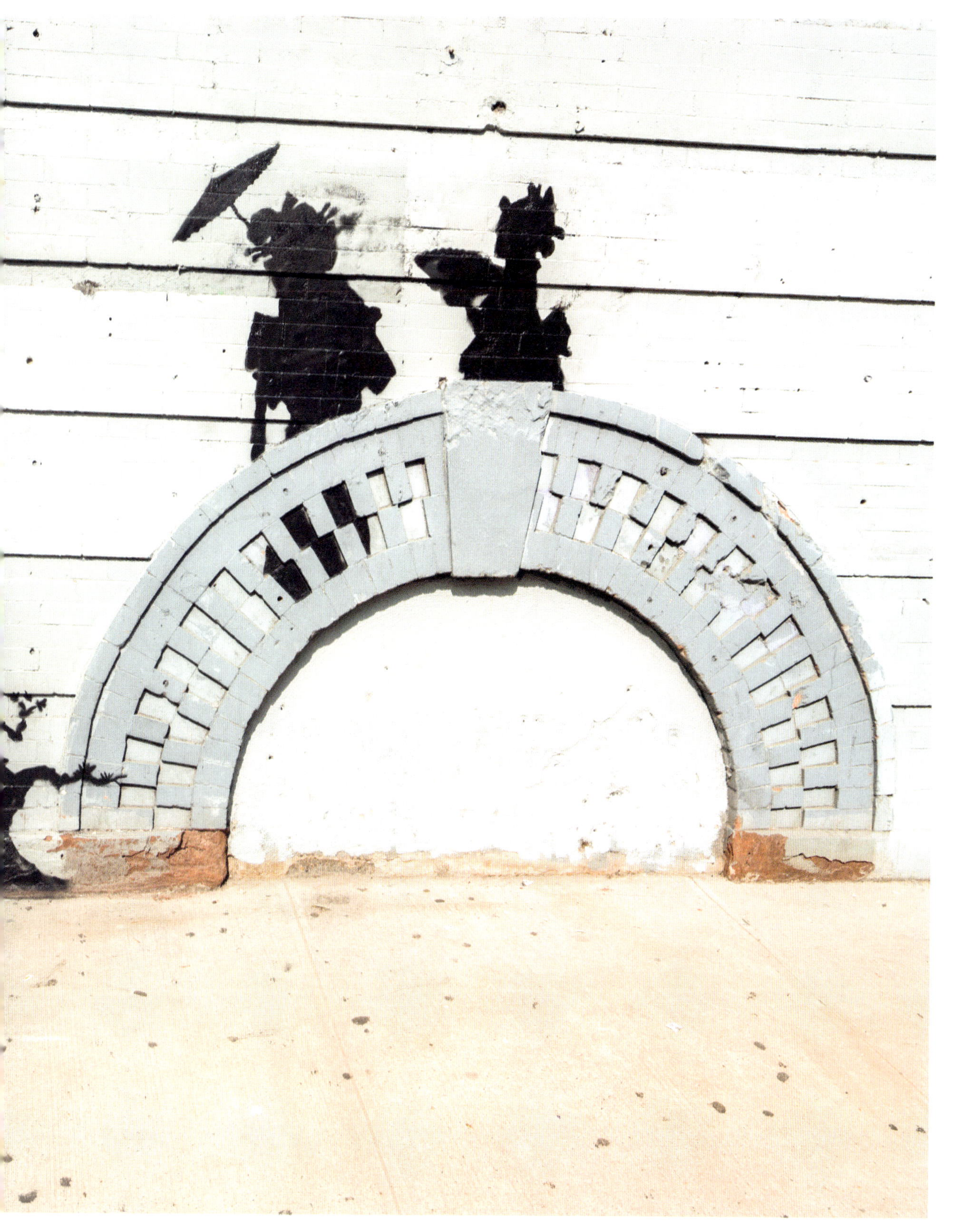

34

THE SPIES
WHO VANISHED

159 FAIRVIEW ROAD, CHELTENHAM GL52 2EX

At Banksy's own retrospective in Glasgow in 2023 he imported a phone box and stencilled on the wall beside it quite a detailed and complicated image of three spies snooping on it. Visitors to the exhibition could enter the phone box one at a time and a friendly gallery staff member would take an instant, if rather dark, picture of you being spied on, which you could take away.

The exhibition is the nearest anyone will ever get to seeing the original piece, which Banksy painted on the side of an end-of-terrace house in Cheltenham, home of Britain's surveillance network GCHQ, in 2014. For in the middle of a bitter row over whether the painting could be taken off the wall and sold, or preserved as 'Cheltenham's Banksy', the wall – or rather its outer surface rendering – collapsed into a pile of rubble, taking with it the Banksy and any dreams of riches.

It was certainly not a happy tale for David Possee, the owner of the house. The work had been scrawled all over with additional graffiti, he had been under fire from some local residents for trying to sell 'their' Banksy, and the local council incorporated the piece into the house's Grade II listing to make it impossible to take off and sell without their consent. He was not a popular man. As he told the local radio station: 'At the end of the day I don't think I've done anything wrong. I've bought a house in Cheltenham and one day Banksy rocks up and I'm the bad guy... If Cheltenham wants it, Cheltenham can have it. So buy the building off me.'

But while efforts were being made to do just that, the Banksy disappeared. The overanxious rumour mill suggested that it had disintegrated in the middle of being taken off the wall to be sold. But the reality was rather more mundane. The owner had been served a notice by the council requiring him to repair the wall where damp had got underneath the render. Although the builder repairing it kept to his instructions not to go closer than a metre from the piece, at some point all the render collapsed.

Poof! Like magic, the Banksy was gone forever.

But not quite. Someone had been enterprising enough to salvage three pieces of wall with the rather cracked heads of the spies on them and they were soon up for sale on Facebook – genuine, but nevertheless no more than souvenirs rather than the real thing.

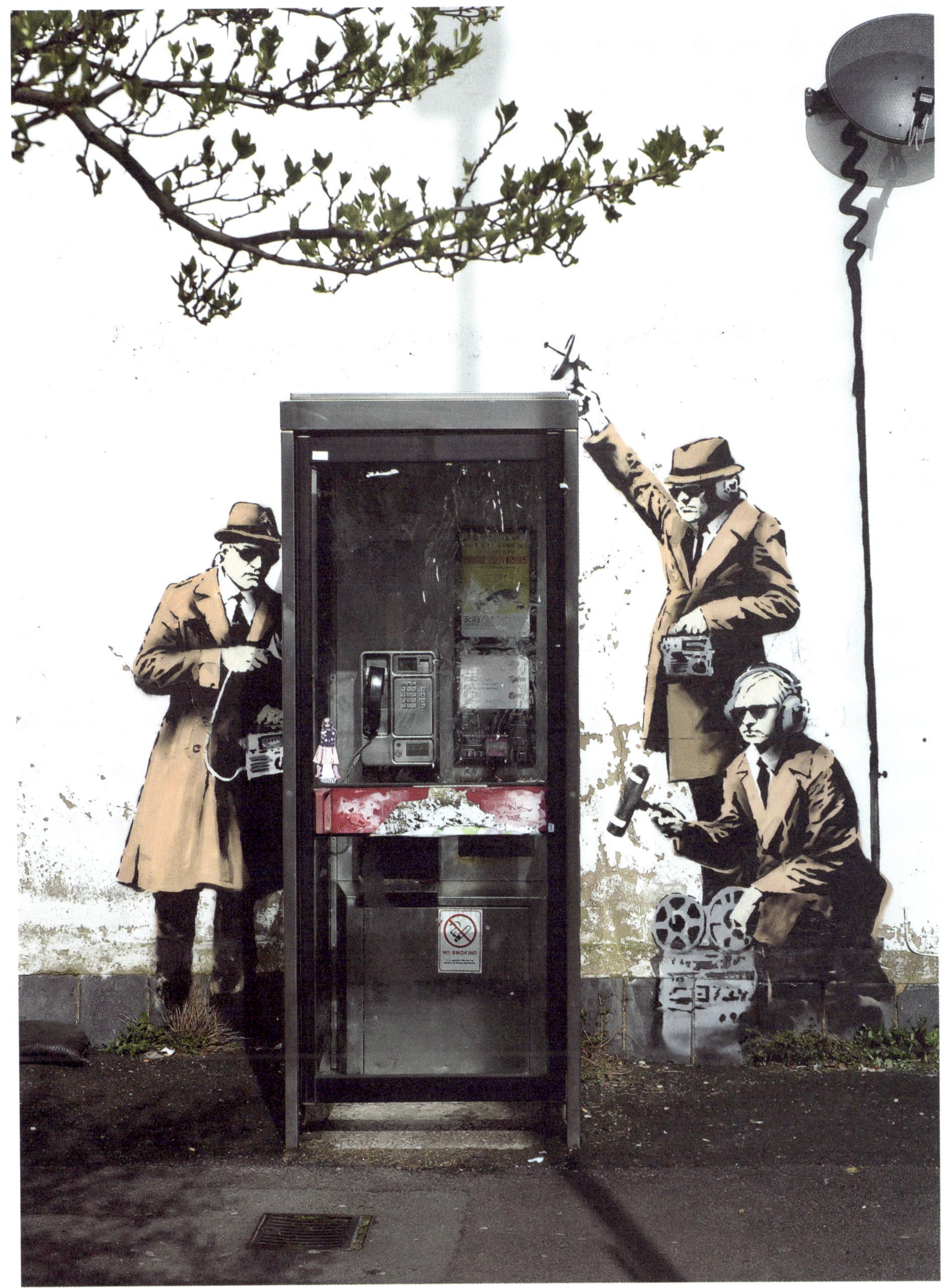

NO SMOKING

35

BEWARE SCAMMERS AT WORK

◉ N. RAMPART STREET, NEW ORLEANS LA 70116

Of all the various attempts to steal a Banksy from a wall, this has to be the cheekiest. *Umbrella Girl* was one of 14 pieces Banksy painted in New Orleans in 2008, three years after the devastation of Hurricane Katrina. It is a poignant piece for, just like the residents of New Orleans who mistakenly thought they were safe behind the city's flood protection system, the girl thinks she is safe beneath the umbrella.

Originally I thought the attempt to steal her was so brazen there had to be a place for her in this book even though she was not actually lost. But in April 2024 the owner of the building where she was painted, a disused rehab centre, had her cut out in preparation for the building's major renovation. So now she too is very much lost to the streets. The owner's lawyer said she would be returned, but the chances of that happening remain very unclear, particularly given that the piece is probably worth more than the building itself.

In 2014 neighbours saw two workmen, protected by a makeshift plywood screen, attempting to cut out *Umbrella Girl*. It was broad daylight and the workmen were not trying to hide. Photographer Charlie Varley managed to clamber through the makeshift cordon, and while he took photographs he questioned the main man: 'He gave me a story about a Tate Modern exhibition coming up on Banksy and this was going to be part of it. "We're going to take it away, we'll make sure it's safely protected, and ship it off to London. When the exhibition is over, we'll bring it back and put it back in place."'

Mr Varley told me, 'it seemed at the time quite plausible, but I thought there's something about this which seems very odd.' The story was a nice try, but completely untrue. One of the residents called the police. The workmen scarpered, making their getaway in the white van they had originally rented to transport the *Umbrella Girl* back to the West Coast. The New Orleans police issued a warrant for the arrest of one of the men, but he has never been taken to court.

Miraculously, the *Umbrella Girl* stayed where she was, but she was attacked – with paint this time – by followers of the rival graffiti artist Robbo (see page 28) over Christmas in 2020. It was one in the morning when a dog walker spotted the damage and called Carlos Fundora, a photographer who, with a friend, has looked after the Banksy for several years. With his own graffiti crew Mr Fundora managed to get off almost all the paint before it dried. And there she stayed, a little faded but good enough for one Banksy follower to advise fellow fans on Tripadvisor, 'You have to go see this. It's truly a spiritual moment standing next to a real deal authentic Banksy piece "in the wild".' Sadly that moment has now gone.

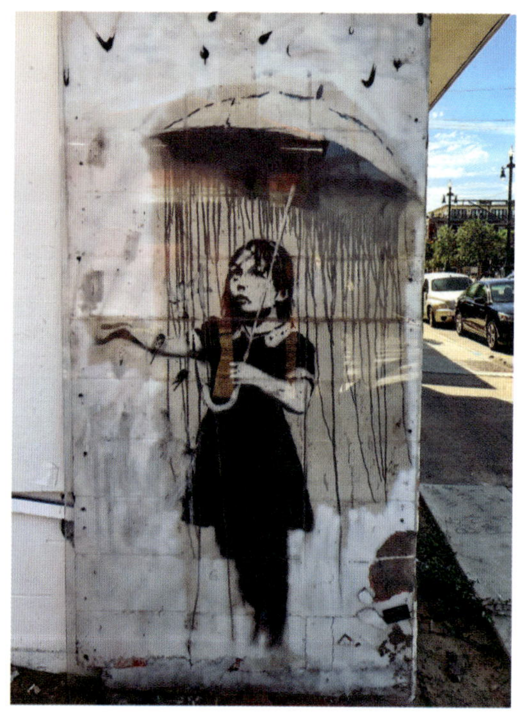

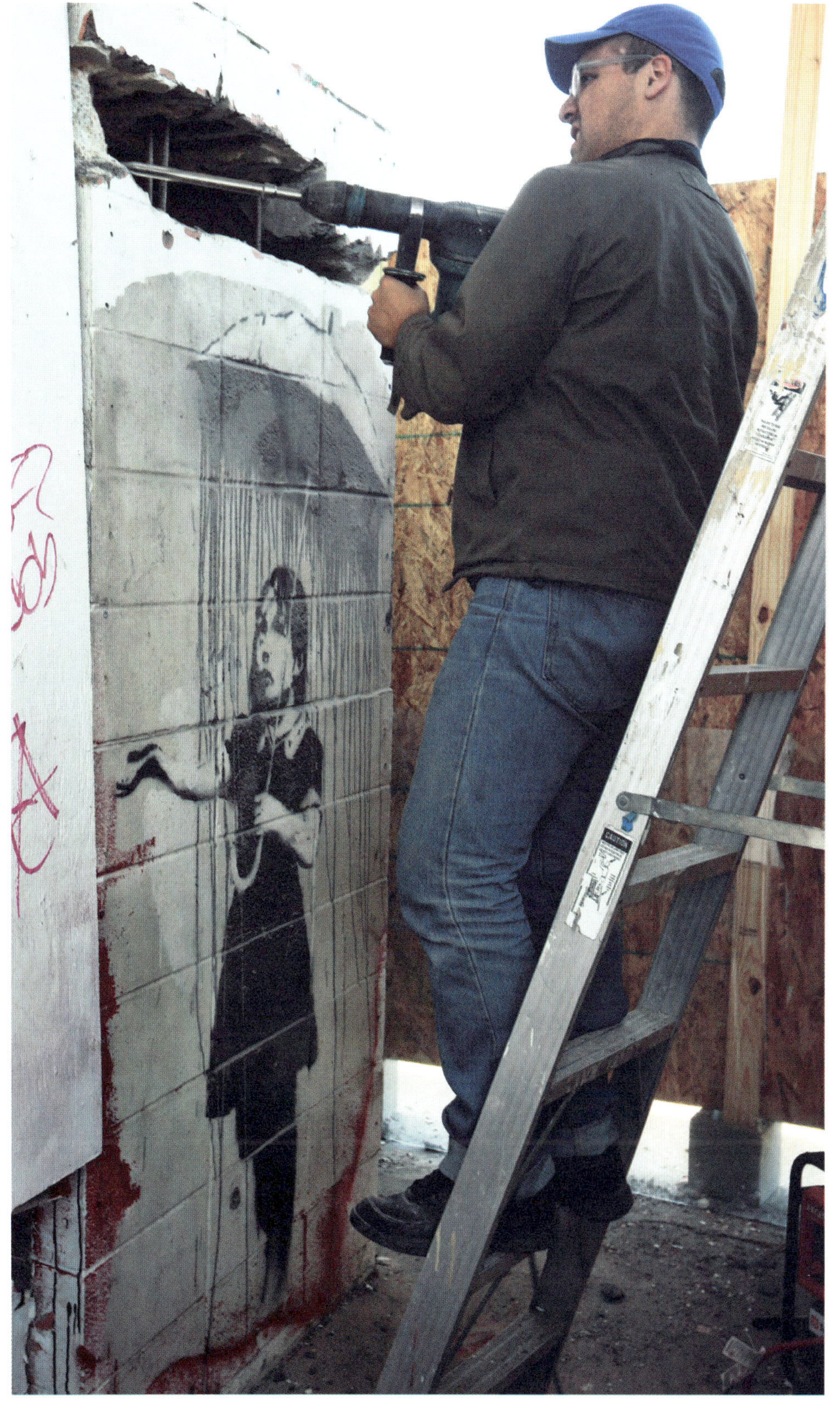

36

HOW SNOW TURNED TO ASH

◉ REAR OF RICHMOND PLACE, PORT TALBOT SA13 1TR

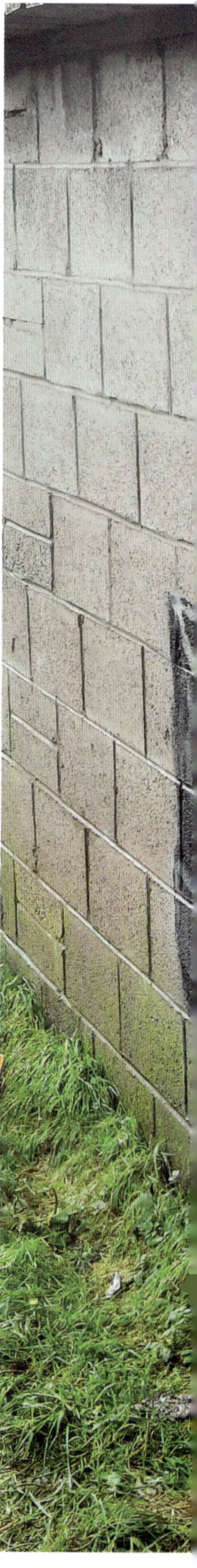

The saga of *Season's Greetings* is a very good example of how Banksy has managed to flip the world upside down and, for him at least, turn civic anger at graffiti into civic pride.

It was Christmastime 2018 when Banksy's work appeared on two walls of a garage on the outskirts of Port Talbot in Wales. It came complete with a gentle little video from Banksy showing a boy, arms outstretched, enjoying the falling 'snow' on one side of the garage while 'Little Snowflake' played in the background. But next the camera moved to a second wall of the garage where a burning fire was spewing out the ash falling on the boy. Finally, there was drone footage of the nearby Tata steel factory, which sits beside the town.

No subtlety there then, but a timely message given that Port Talbot is one of the most polluted towns in Britain. Amid all the excitement – it was almost as though Banksy had paid a royal visit to the town – Essex gallery owner and specialist in all things Banksy, John Brandler, paid more than £100,000 for the piece. He had mega-dreams of it being at the heart of a street-art museum that could bring the town 150,000 visitors a year.

But first the piece had to be moved for exhibition in a former police station in the centre of town, and here the Welsh government came to the rescue.

A Freedom of Information request revealed that the government had spent £53,106 in moving costs and £69,993.95 for security guards to protect it: a grand total of £123,099.95 of taxpayers' money. Although the piece was put on show in the town, the idea of a street-art museum collapsed amid considerable recriminations between Mr Brandler and the town council. So in early 2022 the Banksy was lifted out of the town, headed for storage somewhere in England, but not before a candlelit vigil – yes, a candlelit vigil – was held, complete with schoolchildren singing 'Little Snowflake', to say goodbye to it.

The next time I heard of *Season's Greetings* was in the summer of 2023 when the boy had moved to rather more opulent surroundings: the Orangerie of the Villa Reale in Monza, a sumptuous 18th-century royal palace. (It moved to Venice in 2024.) At the Orangerie, along with a whole collection of Banksy paintings and prints, the boy was on display beside two other pieces taken from the street. The exhibition's curator said these three pieces were being treated as 'archaeological finds' and they were displayed with such reverence they must surely have made Banksy laugh – or perhaps even cry.

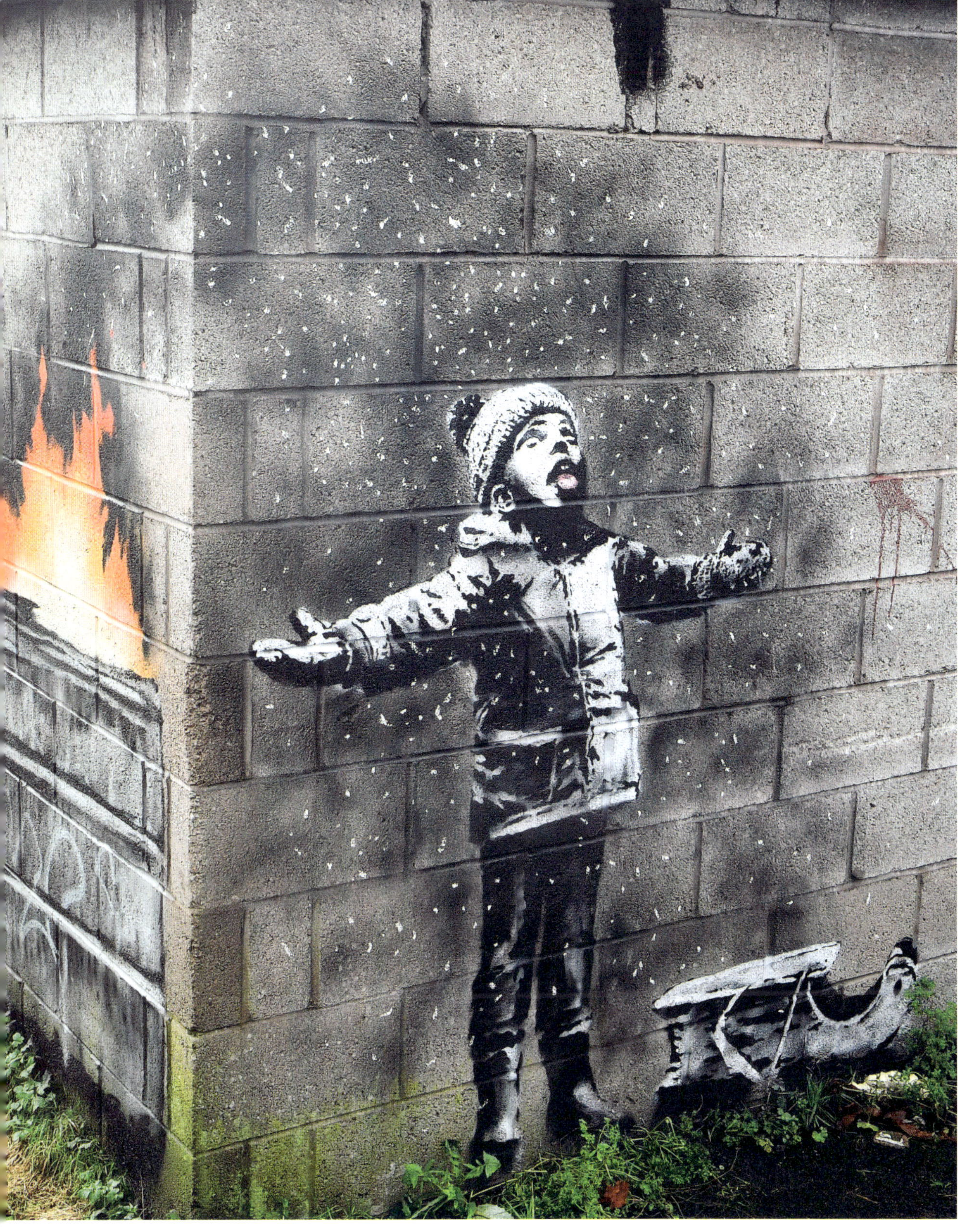

37

A PUZZLING PUNK

◉ BEDDINGTON FARM ROAD, CROYDON CR0 3DY

When Banksy painted his 'LARGE GRAFFITI SLOGAN' on a wall in Croydon in 2009, within walking distance of a large IKEA store, the local council decided that rather than dispatching a street-cleaning team to get rid of it, they would actually ask residents whether it should stay or go.

An election was always going to be a tight race against time because other graffiti artists, bitter perhaps at the soft treatment Banksy was being given, were busy defacing his graffiti by adding their own tags to his work. But within three weeks the verdict of those who had bothered to email the council was clear: the Banksy should be kept where it was.

Only it was already too late: the wall, all four tons of it, had disappeared. Two friends who lived locally, keen Banksy followers, had bought the wall and had no intention of leaving it there. When they started taking it down they were dismayed to discover it was made of reinforced concrete rather than the breeze block they had expected.

So instead of a day or so to get it down, it took them nine days. They fitted the wall into a steel cage and transported it to restorers, who took over a month cleaning off the tags that rivals had put on. The whole operation cost them about £30,000.

Bradley Ridge, one of the owners, who had been collecting Banksy prints since his college days, told me, 'I would love to keep it, but I live in a first-floor flat so that is not going to happen.'

Instead they waited for offers. But again it was very unclear what price to put on a work which Banksy had acknowledged as his, but which he refused to authenticate. Eighteen months after they had dismantled the wall, they appeared on Channel 4's *Four Rooms*, a television series which tried to inject auction-style suspense into the business of buying and selling assorted treasures. There they declared they were looking for £300,000. They meant it, turning down a final bid of £240,000.

Mr Ridge has since become a full-time art specialist, advising on and selling Banksys. But Banksy's *Punk* has been tucked away in storage for 15 years, waiting for the perfect offer, probably still trying to figure out the IKEA-like instructions.

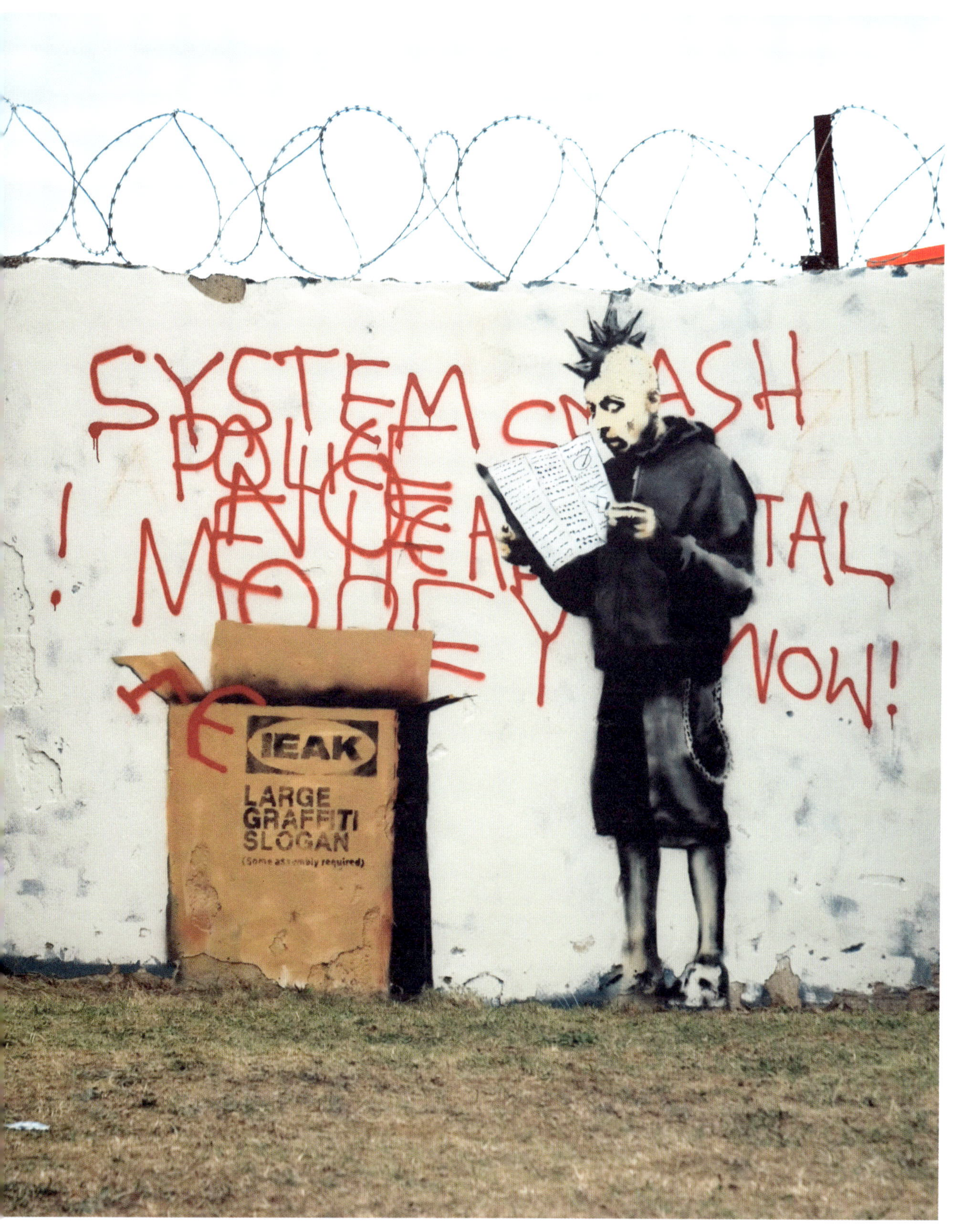

SYSTEM SMASH
POLICE
MENTAL
MONEY
NOW!
IEAK
LARGE
GRAFFITI
SLOGAN
(some assembly required)

SMILING THROUGH

⦿ 99 LOWER LAMB STREET, BRISTOL BS1 5TL

Rewriting a damaged Banksy is like adding your own water lily to a damaged Monet or repairing a Mark Rothko with your own stripe. It just does not work, however good the intentions might be.

Banksy painted this at the back of the Central Library in Bristol in 2011. Again, what it shows is the knack he has for placement. The type, which appears to be his own thought rather than a quote nicked from someone else, was combined with the existing air vents repurposed into eyes to conjure up a smiley face on the brickwork. A great work of art? No, but clever and enjoyable; quite difficult to find but worth it if you were hunting down his work in Bristol.

But four years later, it was decided that the library needed a loading bay at the back, and a roll-top door was inserted right into the middle of the smiley face. You would have thought that would be the end of it, but no, someone involved in the project wanted to keep the Banksy alive.

Where a hole had been punched through for the door, the type had been lost along with the real bricks. So the new roll-top door was actually wallpapered over to give a brick effect, and type almost the same as Banksy's had been found to replace the lost words. Where one of the new lights had got in the way of the type, it was simply written over. Nothing could be done about the missing air vent but at least there was still one air vent/eye left.

So looking at it now, is it still a Banksy? No, but someone deserves ten out of ten for effort.

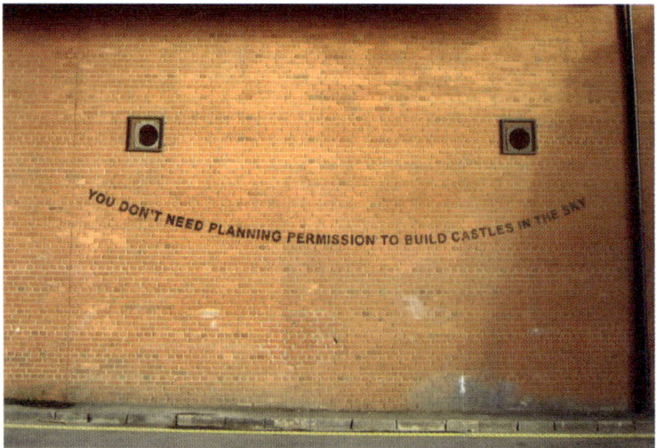

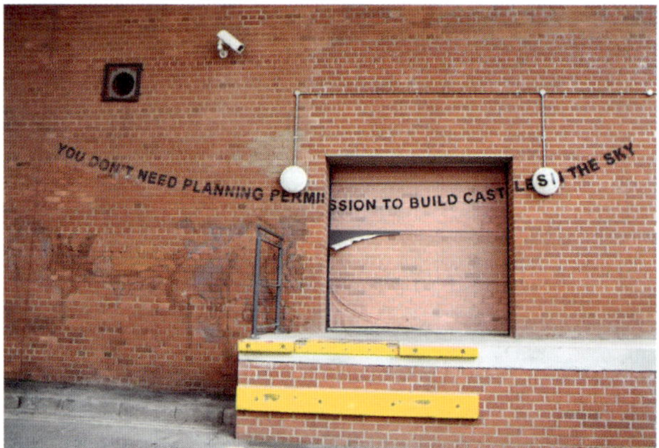

THE ROWING BOAT VANDAL

◉ PAINTED: THE GROVE, EAST MUD DOCK, BRISTOL BS1 4RB;
NOW: M SHED, PRINCES WHARF, BRISTOL BS1 4RN

Banksy started out one night painting an anti-slavery message on Bristol Harbour bridge (painted over the next morning). As he made his getaway in a small rowing boat, he stopped by the *Thekla*, a cargo ship turned floating nightclub moored in the harbour, and painted a squiggly Banksy on the hull. From the one photograph I have seen, it certainly did not look an impressive piece of work.

Banksy writes: 'A few weeks later the harbour master contacted the owners to say he'd toured the docks with some city councillors and they had ordered the removal of the graffiti because it was damaging the harbourside's image.' The boat's owners asked clubbers to vote on whether they wanted to keep the piece or not – no prize for guessing the likely result. But while the votes were being counted the harbour master had the piece painted over. Undefeated, Banksy rowed out again and painted his *Grim Reaper* in the same spot.

It was an arresting sight, at exactly the right height just above the waterline, rowing along, glowering at everyone else in the harbour. Far from 'damaging the harbourside's image' it became a key ingredient in Bristol's slightly alternative message. But *Thekla*, built in Germany in 1958, was growing old and so too was the Banksy. In 2014, when the boat went into dry dock for repairs and renovations, the *Grim Reaper* was cut out before it could rust into oblivion; the owners of the boat gave it on long-term loan to the city. It was an imaginative and generous act – the owners could have sold it for large sums of money – and it is now in Bristol's M Shed museum. But lifted out of context the *Grim Reaper* is now a petrified relic sealed in a display case. It has lost its very reason for being.

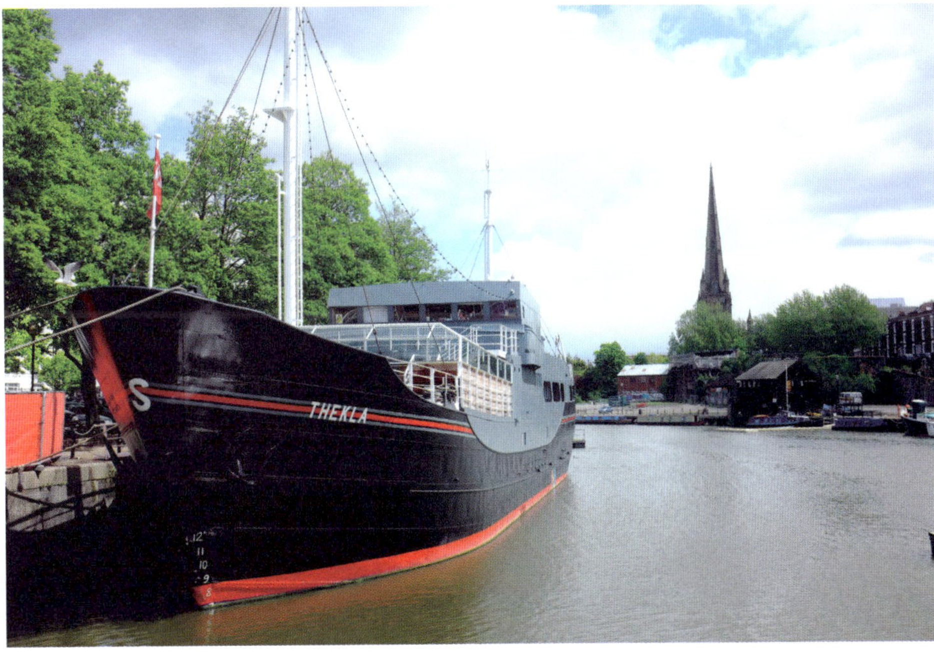

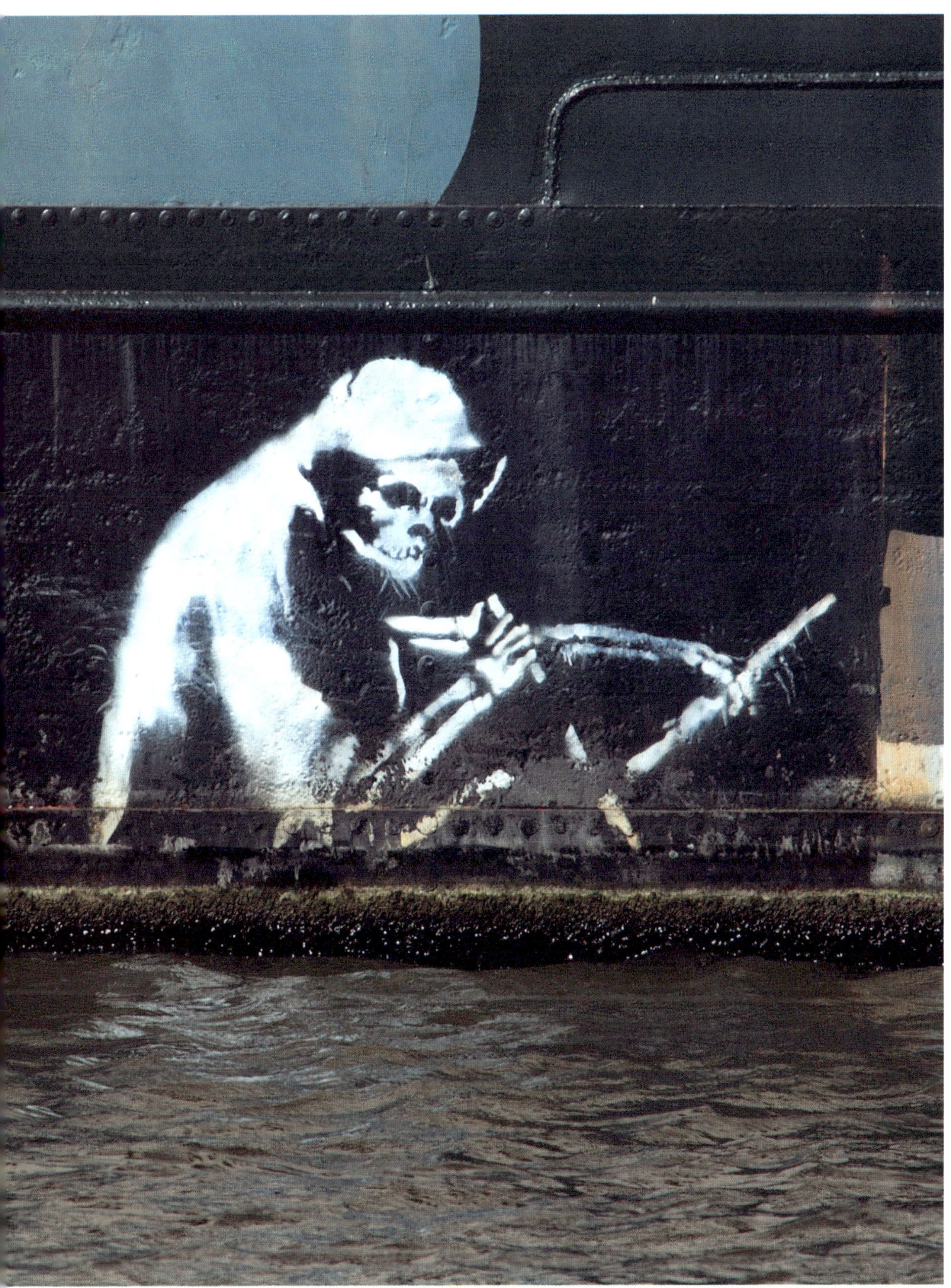

40
STOLEN SPERM

In April 2014 I went to an extraordinary exhibition in the basement of the ME hotel in The Strand called, perhaps unwisely, 'Stealing Banksy?'. Here was a collection of nine pieces, most of them having been removed from walls, much to Banksy's disgust. The only piece that had ever been 'stolen' was *Sperm Alarm,* although it had been recovered by the owner of the building it had been painted on and was now up for sale.

Using as his canvas an aluminium panel on the outer wall of what was then the Hesperia Hotel in central London, Banksy painted 15 sperm circling a large red fire alarm, giving the alarm a slightly weird, sunny face.

It had not been up there long before 32-year-old Leon Lawrence ripped the panel off the wall. What he had not taken into account was the hotel staff's continued interest in 'their' Banksy. They noticed it when it was first put up, they noticed it when it disappeared, and in particular they noticed it when it was put up for sale on eBay priced at a reasonable enough £17,000.

Once they informed the police it was easy enough to track the thief from his eBay account. He appeared to have something of an obsession with art – and stealing it – having been given a community order for stealing a piece of sculpture from a Brick Lane gallery the previous year. His story that a friend had given him the piece was not believed by the jury and he was sentenced to nine months in jail suspended for a year.

Any hopes that *Sperm Alarm* would be put back where it belonged were soon dashed. At the 'Stealing Banksy?' exhibition the price had risen from the original eBay price of £17,000 to a hugely over-optimistic £150,000. Understandably it failed to sell there, but it was shipped off to Julien's Auctions in California where, still unauthenticated by Banksy, it sold for almost $45,000 and has not been seen since.

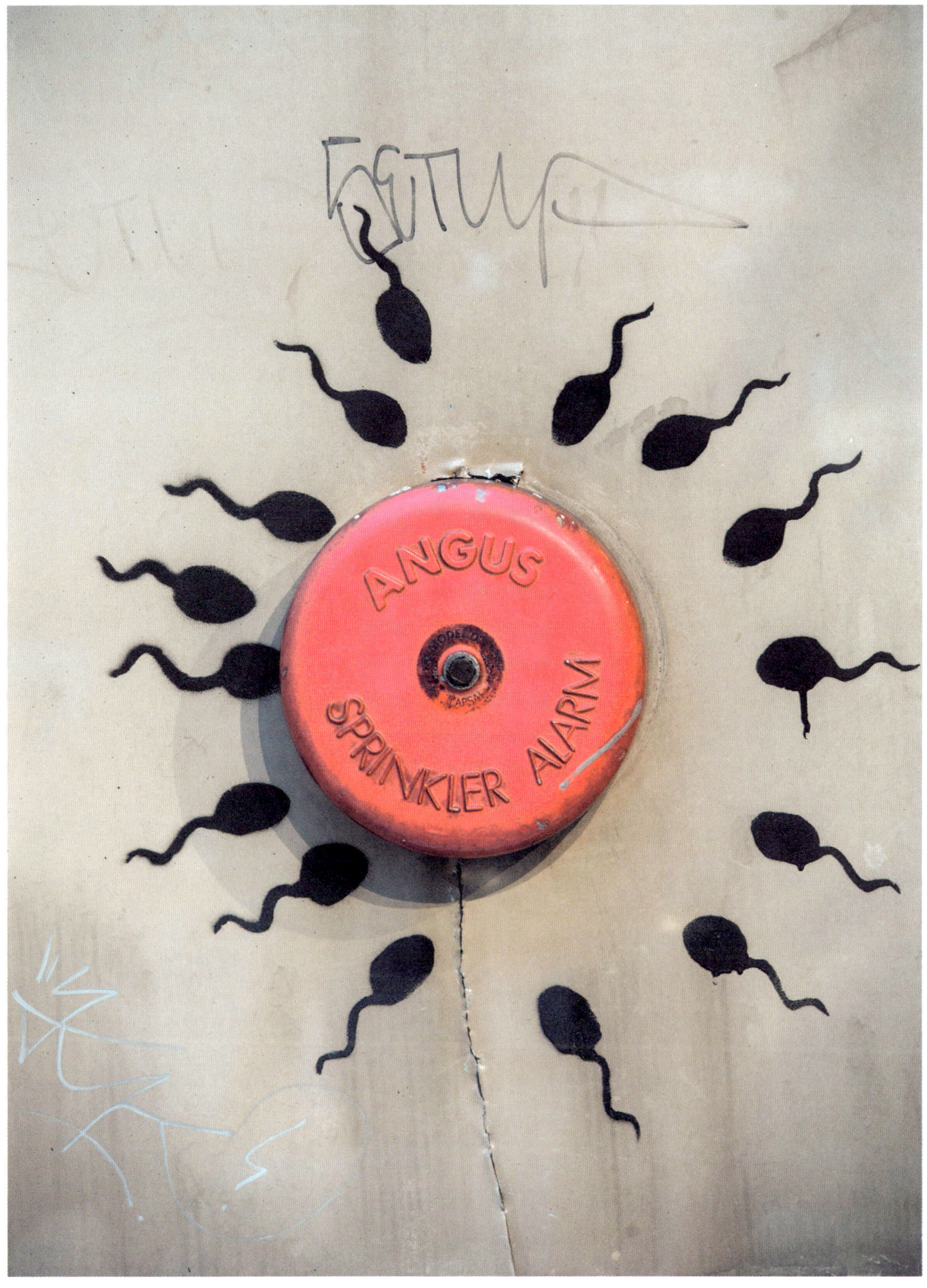

ANGUS
SPRINKLER ALARM

41

THE SPHINX ALSO RISES

📍 35TH AVENUE WITH 127TH STREET, NEW YORK NY 10027

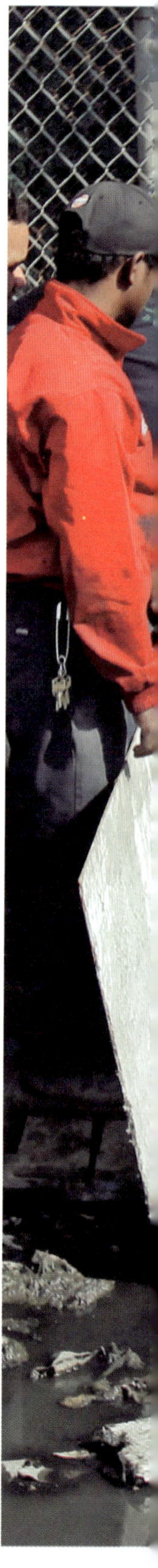

On the face of it the Sphinx that Banksy created three weeks into his 'residency' in New York in 2013 was a candidate for long-term survival. It was well off the beaten track in Queens, it was protected by what at the time was called a moat but was actually a large fetid puddle, and best of all it looked too heavy and fragile to move.

The treasure hunt started as soon as Banksy revealed it on his website, but by the time his followers found the Sphinx amid a jumble of car workshops, it was already too late. Bernardo 'Choco' Veles, who owned an auto-glass shop close by, had arrived for work at six in the morning to find the Sphinx sitting there, and soon he and a couple of friends decided the best thing to do was to get it out of there – fast. As one of them said, 'If we don't take it, somebody's going to do it.'

They found a van, backed it up as close as they could and shoved the Sphinx very unceremoniously into it. They were very fortunate in that the Sphinx was not nearly as heavy as it looked, being made of cinderblocks, Styrofoam and a few bricks.

Watching a video of its departure, there was obviously no thought of numbering the pieces so they could be put back together. Some of the smaller bits were just chucked into the van; one helper sold off a brick for $100. The main bulk was carried into the van on a makeshift stretcher. It seemed inconceivable that there was any life left in the Sphinx.

But there was. The men took it home and hid it in their garage. Then they contacted Stephan Keszler, the key dealer in New York for Banksy's pieces, which were being taken from the streets of New York almost as fast as he was creating them.

Under Mr Keszler's care the Sphinx travelled as far as an art show in Miami with a price tag of $300,000 on its head, but it failed to sell. Eventually Mr Keszler decided to buy it for himself. His theory – totally unproven – is that Banksy had made it largely out of foam deliberately so it would fall apart after a few years, 'so that anyone who paid money for it will have nothing after a while.' (It seems a particularly unlikely theory given that when Banksy hit New York he had no idea of how quickly his pieces would disappear.) It was sent to a restorer who, working on it intermittently, took almost two years to finish the job. According to Keszler, 'It's beautiful now, it's in very good condition and it is not for sale.'

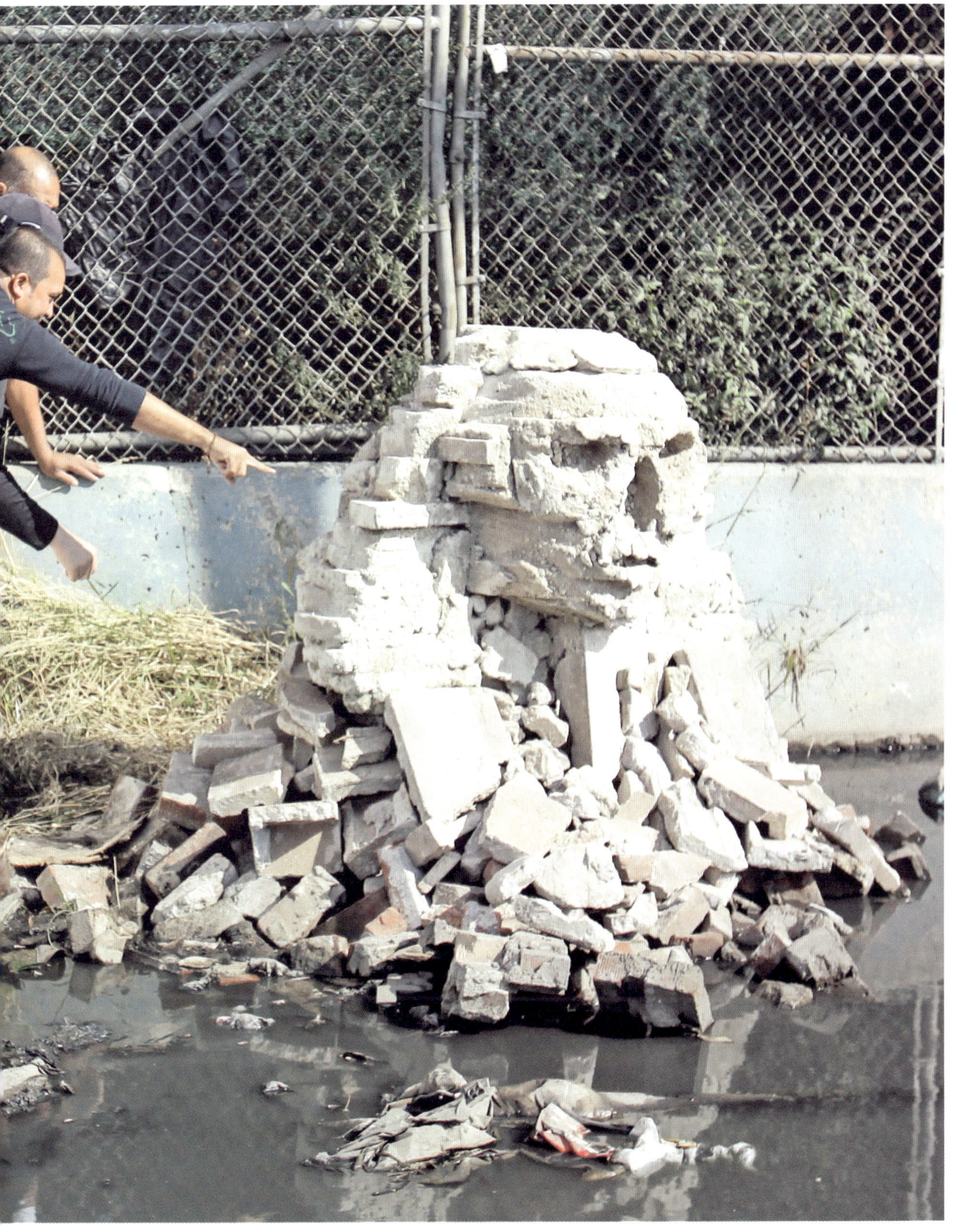

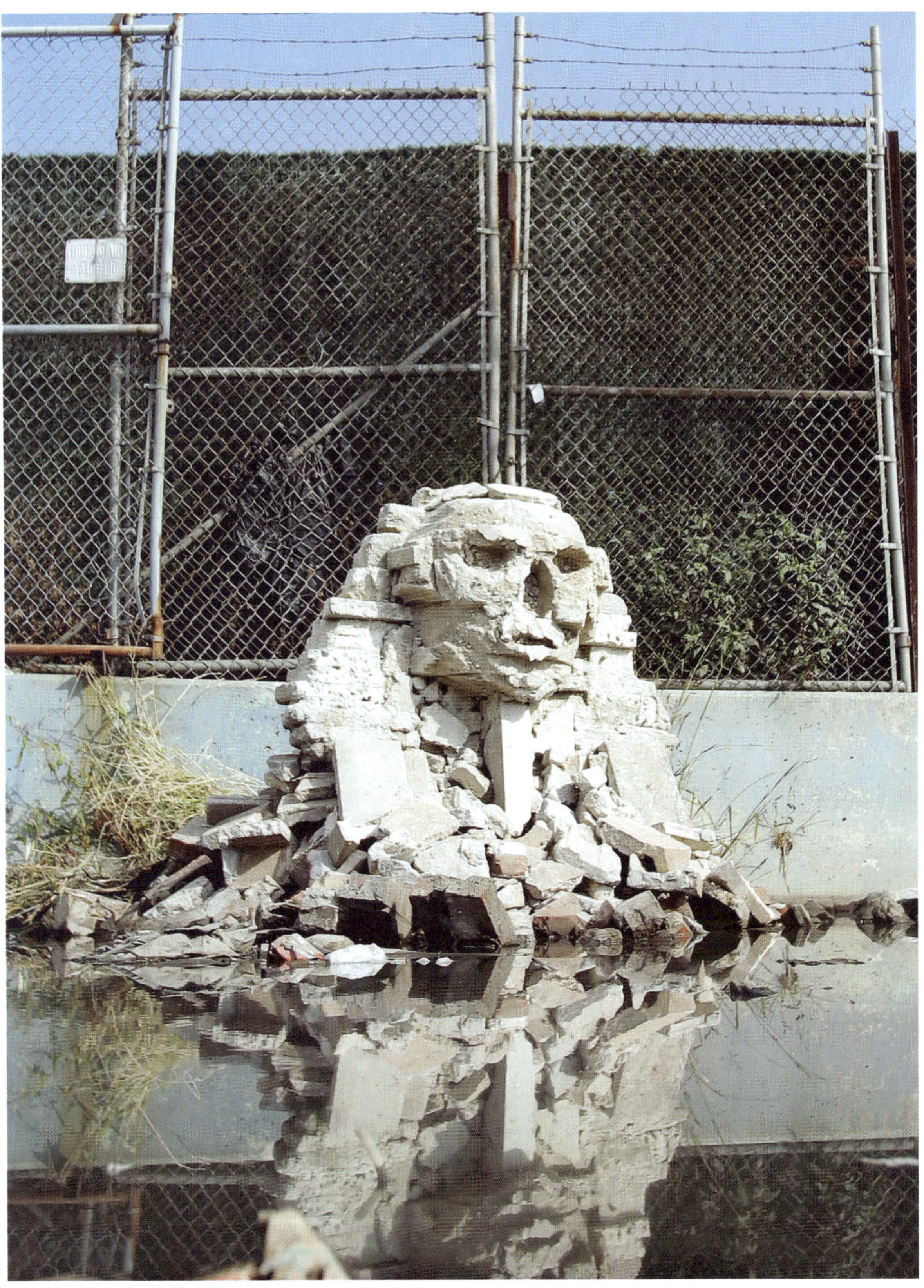

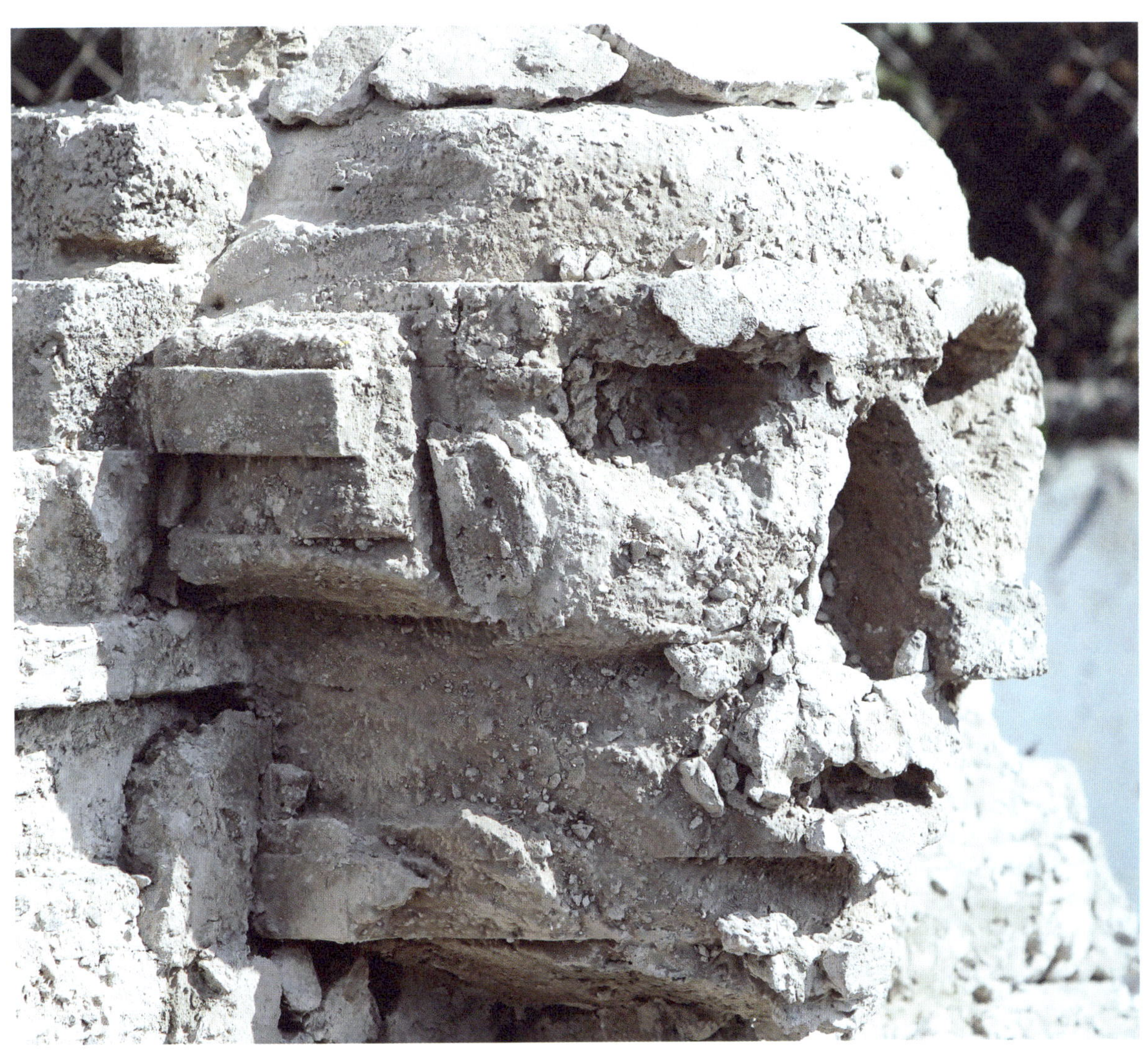

42

NEIGHBOURHOOD WATCH

◉ THOMAS STREET NORTH, BRISTOL BS6 5TN (*MOUSETRAP ROSE*);
◉ 79TH STREET AND BROADWAY, NEW YORK NY 10024 (*HAMMER BOY*);
◉ ROSEBERY AVENUE, LONDON WC1X 0DW (*CASH MACHINE*)

If a Banksy lands on your wall, is it worth trying to protect his work with a proper frame and Perspex, or do you simply leave it open to determined taggers? Successfully preserving a Banksy depends not only on how good the frame is and how out of the way the piece is, but also on how much the local community is involved in trying to protect it.

Take two survivors. In Bristol it was local residents who clubbed together to pay for a frame and Perspex to protect a small and rather delicate piece, *Mousetrap Rose*. That was in the early 2000s and it worked well until 2019 when Rob Dean, director of the Bristol tour company Where The Wall, was walking past and saw the frame was broken and the Perspex ripped off. 'Anyone with a spray can in their pocket could get rid of it within a few seconds. I felt that the Banksy story in Bristol needed to be preserved for future generations.' So he arranged for a carpenter friend to come and put up a new frame – the only slight problem being one local resident who thought they were trying to take it *off* the wall, not keep it on. In 2024 *Mousetrap Rose* was still there.

In New York in 2013 Banksy painted *Hammer Boy* on a building owned by the Zabar brothers, who run a famous deli on the Upper West Side of Manhattan. On a Sunday morning fans started to arrive to see the Banksy. 'It was a magical moment,' Saul Zabar told a New York writer. 'There was so much positive feeling... I'll never forget it.' Up went the cover and frame as well as a CCTV camera and a gentle ad: 'Help Zabars save this Banksy.' There was even a complaint from one neighbour who started cleaning the Plexiglass himself, claiming that the Zabars were not good enough guardians. But they have certainly looked after it well enough for it to be the one remaining piece from Banksy's 2013 stay in the city that is still on display on the street.

Compare this with a piece in north London where a frame did nothing to deter the taggers. On Rosebery Avenue Mark Ellis discovered a Banksy underneath a piece of rusting metal next to the shop he was renovating. It was, he says, 'absolutely mullered', with two white lines rollered down it. But he and his daughter cleaned it up, added a frame and Perspex and opened the renovated shop, calling it Banksy's Bagel Bar. The result? It was soon an unhappy mess. No one else seemed to care. The Banksy has all but disappeared under a storm of tags on the Perspex, and the Bagel Bar has gone too.

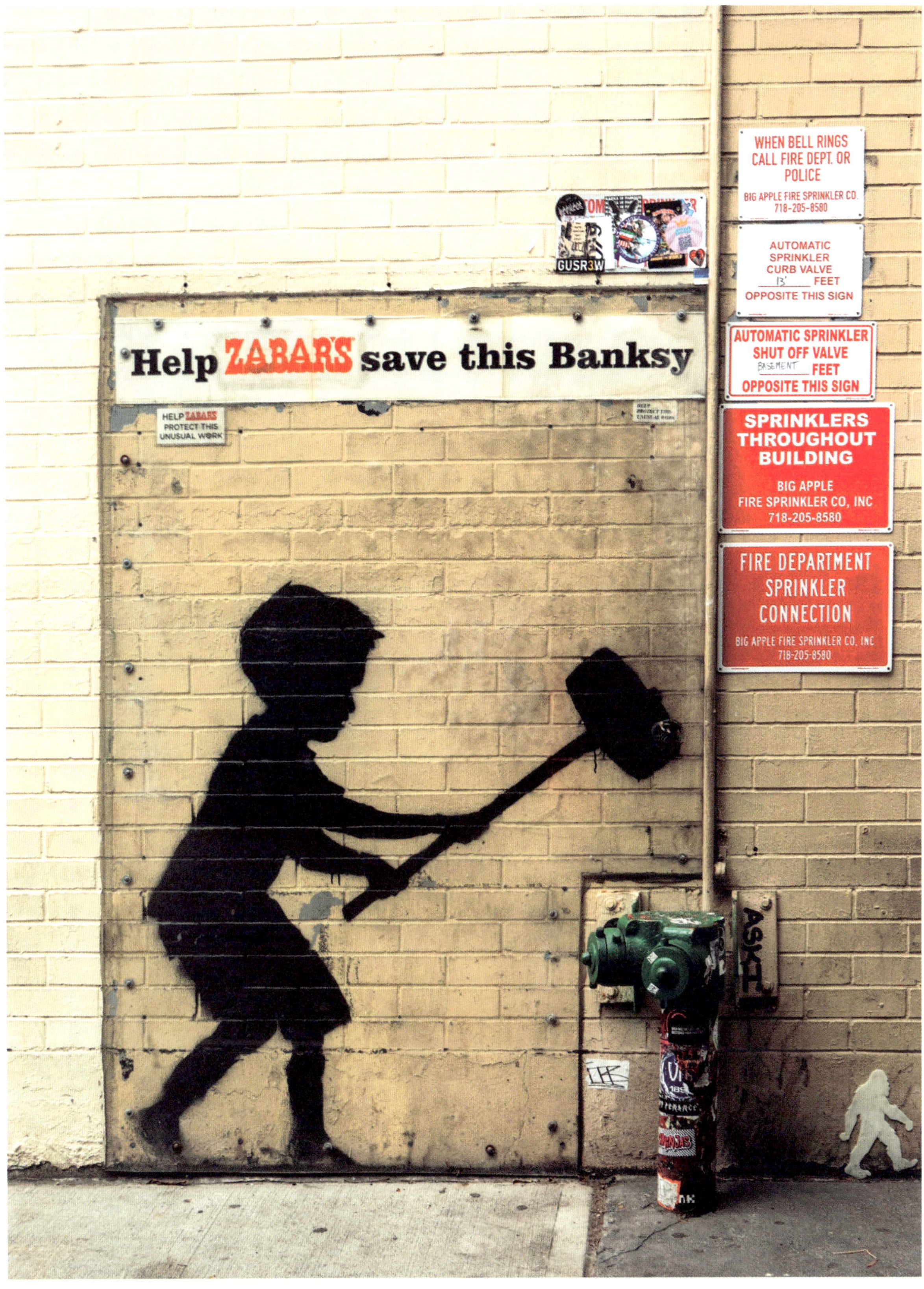

Help ZABARS save this Banksy
HELP ZABARS PROTECT THIS UNUSUAL WORK
WHEN BELL RINGS CALL FIRE DEPT. OR POLICE
BIG APPLE FIRE SPRINKLER CO.
718-205-8580
AUTOMATIC SPRINKLER CURB VALVE
13' FEET OPPOSITE THIS SIGN
AUTOMATIC SPRINKLER SHUT OFF VALVE
BASEMENT FEET OPPOSITE THIS SIGN
SPRINKLERS THROUGHOUT BUILDING
BIG APPLE FIRE SPRINKLER CO, INC
718-205-8580
FIRE DEPARTMENT SPRINKLER CONNECTION
BIG APPLE FIRE SPRINKLER CO, INC
718-205-8580
ASK!
GUSR3W

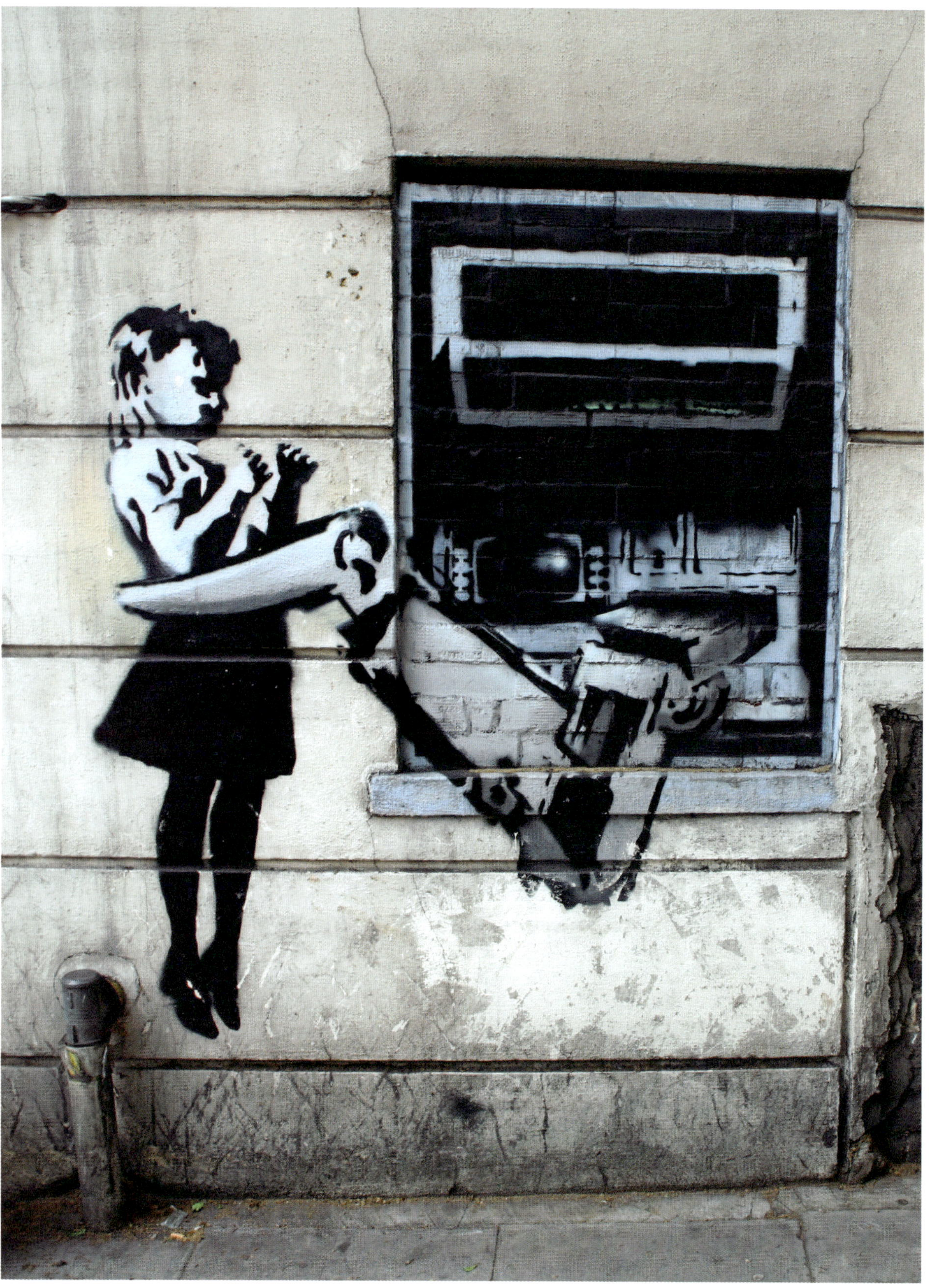

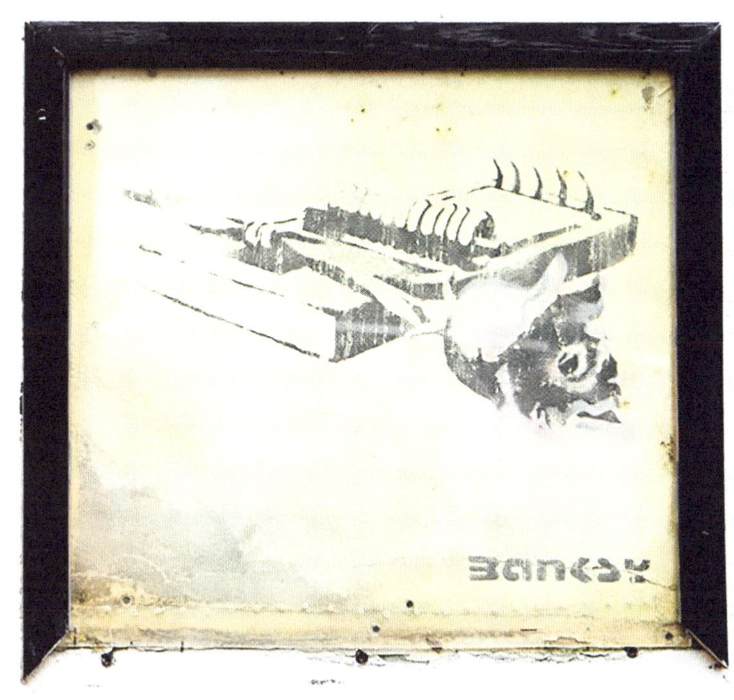
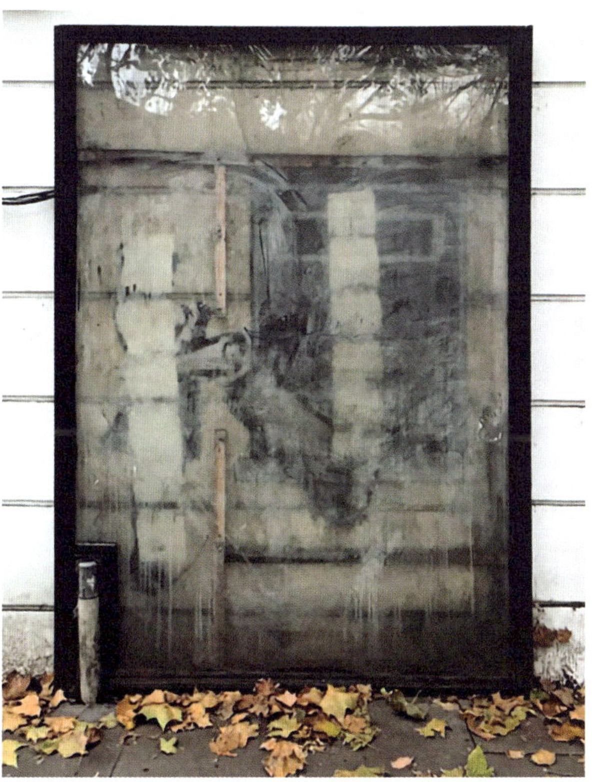

43

SEEN AND GONE

YORK STREET, DOVER CT17 9FA

This piece in Dover was a classic example of Banksy hiding in plain sight, making the whole operation so visible no one would ever have conceived that it might have been him at work. The building he chose, near the cross-channel ferry terminal, had been derelict for several years, so when, in the spring of 2017, nearby residents saw scaffolding going up along its flank wall, they assumed it was for repairs.

There were no repairs, just Banksy. When the scaffolding and its covering were taken down, there it was: a workman on a long ladder chipping away at one of the yellow stars in the giant, blue EU flag. It was a powerful piece, albeit a poignant one for anyone who the year before had voted against Brexit.

Two years later the scaffolding was up again, but this time it was not for Banksy but for the owners of the building, who ordered that the whole thing, including the workman's ladder, should be painted over. Why? It remains unclear, but the family who owned the building had lost out badly in an expensive legal struggle over Banksy's *Art Buff* (see page 88) which he painted on a building in Folkestone where they were tenants; perhaps they just wanted to (white)wash their hands of him before he gave them any more trouble.

If they were worried that someone might start a campaign to 'save' the Banksy, they had every right to be. As the blue slowly began to peek out from under the whitewash, 70 shopkeepers in the town, led by the owner of a fish and chip shop, launched a petition asking the local council to retain the piece as part of a plan to revive the town centre. This in a town where 62 per cent voted Leave.

They were too late. The local council had already bought the site as part of a huge re-development plan and down came the building and thus the Banksy, plus the other buildings alongside it. As for the Banksy itself, DDS, the demolition company, has managed to salvage most of the workman on his ladder and the EU stars he was chipping away at, but not much of the blue flag itself. By Easter 2024 restorers reported that the whitewash over the stars could be removed and they hoped to be able to do the same to the workman. So they are confident they can restore most of the work, although it will survive in chunks, never in one piece again.

Yet without the Channel by its side, how much will the stars and a workman plus his ladder mean to anyone?

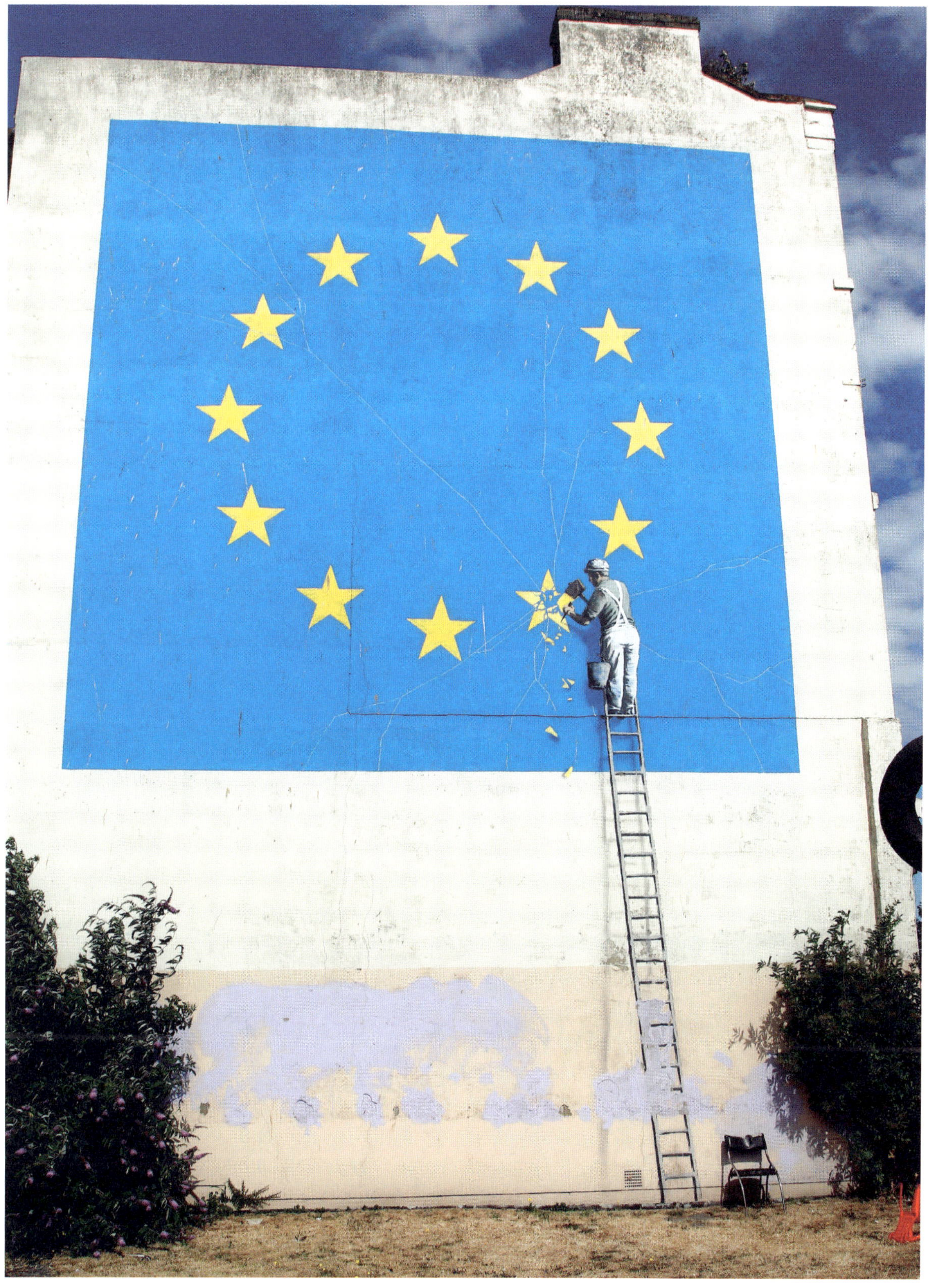

44

EVERY BRICK IN THE WALL

◊ BEVERLY BOULEVARD AND LA BREA AVENUE, LOS ANGELES CA 90036

Back in 2008 the owner of a gas station in Hollywood had a visit from a good customer, Thierry Guetta, now known as the street artist Mr Brainwash, who pulled up in his truck with two friends. He wanted to know if he could borrow a wall on the gas station to paint on. What they painted would be 'tasteful, nothing risqué'. One of his friends was an Englishman wearing a black hoodie with paint under his fingernails and paint all over his jeans.

So was it Banksy? Eytan Rosenberg, the owner of the gas station, had no idea who Banksy was let alone what he looked like. But a few weeks after giving his permission, he arrived for work to find the *Flower Girl* on the wall, and already fans were there taking pictures of it. There was no doubt, this was Banksy.

After his father died Mr Rosenberg and his sister decided to sell the gas station but keep *Flower Girl*. 'I wish I could keep it, but it was out of my pay grade,' he said at the time. It was taken to Julien's Auctions in Beverly Hills in December 2013, where it was the star of their first Street Art auction, selling for $209,000 to an anonymous bidder. It was a bonanza for Mr Rosenberg, but it was also a game changer for Julien's, which is called 'Auction House to the Stars' but is still a minnow compared to the likes of Sotheby's or Christie's.

It was the first Banksy Julien's had auctioned off, and Martin Nolan, co-founder of the auction house, said 'it was a massive undertaking, because we had to figure out how do you extract it, keep it intact and protect it. We couldn't risk losing even one brick from the artwork, it would have lost its meaning.'

Julien's never looked back. 'We always reflect back on this project which was daunting at the time. We are a small company. We are the disrupters in the art auction industry. We thought this will really put us on the map if we cut down a wall and bring it to auction... without doubt it definitely changed gears for us.'

Julien's became the major international auction house for works that were taken off the street and there is no doubt there have been works by Banksy, although he has refused to authenticate them. Mr Nolan estimates they have sold between 30 or 40 pieces like this over the last decade.

And what happened to *Flower Girl*? The winning bidder was building a house at the time, and Julien's had to store the piece in their warehouse for almost four years before the house was ready for the artwork. 'If it came back to auction now,' says Mr Nolan, 'we would probably sell it for $1,000,000.'

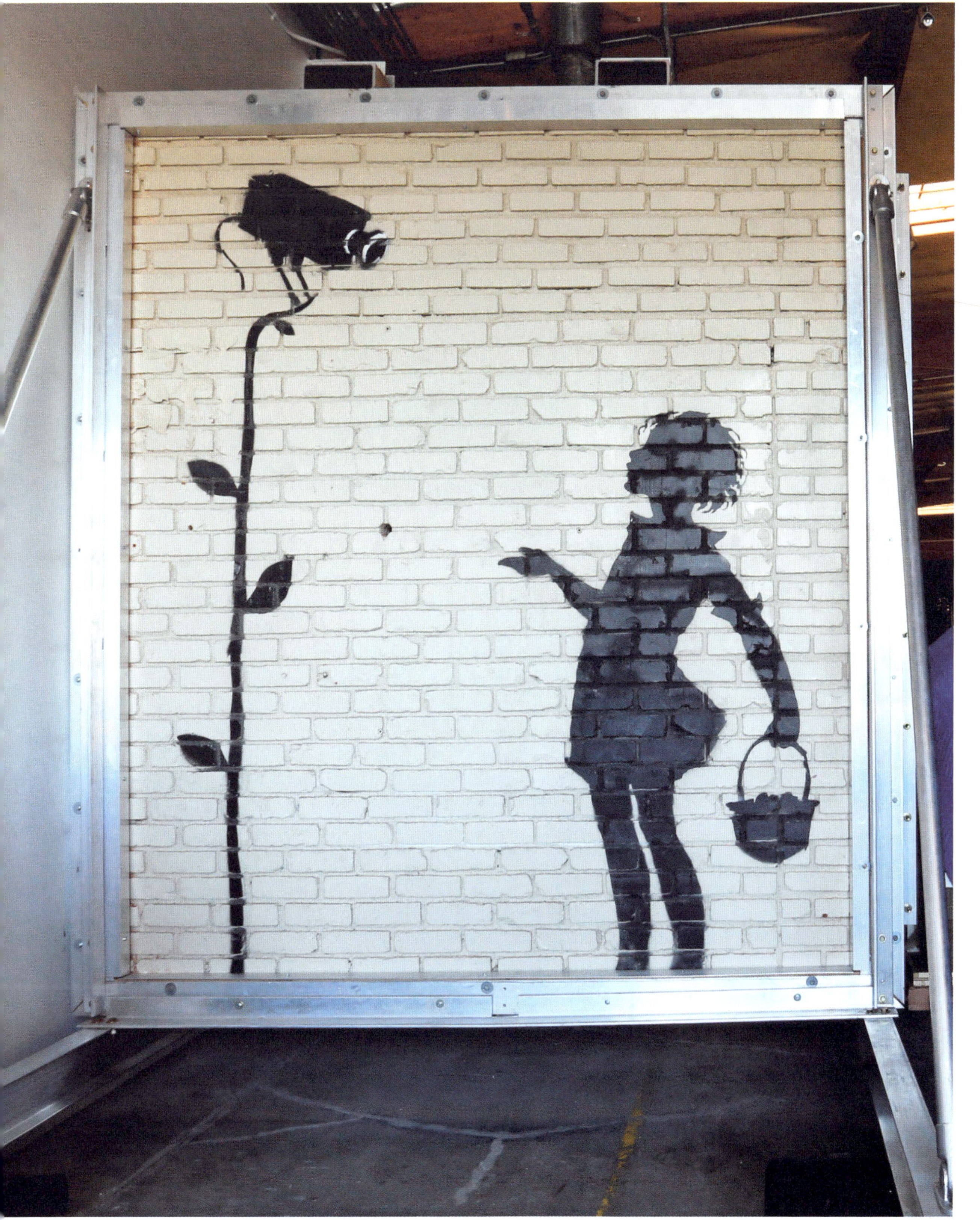

IN AND OUT OF THE BRONX

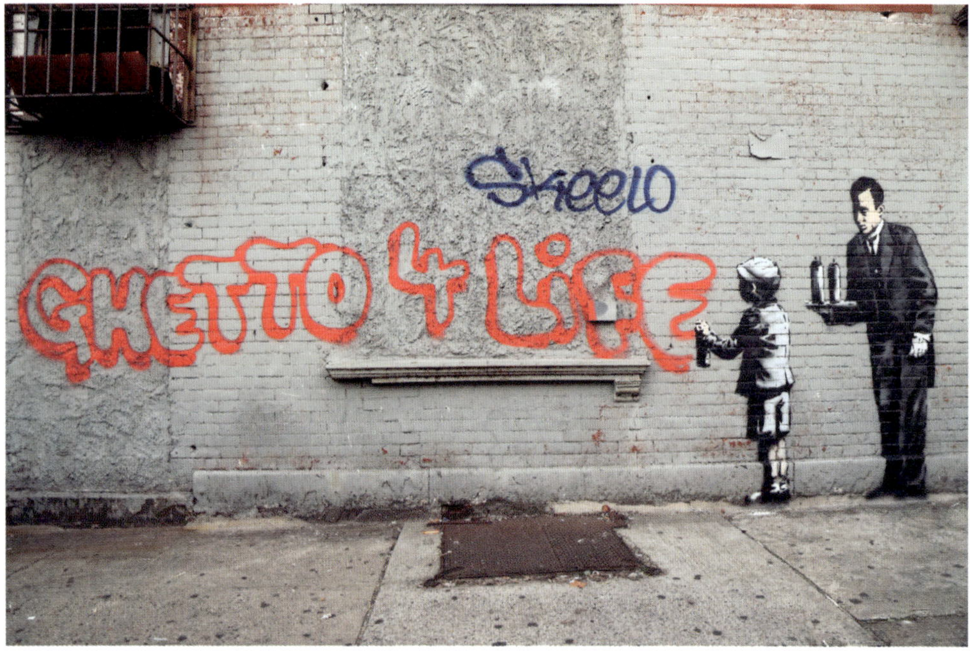

Picture the scene in October 2013: Banksy strolls into New York for his month-long residency and on day 21 he paints this in the South Bronx. Here, in a borough which was trying to shrug off its reputation as a place where outsiders feared to tread, it was not a popular piece.

The borough's then President, Rubén Díaz Jr., lectured Banksy, 'We are a place where people are living the American Dream. To 1.4 million people we are home, and Banksy would do well to remember that before he traffics in ancient stereotypes about our borough.'

Now fast forward eleven years and New York was losing one of its last remaining Banksys.

Ghetto4Life was being shipped off to storage in Connecticut and an uncertain future. Good riddance? Not at all – the residents of the Bronx were not happy. Steve Jacob, who owned a store across the street from *Ghetto4Life*, told the *New York Post*, 'Everybody was crying around here. This is art. The gentleman made it for us, the community. I've lived all my life in the Bronx and this was made for the Bronx people. And now someone's taken it away from us.' Another resident told the *Post*, 'They really took a piece of my heart.'

The irony is that for most of its life in the Bronx this piece was seldom ever seen. Shielded by the owner of the desolate building where it was

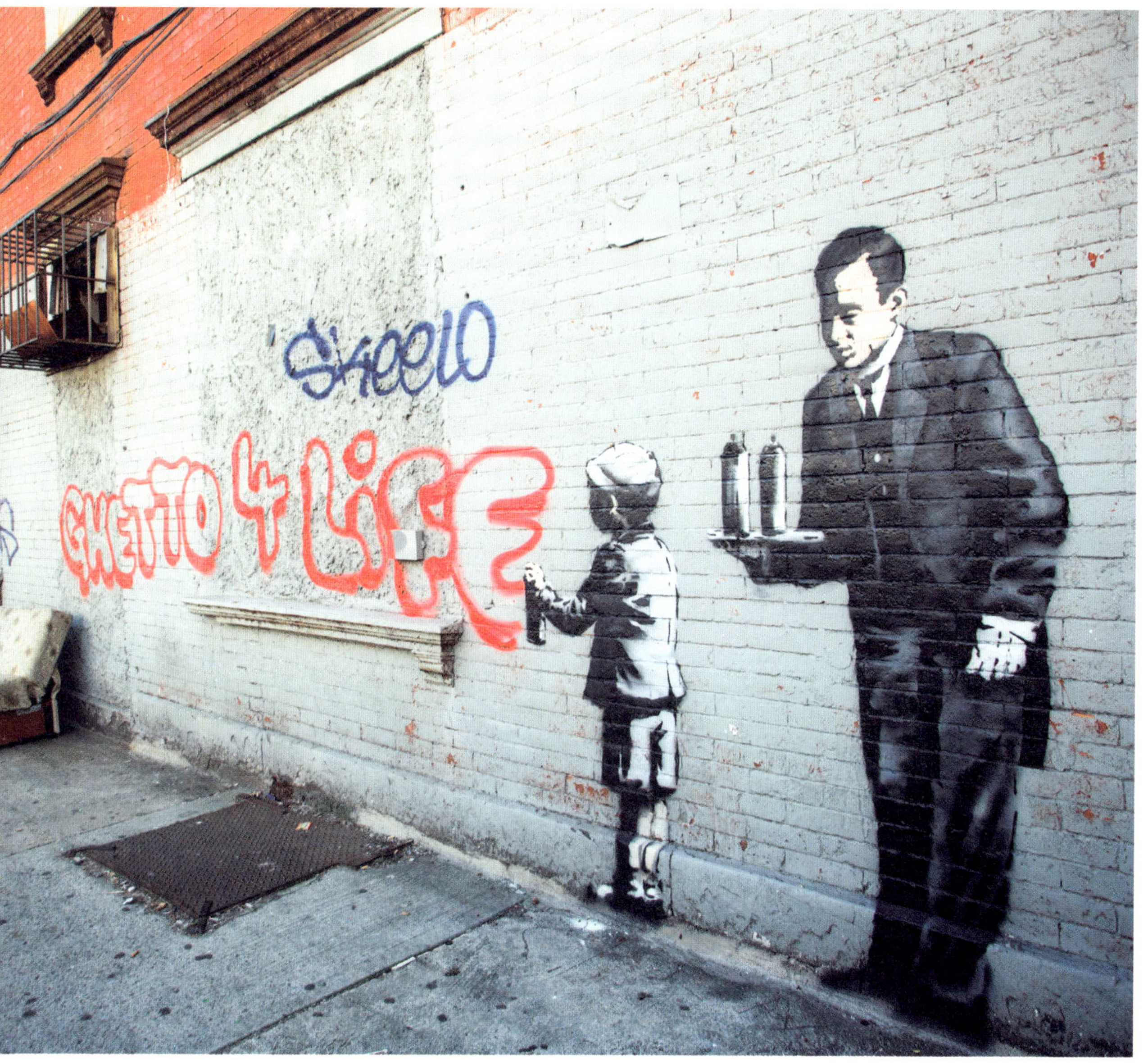

painted, first by makeshift curtains and then both by Plexiglass and a roll-down steel shutter, it was surely not so much that *Ghetto4Life* had grown on the Bronx, but that Banksy's fame had grown so big, people enjoyed having a slice of it.

The Banksy had to go because David Damaghi, a property investor who owned the building, needed it demolished in order to build a school in its place. In a delicate operation the wall was carved off the side of the building and put on a lorry bound for Connecticut. After the move Mr Damaghi was not taking any calls but his representative told me 'it was more expensive to preserve it than to demolish it.' In Connecticut the wall 'will be safely stored until we decide what to do with it... we have no plans to sell it, we want to preserve it.' But sold or not, *Ghetto4Life* is gone from New York. Now of the 30 pieces Banksy created in the City during his month-long residency (one day was blank due to 'police activity'), only two are left: one under Plexiglass and the other behind a shutter. But then the lifespan of graffiti is counted in days not years.

46

MISTAKES DO HAPPEN

If only the plumber in Melbourne, Australia, had drilled the hole in the wall 20 centimetres higher and to the side, then Banksy's *Parachuting Rat* would still be there. If only the cleaners paid to keep London's tube trains free of graffiti had known that the 'rat thing' they had discovered in one carriage of the tube was rather more than that, then Banksy's rats might still be riding London's Underground.

It was in 2012 that the unfortunate plumber in question was installing pipes ready for the opening of a new café in Prahran, Melbourne. The city was so pleased to be called Australia's street-art capital that people who knew where the Banksys were in the city often kept quiet about them in the hope that this would protect them. Too quiet, perhaps, because the plumber, completely unknowingly, drilled through the centre of Banksy's parachuting rat, which had been untouched on the outside wall ever since he painted it nine years earlier.

Someone working at the Signed & Numbered gallery across the road posted: 'This is what happened to me 10 minutes ago... I glanced over to the building across from us to see that Banksy's *Parachuting Rat* had (the very moment before) been drilled through and replaced with a drain pipe!!! I rushed across to talk to the construction worker, who had no clue of its importance or even what a Banksy is. Isn't there some street art register to prevent things like this happening?'

The answer is that Melbourne did have a street art permit system, but Banksy was not on it. To make matters worse, two years earlier a council clean-up team had painted over another *Parachuting Rat* after being instructed to clean over all 'unapproved areas.'

In this they were as blameless as the London Underground clean-up team who went to work in July 2020 after Banksy painted his rats inside a London tube train. The problem was they worked so fast they had cleaned off all the rats before Banksy had even gone on Instagram to announce it was his work. Mayor Sadiq Khan, who said he was a 'bit crestfallen', explained 'our brilliant cleaners, and they are brilliant, did the right thing – they saw a piece of graffiti and they cleaned it off.'

And from London Transport's point of view, they certainly did do the right thing. Imagine if Banksy had revealed that the rats were his before they were cleaned off. There would have been a clamour to keep them, making them a tribute to Banksy and a target for every other graffiti artist whose work had been cleaned off the trains.

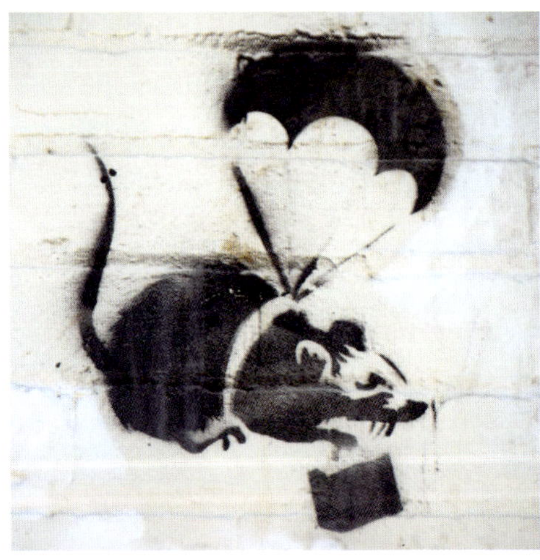

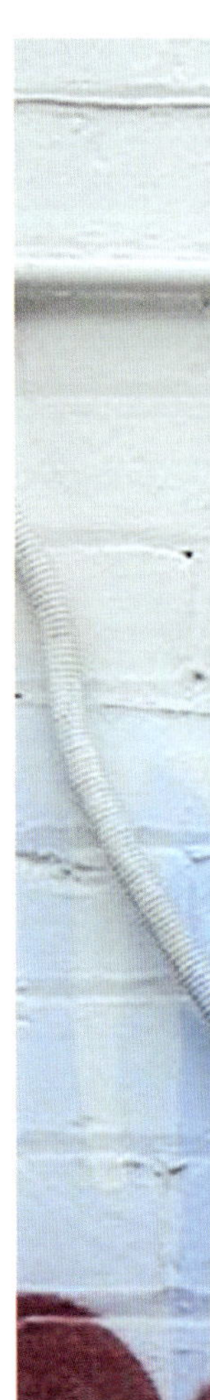

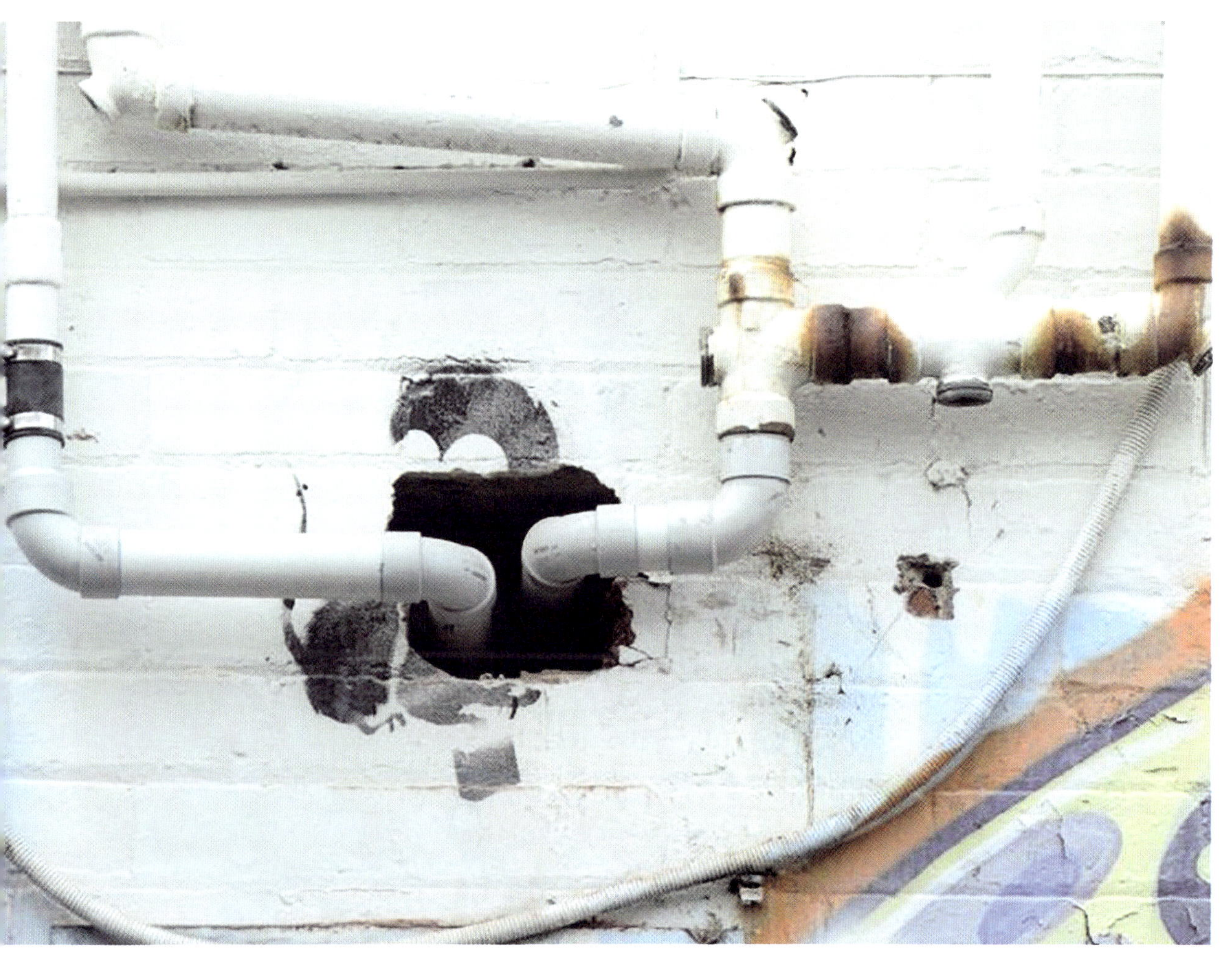

SKIP AND CHIPS

When parking in a street close to Banksy's *Seagull* in Lowestoft, I noticed a classy looking butcher's shop with a sign that read 'A&S Dawson and daughter, Traditional Family Butcher.' The queue stretched out of the door and onto the pavement. This seemed, for a moment, to be a curious part of town for Banksy to be painting in; usually he operates in more run-down areas where people are less likely to bother him. But looking closer I realized that it was no longer a butcher's shop that people were queuing for, but a food bank – the butcher had long since gone out of business.

Lowestoft seemed like a decaying seaside town that needed all the help it could get, and what better man to do it than Banksy. On his seaside 'Spraycation' in 2021, he sprayed two pieces in the town and one on the beach. Yet visiting the town two years later, there was hardly a trace of Banksy left. The *Rat in a Deckchair* sprayed by the beach had been whitewashed over very soon after he acknowledged it was his. Now it was covered in Perspex, but the bolts were beginning to go. A few more gales and the whole thing would be wiped away, perhaps a good thing given the state it was in.

In the High Street *Sandcastle Girl*, painted next to a closed-down Tesco, lasted just three months before it was extracted from the wall ready for sale. I caught up with her at an exhibition in Bury St Edmunds, where she had pride of place. Even the elaborate sandcastle newly built in front of her, reflecting the one that Banksy had built on the pavement, could not disguise the fact that this was not her proper home.

That left two down and one to go, the menacing *Seagull* looking for 'chips' in the skip. The lure of Banksy is such that the dealer John Brandler was offered a few of these polystyrene 'chips', but since he knew they must have been stolen from the skip, he called in the police. The seagull itself was so large it seemed impossible it could be taken off the wall. But in April 2023, just a month after builders had reassured the town's mayor that they were not taking down the wall, only 'stabilizing' it, the seagull had gone. The owners of the house told *The Times* that the seagull had been a 'living nightmare' and it had cost them more than £50,000 to get it off the wall and into storage.

When I arrived the builders were still finishing off this extraordinary undertaking, building a whole new wall for the house, which had been pinned with steel rods to keep it together. The *Seagull*, inevitably, is now for sale with an asking price of around $3.5 million. For that you get not only the seagull but also the skip and the chips.

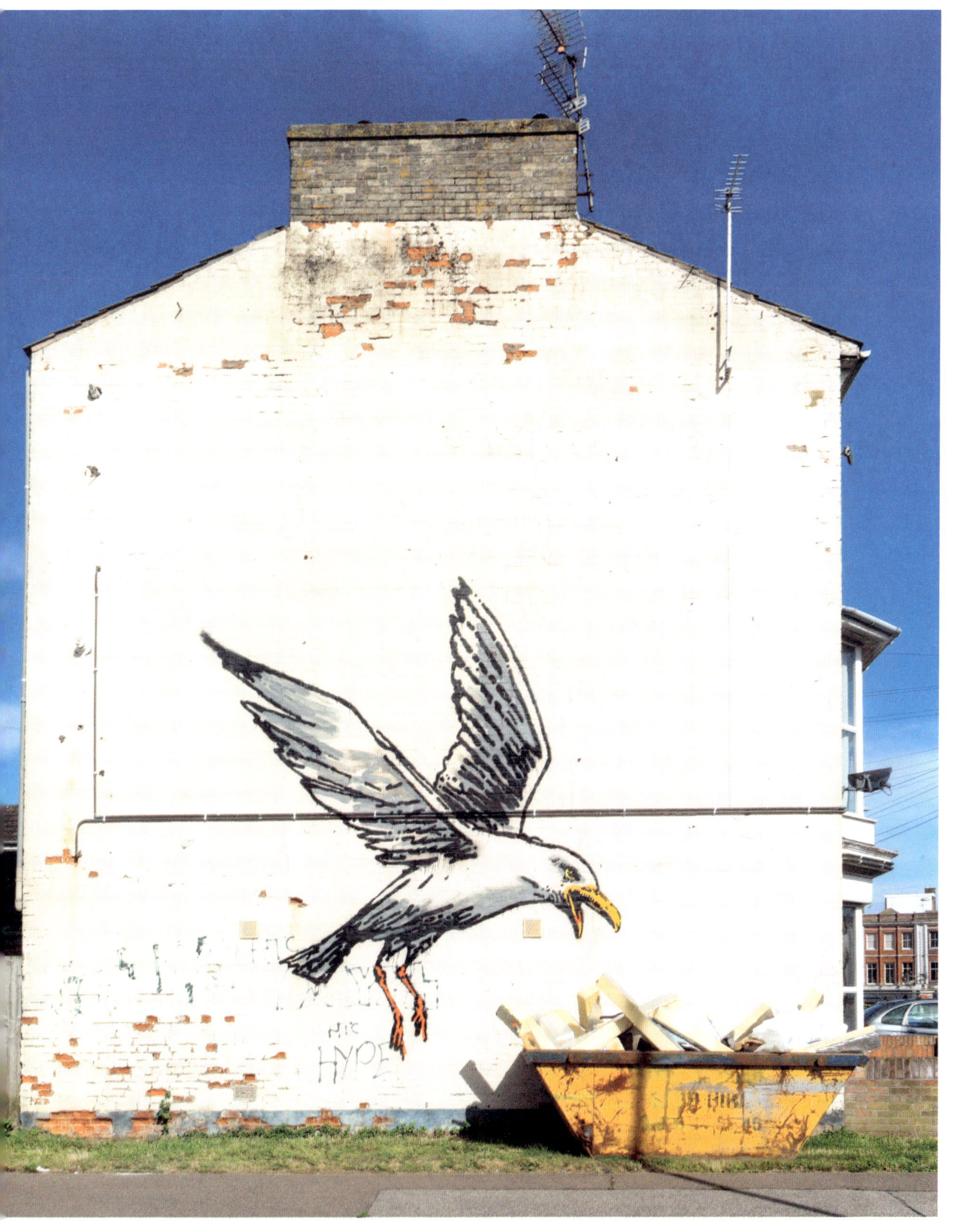

HYPE

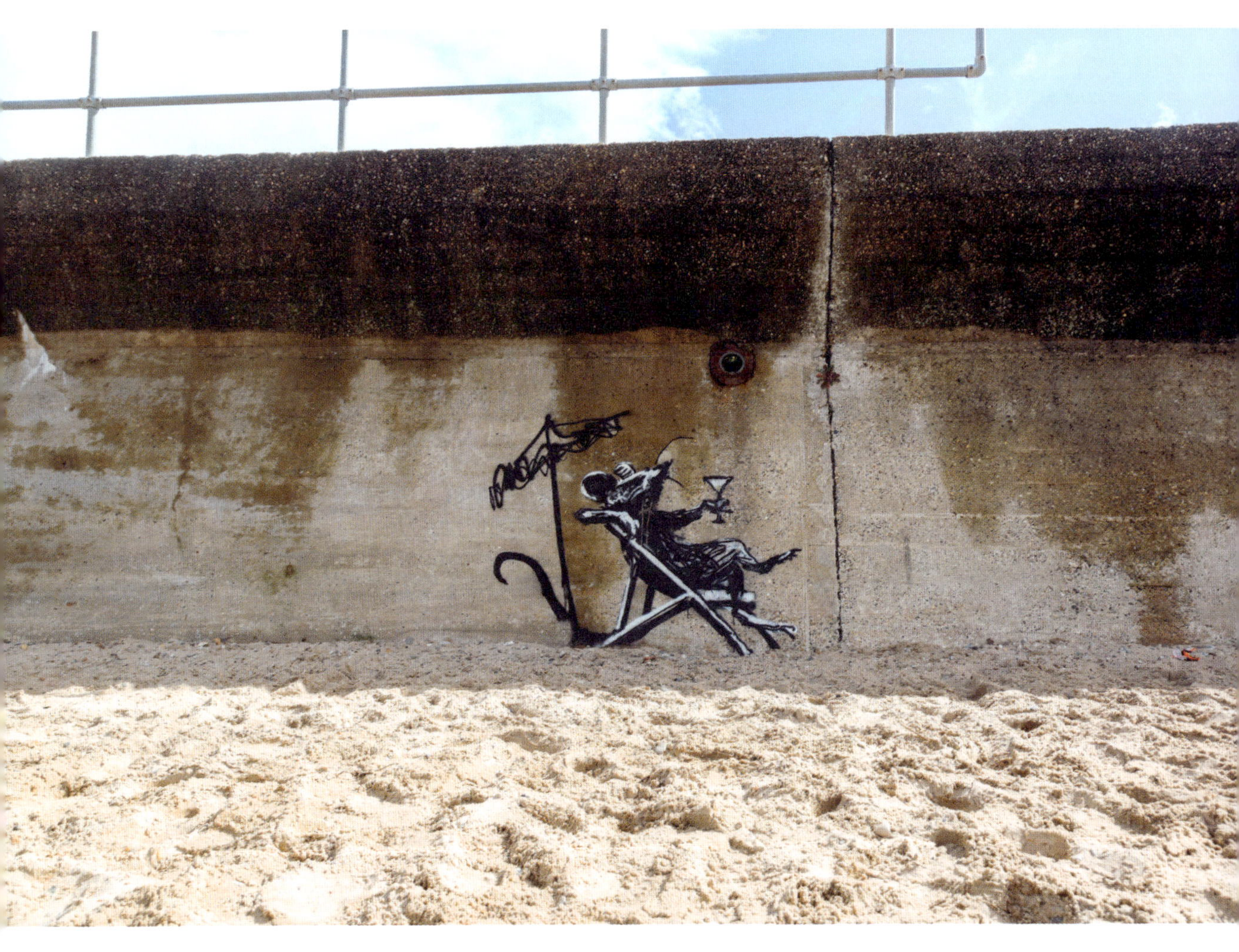

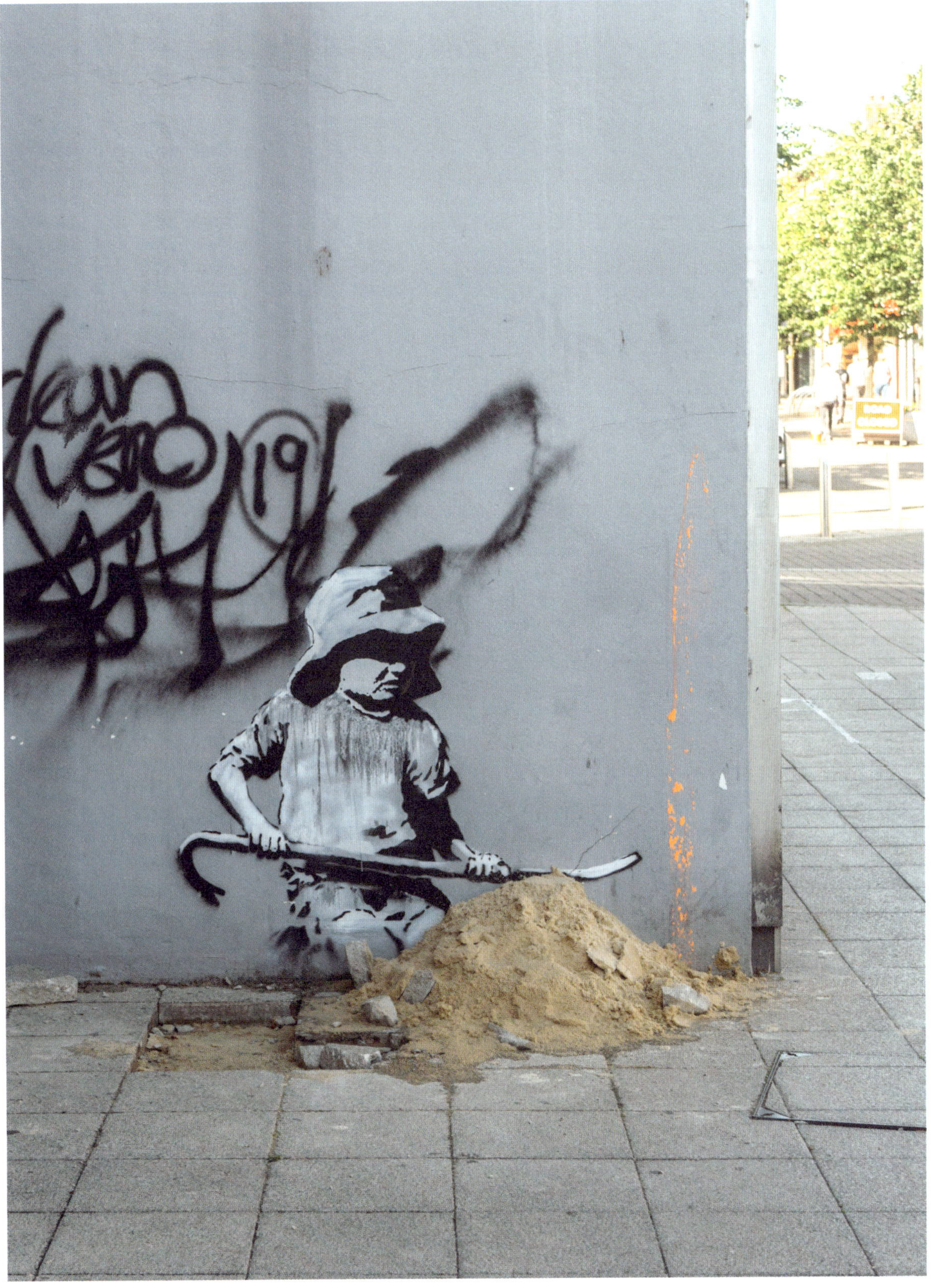

48

SINK OR SWIM

📍 PALAZZO SAN PANTALON CAMPO SANTA CROCE 1

What should be done with Banksy's *Migrant Child* standing only just above the waterline on the Rio Novo in Venice? The child has been gently fading away ever since he painted it six years ago. Restore it so it looks like new or leave it to die a natural death, hurried on by the *moto ondoso* caused by the swell of passing boats?

Until 2023 it seemed that inertia, caused by bureaucratic doubts about who had the right to restore it and a lack of money to do the job, meant that disappearance was the inevitable answer. But then a Venetian bank, Banca Ifis, stepped in. First they bought the 17th-century Palazzo San Pantalon on which it was painted, a building very badly in need of complete restoration. Not only would the bank restore the building, they would also fund the restoration of the *Migrant Child*, which would become part of Ifis Art, a project conceived by the Bank's president, who said, 'we have the responsibility, in the collaboration between public and private institutions, to preserve art and culture in Venice.'

Cue for universal praise? Well not exactly. Quite apart from Banksy's well-known sentiment that his pieces should be left just as he painted them – a very unlikely hope at this stage in his career – this piece was particularly site specific. The Venetian Architects' Association argued that the point of the piece was that 'in time it will be submerged by water and will, alas, come to the same end as the many children who have died in the Mediterranean over the last ten years.'

The street artist Cristiano Bovo, who is known as Joys, told *La Repubblica*: 'You save an artwork, or remove it from a wall, if the artist is dead or if it's his most important work. Banksy has used colour for 30 years, he knows how long they last, and I don't think he would be so presumptuous as to believe his work lasts for ever.'

Banksy himself said nothing about the possible restoration, but even if he had, Vittorio Sgarbi, Undersecretary in Italy's Ministry of Culture, would have been very unlikely to listen to him. He made it clear that the ministry wanted it restored and it did not matter whether Banksy agreed or not. 'We are not interested in having the artist's consent, the mural was created illegally. I take responsibility.' Banksy might have wanted his work left to fade gently away but the ministry's task, Mr Sgarbi argued, was to 'save what can be saved.' So, even though the *Migrant Child* will not drown, he will not be the same child that Banksy originally painted.

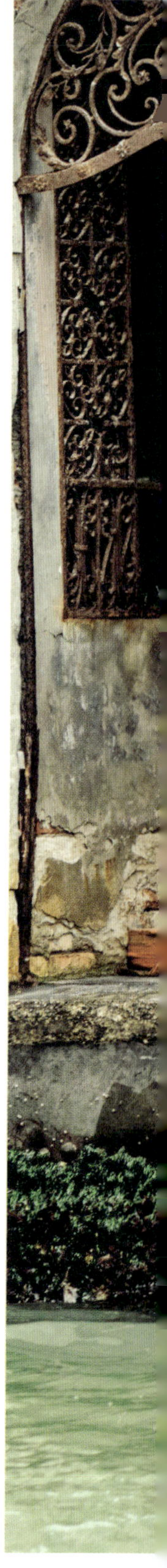

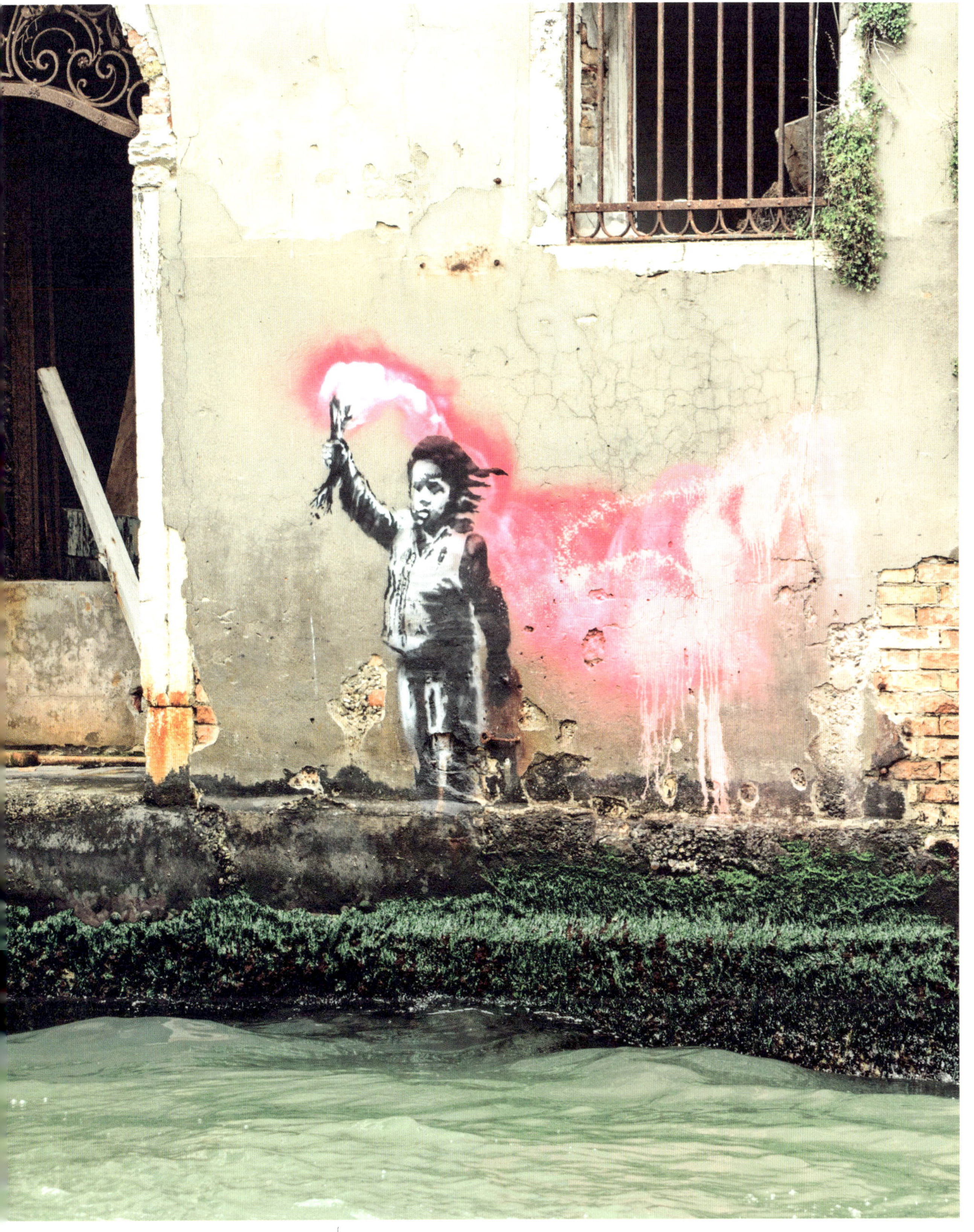

49

THE SAME BUT DIFFERENT

📍 HARBOUR STREET, TORONTO, ON M5J (*GUARD WITH BALLOON DOG*);
ELYSIAN FIELDS AVENUE, NEW ORLEANS LA 70117
THEN INTERNATIONAL HOUSE HOTEL, CAMP STREET, NEW ORLEANS LA
70130 (*LOOTERS*)

Two pieces, one in Toronto, the other in New Orleans, both surviving in good condition, illustrate the problem with Banksy. Are the men who 'saved' them saviours, art villains or somewhere in between? One piece has ended up in in a boutique hotel in New Orleans and the other stands in a glass box on show beside the PATH network, a largely underground walkway connecting downtown Toronto.

Banksy painted *Guard with Balloon Dog* in Toronto in 2010. The building was demolished a year later, but the company developing the site salvaged the three pieces of limestone it was painted on. The developer 'really wanted to give it back to the public' and the *Toronto Star* explained that developers, could use the planning laws to trade community benefits for an increase in the height of the high-rise building they planned. So Banksy, appraised at a value of $850,000 dollars (plus other perks, including a $10 million cash payment for area improvements), became a community enhancement, and the towers duly increased in height.

In New Orleans *Looters*, where two National Guardsmen made off with their spoils, was painted in 2008 three years after Hurricane Katrina hit the city. The National Guard were called in to help and there were reports they had been looting. It was painted on an empty warehouse and when the owner, Sean Cummings, and his partners sold the warehouse six years later they kept the Banksy.

Once it had been conserved he displayed it, at the International House Hotel which he owns. I asked Mr Cummings about Banksy's view that his work should be left in the context in which it is painted. He replied by email: 'I understand, respect and admire Banksy's opinion. But there was no way to protect the stencil if left on the street. So, I did the next best thing: moved it to a hotel lobby that offers security and, importantly, is accessible 24 hours a day to all visitors and at zero cost of admission. *Looters* remains public art – free of charge.'

He has always said that the hotel is not its permanent home. So where does he hope it will end up? 'I don't know yet,' he replied, 'but I think about it a lot. Any ideas?' (Answer: No).

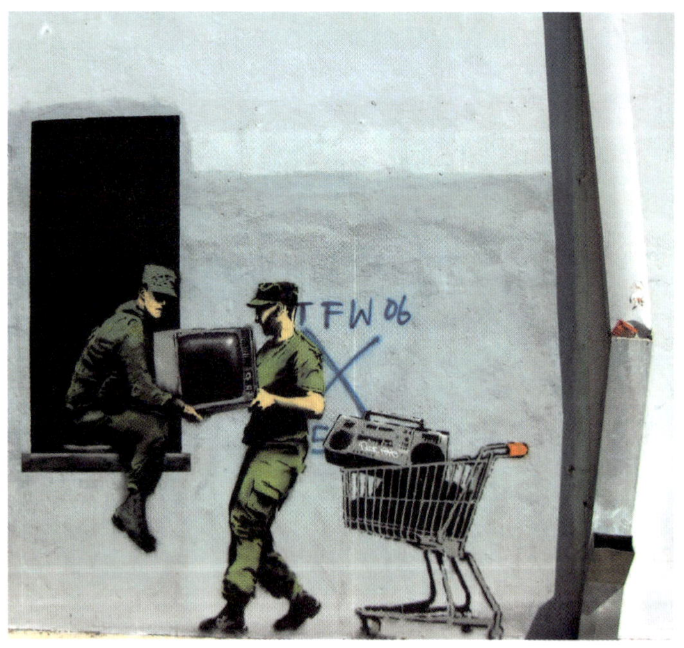

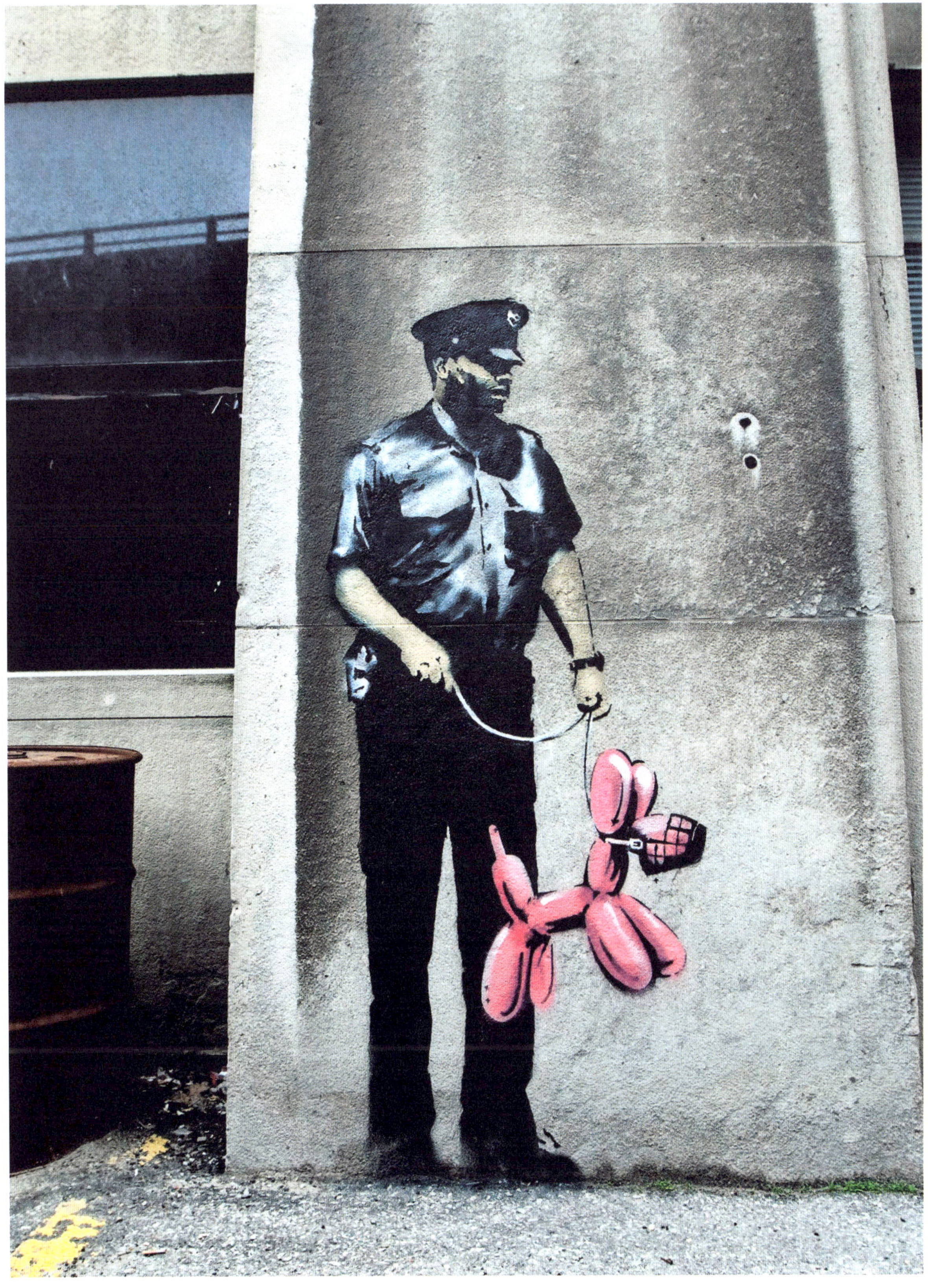

TEMPTATION AT THE BUS STOP

📍 FARRINGDON ROAD, LONDON EC1R 4SQ

It's all very well to believe that it is totally wrong to rip street art off the wall and try to sell it at a huge profit; but what happens when you are given the possible chance of doing just that? I thought I had that chance a few years back and I have to confess I was mightily tempted.

Banksy likes nothing better than a rat, and on a stone pillar next to a bus stop on the Farringdon Road, north London, there is, or was, a Banksy rat. The rat, as often with Banksy, was wearing a CND badge round his neck and held up a placard reading (originally) 'Always Fail', which was somewhat appropriate given the pillar was marking the outer boundary of the Mount Pleasant postal sorting office.

Although the piece was faded, I knew it well, having often waited for the bus alongside it. So it was with considerable excitement when one day I arrived at the bus stop to find no pillar and thus no Banksy. Mount Pleasant was being redeveloped and the railings and the pillar had to go. The bulldozers were still working nearby on site and maybe, I hoped, there was a chunk of stone with the Banksy on it lying around. Maybe I could talk to the foreman, maybe he had never heard of Banksy, maybe I could walk away with a Banksy for a fiver, maybe, maybe … and then what?

I found the foreman. Of course he knew who Banksy was. However, he had no idea that Banksy had painted on a pillar his men had just destroyed. The pillar had been broken up and lay amid a nearby pile of rubble. He was sorry, but health and safety and all that meant I could not go digging for it. So another Banksy bit the dust – apologies for too tempting a pun – and my chance of selling off an original if not very interesting

Banksy for hundreds of thousands of pounds was gone. Would I have taken the money? Who knows, but the fact that I was prepared to go to quite an effort to discover the fate of the pillar suggests, I fear, that I might have done.

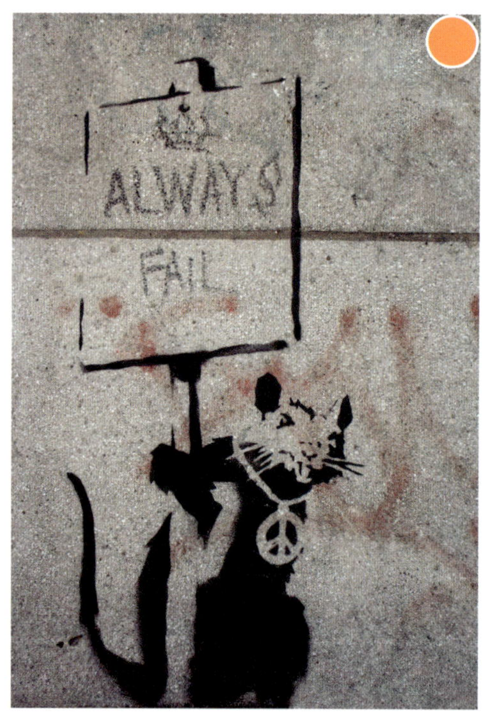

NOTHING LASTS FOREVER

18 ALLEN STREET, CHINATOWN, NEW YORK NY 10002

This was the first piece that Banksy put up when he swaggered into New York in October 2013. The two urchins daring to steal the spray can from the middle of a permanent anti- graffiti sign said all that needed to be said about what he was doing in the city.

But within a few hours the sign and half of one lad's arm had gone and he was left clutching at nothing. Not for long. The sign was rapidly replaced by another one from Smart Crew, a collective of graffiti artists from Queens, and now the boys were clutching at a different sign, one which gently mocked Banksy, reading 'Street Art Is a Crime.' The next day, the second sign and the boys had all gone, stolen or whitewashed out of existence. The original sign has never resurfaced and it has never been near a saleroom.

Banksy himself had a pretty good idea of what was in store. He had stencilled on the wall alongside the boys an 800 toll-free phone number. If you used it you were treated to a commentary dripping in fairly heavy-handed satire. 'Hello, and welcome to Lower Manhattan,' the commentator says. 'Before you, you will see a "spray art" by the artist "Banksy". Or maybe not; it's probably been painted over by now.'

How right he was. But does it matter? Like so much of his work it had been seen by the fortunate few who found it first, and then by millions on the web. It was created in the full knowledge that its street life was going to be short – that is the way graffiti artists think. Perhaps it is the audience that has to change, to move from what we are accustomed to, the idea that a painting needs to be hung on the wall of a gallery to make it important, and accept that some art is immediate and live, existing for the now, not for the forever.

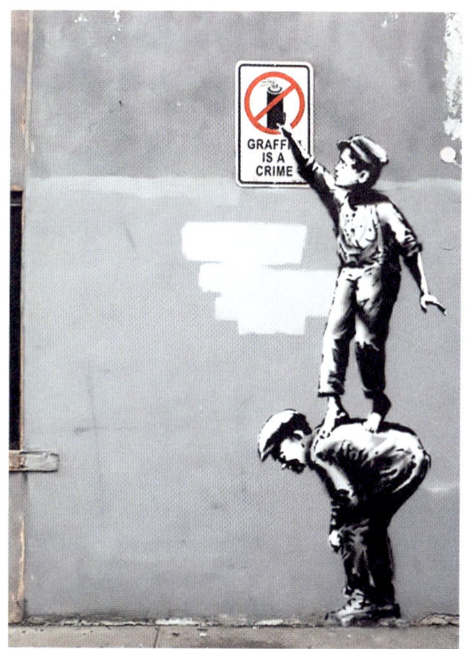

INDEX

ACKNOWLEDGEMENTS

One of the things that surprised me about Banksy was how there would always be an enormous flurry of stories whenever he confirmed any new piece was his, but then the story would often stop. I would then have to rely on people in various parts of the world to help me find out what happened next.

The first people I would like to thank are in Ukraine. It is easy to imagine how strange it was to ring or email someone there in the middle of a horrifying war, apologize for interrupting them when they had more serious things on their mind and then ask about the whereabouts of a Banksy.

My first point of contact was Olha Stefanishyna. From her I went from Iryna, to Olha and finally to Ilyha, and they were all as helpful as they could possibly be.

Naturally enough it was simpler in other parts of the world. In San Francisco Jesse Leake kindly went out to photograph what was left on the wall of the Eastern Bakery. Since the owner of the bakery did not want to talk to someone in England who he had never met, Jesse went back and interviewed him for me.

In New Orleans photographers Charlie Varley and Anthony Turducken both spoke about the pictures they had taken years ago. Carlos Fundora talked about his and others' efforts to preserve Banksys in the city. Sean Cummings, the owner of a Banksy as well as a hotel which he put it in, was refreshingly direct, dispensing with any PR guards. In Detroit both Pete Senteris and Shane McMurphy were very helpful in putting together the last hours of *Diamond Girl.* Brian Greif was of help in San Francisco and so too were Cara Tabachnick, who had a Banksy painted on her family's building in New York, and Steve Spina in Los Angeles, who bought an unauthenticated Banksy. In Toronto Tim Rostron checked out *Guard with Balloon Dog.* In Paris Annabel Courage uncovered what eventually happened to the Bataclan door and the person who is now its owner.

Closer to home I would like to thank David Graham for his continued faith in me when he became Managing Director of Batsford. And at Batsford my thanks go to Rebecca Armstrong, Eoghan O'Brien and Nicola Newman, both for their help and their patience. Special thanks too to Graham Coster, my former publisher who now runs his own publishing company, Safe Haven Books, and was a major help to me in shaping this book in the early days.

I would like to thank James Dawe for help both with graffiti and design, John Nation and Waliur Rahman in Bristol; Chris Marks for help with NFTs; David Samuel, who first introduced me to Robbo and has helped me ever since; Maeve Neale in Norfolk; Colin Darlow in Great Yarmouth; Alex Georgiou in Camden and Ashley Ovenden, who helped demolish – and photograph – the Banksy in Herne Bay. The dealers Richard Hessink, John Brandler, Julian Usher and, in particular, Robin Barton, who I disagree with completely on Banksy and in particular on what should happen to his work, but who has always been very helpful whenever he could be.

Finally then, to Lara Guyoncourt for her continuing vital support and occasional key interventions, and to Elizabeth Grice, who has gone through every word and every thought in this book with such care and attention to the smallest detail. I owe you both so much.

PICTURE CREDITS

Cover: © PA Images / Alamy; Page 2: © Photozaic / Alamy; Page 8: © Dan De Kleined / Alamy; Page 10: © Dave Ellison / Alamy; Page 12: © Matjaz Tancic / Alamy; Page 14: © Associated Press / Alamy; Page 16: © Chloë Chapman / Alamy; Page 18: © Matthew Lambley / Alamy; Page 19: © Rod Olukoya / Alamy; Page 21: © Dan De Kleined / Alamy; Page 23: © dpa picture alliance / Alamy; Page 24: © Associated Press / Alamyl; Page 25: © Associated Press / Alamy; Page 27: © Ted Soqui / Getty; Page 28: Dave Stuart; Page 29: © PA Images / Alamy; Page 29: © Julia Fogg; Page 30: © Eva Blue; Page 31: © Peter Tsai Photography / Alamy; Pages 32–34: © Jesse Leake; Page 34: https://www.flickr.com/photos/shell-shock/6591449589/in/photostream/; Page 35: © Barry Lewis / Alamy; Page 37: © Stefano Baldini / Alamy; Page 30: Geoff Walsh; Page 39: © Guy Bell / Alamy; Page 40–41: © PA Images / Alamy; Page 42: City Nature; Page 43: © Peter Senteris; Page 44: © PA Images / Alamy; Page 45: © PA Images / Alamy; Page 46: © PA Images / Alamy; Page 47: © PA Images / Alamy; Page 48: © Sipa US / Alamy; Page 49: © Associated Press / Alamy; Pages 50–51: © Associated Press / Alamy; Page 52: © Refluence / Shutterstock: Page 53: © Raj Valley / Alamy; Page 55: © Photozaic / Alamy; Page 56: © Associated Press / Alamy; Page 57: © Rob Corder; Page 58: Street Art Utopia; Page 59: Steve James; Page 61: © manwithacamera.com.au / Alamy; Page 62: © Anthony Turducken; Page 63: © PA Images / Alamy; Pages 64–65: © PA Images / Alamy; Page 66: Dave Stuart; Page 67: © Frank Kinch / Alamy; Page 69: Thomas Hawk; Pages 70–71: © Ted Soqui / Getty; Page 72: © Ashley Ovenden; Page 73: © Ashley Ovenden; Page 75: © Associated Press / Alamy; Pages 76–77: © Associated Press / Alamy; Page 79: © Associated Press / Alamy; Page 80: © Matthew Chattle / Alamy; Page 81: © Graham Bridgeman-Clarke / Alamy; Page 82: © ZUMA Press, Inc. / Alamy; Page 83: © Associated Press / Alamy; Page 84: © Ocky Murray; Page 85: © Jamie Gladden / Alamy; Pages 86–87: © Paul Carstairs / Alamy; Page 89: © PA Images / Alamy; Page 90: Trixie Delite; Page 91: Trixie Delite; Page 93: © Roger Bamber / Alamy; Page 94: © Christiane Michel; Page 95: JOHN19701970; Page 96: © AFP / Getty; Page 97: © Brendan Bell / Alamy; Page 99: © Richard Levine / Alamy; Page 101: © PA Images / Alamy; Page 102: © james anderson / Alamy; Page 103: © Sipa US / Alamy; Page 105: © PA Images / Alamy; Page 107: © JCB-Images / Alamy; Page 108: © Ben Hockman; Page 108: © Miriam Ferrarin; Page 109: © Jonny White / Alamy; Page 110–111: © christopher jones / Alamy; Page 113: © Nick Moore / Alamy; Page 115: © UPI / Alamy; Page 116: © UPI / Alamy; Page 117: © UPI / Alamy; Page 119: © Randy Duchaine / Alamy; Page 120: © Coaster / Alamy; Page 120: Steve Cotton; Page 121: Alexinwanderland; Page 123: © Eye Ubiquitous / Alamy; Page 125: © Associated Press / Alamy; Page 126: © Richard Levine / Alamy; Page 127: © Frances Roberts / Alamy; Page 128: Megan David; Page 129: © Julian Smith/EPA/Shutterstock; Page 131: © Photozaic / Alamy; Page 132: © Photozaic / Alamy; Page 133: © Photozaic / Alamy; Page 135: © BasPhoto / Alamy; Page 136: Katiekay88; Page 137: © Associated Press / Alamy; Page 138: Daddy W; 139: https://www.gallerymonkey.com/Banksy-Graffiti-Is-A-Crime-Art-Print; 143: © Raj Valley / Alamy

Batsford is committed to respecting the intellectual property rights of others. We have taken all reasonable efforts to ensure that the reproduction of all contents on these pages is done with the full consent of the copyright owners. If you are aware of unintentional omissions, please contact the company directly so that any necessary corrections may be made for future editions.

FOR CARLO, LUKE, VINIA & ETHAN

First published in the United Kingdom
in 2025 by
Batsford
43 Great Ormond Street
London
WC1N 3HZ

An imprint of B. T. Batsford Holdings Limited

Copyright © B. T. Batsford Ltd, 2025
Text copyright © Will Ellsworth-Jones, 2025

All rights reserved. No part of this publication may be copied,
displayed, extracted, reproduced, utilized, stored in a retrieval
system or transmitted in any form or by any means, electronic,
mechanical or otherwise including but not limited to photocopying,
recording, or scanning without the prior written permission of
the publishers.

ISBN 9781849949057

A CIP catalogue record for this book is available from the British Library.

10 9 8 7 6 5 4 3 2 1

Reproduction by Rival Colour Ltd, UK
Printed by Toppan Leefung Printing International Ltd, China

This book can be ordered direct from the publisher at
www.batsfordbooks.com, or try your local bookshop.